D1329497

STARLIGHT TOUR

SUSANNE REBER AND ROBERT RENAUD

STARLIGHT TOUR

THE LAST, LONELY NIGHT OF NEIL STONECHILD

VINTAGE CANADA

www.randomhouse.ca

Library and Archives Canada Cataloguing in Publication

Reber, Susanne

　　Starlight tour : the last, lonely night of Neil Stonechild / Susanne Reber and Rob Renaud.

Includes index.

ISBN13: 978-0-679-31308-3
ISBN10: 0-679-31308-7

　　1. Police misconduct—Saskatchewan—Saskatoon.　2. Stonechild, Neil, 1973–1990— Death and burial.　3. Indians of North America—Crimes against—Saskatchewan— Saskatoon.　4. Saskatoon (Sask.).　Saskatoon Police Service.　I. Renaud, Rob　II. Title.

HV8160.S27R42 2006　　　　　363.2'097124'25　　　　　C2006-902080-9

The four panels from Kilburn Hall and the drawing of the wheel of life turning backwards are used courtesy of the artist, Jeffrey "Bluesky" Crowe.

Photographs of the panels and the Queen Elizabeth power station by the authors.

Photographs of Neil Stonechild and the Stonechild family, and various images and documents are used courtesy of Stella Stonechild Bignell.

Neil Stonechild: A Founding Champion DVD used courtesy of Geoff and Gail Wright.

Book design by CS Richardson

Printed and bound in the United States of America

10 9 8 7 6 5 4 3 2 1

To the families

Contents

PART I

SWEET CHILD

Prologue

Early on the frigid morning of January 9, 1964, a curious four-year-old wandered about his new house, scouting his surroundings. The plain one-storey stucco bungalow at 922 Avenue J North, Saskatoon, consisted of just two bedrooms, a bathroom, front room, kitchen and basement, but after the cramped rental suite where the boy and his family used to stay, it seemed enormous.

Four people lived with the boy, whose name was Donald, although people usually called him Donny. His mother, Margaret Worme, was thirty-eight years old. Donny loved everything about her. He liked the way she dressed, neatly and carefully, even though her life had been tough. Born and raised on the Kawacatoose reserve, an hour's drive southeast of the city, she'd had four children before Donny's father had abandoned her. Donny didn't remember him. Nor did he remember his brother Darren, born almost three years ago and put up for adoption at nine months old. Margaret knew the people who had happily taken Darren in—a German couple named Winegarden—but the families soon lost touch, even though they lived only a few kilometres apart. Donny's mother had made an excruciating choice: she'd decided that the best thing for the rest of her children, and for Darren too, was to give her son up, because the money she got from social assistance and the odd cleaning job would never stretch to feed, clothe and house them all.

Donny still had one older brother, Dale, a rambunctious seven-year-old who, as dawn approached, was busy getting ready for school. Also, their Uncle Hilliard was visiting from the Quinton reserve. And Donny's seventeen-year-old sister, Pat, and her eighteen-month-old toddler, Kim, had moved in.

Donny, an observant little boy with cropped raven hair and intense dark eyes, knew that his sister was sad right now, though she was doing her best to hide it. She'd had a baby girl just four weeks earlier, but she had reluctantly decided to give her daughter up, thinking that surrendering her child might make it easier for her to flee from her husband, Francis Littlechief, who beat her in his frequent drunken rages. When Pat brought Kim to the new house, she left her husband behind, hoping it would be for good.

Dale, for one, was glad Francis hadn't come; he didn't like his sister's husband. Donny had no opinion about Francis one way or the other—Francis had never paid that much attention to him—but he did know that his mother was happy Francis was gone. Even though he had trained as a welder and mechanic's helper, Francis was often unemployed. But in mid-November he'd left his pregnant wife and their son behind to take on a short-term mill job in Thompson, Manitoba. Margaret had hoped her son-in-law wouldn't come back. But he'd returned to Saskatoon on Christmas Eve, showing up at the old place and berating Pat about giving up their daughter in his absence.

Francis had made a strange appearance at the new bungalow just a couple of nights ago. As his wife and her family were sitting down to supper, he had barged through the back door and stood by the table for the rest of their meal.

"I want to talk to Pat about the children," he had said more than once, staring fixedly at Margaret even though Pat was right there. Donny had sat quietly watching. His sister was having none of it. "I don't want anything to do with you," she said. Francis didn't move. When she finally retreated to the bedroom, he followed her. They stayed in there talking for well over an hour, but there was no yelling, and Margaret decided to leave them be. When Francis had come out, he'd sat quietly with Hilliard in the front room watching television for a bit. Then, as abruptly as he'd arrived, he said, "I have to go," and took off.

— — —

Margaret and Pat were bustling around now, getting ready to face the cold dawn and a day of cleaning houses. Even when she was dressing for menial work, Margaret wore something nice, and that morning she put on the dark brown blouse she liked to wear with her tan skirt and jacket.

In the past twenty-four hours the temperature had sunk to minus twenty-five degrees Celsius. A thick crust of ice had formed around the frame of the back door, sealing it shut. Not even Uncle Hilliard had been able to budge it. Forty years later, Donny would still vividly remember the way the cold forced its way into that little house like something alive.

At about seven-thirty there was a knock at the front door. Margaret's niece, Marleen, who lived a few blocks away with her husband, John Goosenose, had arrived to babysit Don and Kim while Margaret and Pat went to work. Nineteen years old and nine months pregnant, Marleen headed straight for a chair at the kitchen table; the slightest exertion exhausted her. Once her aunt and cousin were out the door, Marleen packed Dale off to his grade one class at Westmount Community School. Hilliard woke up a little later and, after picking up a few groceries for the house, headed out for the day, leaving Marleen alone with the two little boys.

Much to her relief, the children were content to amuse themselves. Pat returned in the early afternoon. Having given birth so recently, she hadn't been able to make it through a whole day of house-cleaning. Around four o'clock, Dale came tearing through the front door with the pent-up energy of a seven-year-old who had been cooped up all day in school. Despite the very cold weather, Dale and the little boys pleaded to work on the snowman they had been building in the front yard. Marleen bundled them up well. They lasted twenty minutes outside before they paraded back into the house, trailing snow, wet mitts and icy boots.

Marleen started supper early, frying up slices of bologna and heating some canned tomatoes to go with bread and butter. The vinegary, sweet scent of the tomatoes drifted through the house. Margaret was expected home around six.

— — —

About the same time as Marleen was laying bologna slices in the frying pan, Hilliard was heading to the Ritz Beer Parlour, near the railway station. The winter darkness had already descended. At first he sat by himself, with two glasses of beer in front of him for company, but then he saw Francis Littlechief at a nearby table. Littlechief waved him over to join him and a taxi driver named Fred Peigan. William Popowich, a bartender and a friend of Hilliard, sat down a little later. Each of the four took turns buying rounds for the next hour or so, except for Littlechief, who claimed he was broke.

Littlechief pulled a photo out of his shirt pocket and showed it around the table. "Look at her." He pointed to Pat, who cradled the newborn baby and had one arm around Kim. "See how pretty she is," he said, slurring his words and draining his glass. "You know, I just want her back. That's all. I just want my family back." Hilliard thought he sounded more concerned than angry. Littlechief had been drinking since eleven in the morning—quite a feat for a guy with no cash. Eventually, not wanting to stand him another round, Hilliard and Popowich made excuses to leave. Littlechief tried to follow his uncle-in-law out, but Hilliard had ducked into the café next door and ditched him.

Peeking out into the street, he watched Littlechief look around, puzzled, until he gave up and staggered away.

— — —

Donny and the other kids had almost finished supper by the time Margaret got home a little after six. Donny always loved the moment when she came through the door, and he ran to bury his nose in the fur of her coat sleeve. She shucked off her coat and held it over her right arm for a while before hanging it up, her head cocked as though she were really listening closely to Donny's animated account of his day. Tired from babysitting and too content in the happy company of her aunt's family to rush home, Marleen stayed seated at the kitchen table. Margaret warmed up leftovers from the kids' dinner and had just sat down to eat when two loud knocks rattled the front door. It slammed open. Littlechief stormed into the house.

"Get out," Pat and Margaret shouted at almost the same time. Margaret rose from the table and stepped toward him. "Now!" she commanded. "You don't belong here." Donny backed up against a side table in the kitchen. He wasn't scared, though, not yet.

"I have as much right to be here as you," Littlechief slurred back. "I want to talk to Pat." His voice was loud and his eyes were red from drink and lack of sleep. He was staring straight at Margaret.

"Get out. I want you out. Don't you understand? You don't belong here," Margaret insisted. "Why are you here? Tell me why you're here."

Oddly, Littlechief made a move toward the basement. "I want my green shirt. I know it's downstairs, and I'm going to get it."

Margaret blocked the way. "Stay where you are," she warned him. "I'll get it for you."

When she came up from the basement she had the green shirt in one hand and an axe in the other. "Here's your shirt," she said, throwing it at him. "Now get out."

In one lunge, Littlechief covered the three metres to the knife rack and grabbed both a bread knife and his wife. Donny tucked himself under the little side table. He heard someone yell, "Call the police." Marleen tried to get up from where she was sitting, but pregnant and terrified, she couldn't seem to move.

"Help me, Mum," his sister pleaded as Littlechief backed with her toward the living room. Then everything became very quiet. Donny realized he was crying, and so were Dale and Kim, who was screaming uncontrollably. But, strangely, Donny couldn't hear anything, didn't feel anything, his senses had shut out everything but the sight of his horrified sister in her husband's grip.

Littlechief stabbed at his wife; the bread knife bent under the force of repeated blows. When he dropped it to grab another from the rack, Pat crawled toward the front door, bleeding. When he chased her, Margaret ran after him, still carrying the axe, and Marleen managed to stagger to the phone on the wall to call the police.

Donny saw his brother slowly following their mother and he wanted to warn Dale to stay back, but the words wouldn't come out of his throat. Pat was on the floor, her right arm raised to ward off her husband as he attacked again with a new knife. His mother swung the axe at Littlechief, but he grabbed it out of her hands, and the four-year-old boy watched in eerie internal silence as his sister's husband smashed the axe into his mother's head. Donny screamed, but he still couldn't hear himself.

Marleen dropped the phone and turned toward the back door. When she didn't see him under the table, Donny wondered if he really wasn't making any noise. Francis started for the kitchen and Marleen began to run, hurling her pregnant body forward with enough force to slam through the ice that had sealed the back door. Littlechief found his way blocked by Dale, and he hit the seven-year-old in the head with the knife. Donny's brother dropped to the floor, unconscious.

Littlechief loomed, wild-eyed and bloody, over Dale's prostrate figure. He noticed Donny cowering beneath the little table and locked on the boy with his eyes. Sound rushed back to Donny. Kim was sobbing hysterically, but remained mercifully unscathed. "Don't hit me," Donny yelled, and Francis vanished past him, following Marleen out into the snow and the dark.

Donny crawled out from under the table. Kim was still frozen in place, crying. Though he wasn't much bigger than his nephew, Donny hugged Kim and tried to get him to walk. Nothing worked. "I'm going for help," he finally said. Drifting snow pooled at the back door and the alley was dark—Littlechief was out there, somewhere. Three bodies lay between him and the front door; Dale, not moving; his mother, who was face down in the middle of the living room; and Pat, on her back, by the door. Somehow he steeled himself and stepped past them.

The Cumpstones were sitting at the supper table when the little boy who had just moved in next door came flying through their front door, screaming. What he was yelling seemed un-believable—they hadn't heard a thing from next door. "My mum and Pat and Dale are killed by an axe. Mummy got chopped with an axe in the eye. The bad guy, he killed my mummy, Pat and Dale." Mrs. Cumpstone held the boy against her hip to comfort him while her husband called the police.

"You're okay now," she said. "You're safe here."

"I hid under the table," Donny said when he was able to catch his breath, as if he were trying to understand how he was still alive while everyone he loved most in the world was dead.

Somewhere in the lane Marleen's slippers had come off. When she pounded on the back door of the neighbours' house on the other side, their little boy let her in and she almost ran him over. Barefoot and shaking uncontrollably, she lunged for the phone, shouting, "Lock the door, for God's sake, lock the door. He tried to kill me with the axe, too. He's coming. He's coming. We have to shut the door." She started to dial the police but fainted outright. The boy's father ran into the street and flagged down a police car headed for another call.

When the police entered Margaret's little house, it took a while for them to realize that there was one small piece of good news: Dale was still alive.

— — —

Two officers arrested Francis Littlechief an hour later outside the Adilman's department store on 20th Street, where he was standing in a daze. When they asked him where he was headed, he held out his hands and said, "I am under arrest. I am Francis Littlechief. I killed my wife." The next day the newspaper ran stories about the bloody double murder, along with a huge picture of Donny sitting on the Cumpstones' living-room couch trying to read a story to Kim, whose wide-eyed stare betrays his shock.

When Littlechief went to trial on second-degree murder charges a few months later, Donny, Kim and Dale were in the care of social services. Marleen was a nervous wreck, and could barely frame a coherent account of the murders. Seven-year-old Dale had taken a long time to recover from his injuries and was able to recount what had happened that night up to the moment Littlechief hit him. But it largely fell on four-year-old Donny's shoulders to stand up in court—unheard of in a murder trial— and describe what had happened in his house that cold January night, to tell the truth for his mother and sister. He had lost them, but at least he could have justice. Francis Littlechief was convicted.

When the trial was over, Donny, Dale and Kim went to live with their maternal grandfather on the Kawacatoose reserve. The reserve was named after a brave warrior who went into battle armed with only a lance. Thirty-five or so years later, Don Worme would strive to embody such courage and to honour the warrior tradition in his own way.

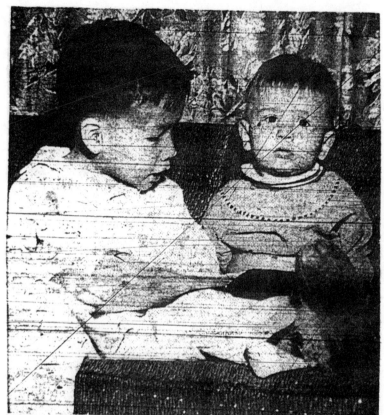

FOUR-YEAR-OLD Donald Worme and his 18-month-old nephew, Kim Little-chief, are shown here looking at a children's story book at the home of Mr. and Mrs. J. E. Cumpstone, shortly after their mothers were killed in a hatchet slaying earlier Thursday night.

VANISHED

IT WAS A SCHOOL NIGHT TOWARD THE END OF November 1990. Stella Stonechild sat staring at the little red-flower pattern that circled her Arborite kitchen table top, drinking tea and worrying about her son, Neil, who seemed to be going from bad to worse. He was her second youngest, seventeen years old, a boy with a quick wit, a big smile and a lot going for him. Even Pat Pickard, who ran the community home where Neil was supposed to be serving a six-month open-custody sentence for yet another petty crime, thought he had a lot of potential. And until two weeks ago, Pickard had been cutting Stella's boy some slack.

Stella herself had been thinking that Neil was finally getting it together. He was going to school with the other boys from Pickard's home, getting passable grades, doing his community-service hours at the native friendship centre downtown, heading dutifully back to Pickard's after visiting his family on day passes, and even talking about taking up wrestling again. From the age of fourteen, Neil had competed and won tournaments at the local and provincial level. His coaches thought he had the stuff to be a real contender, that extra competitive grit that never let him give up. But after a couple of years he had suddenly dropped the sport. Neither his mother nor his coaches really understood why. Drinking, hanging out with bad company and one run-in after another with the cops had followed.

Boozing, smashing car windows to steal radios and selling them for a few bucks to buy more booze, then breaking probation: Neil's escalating bad behaviour had led to several stints at Kilburn Hall, a youth detention centre, a much tougher place than Pickard's. Many of the other boys at Kilburn were in deeper trouble than he was, so Stella hoped that his time there had smartened Neil up a little, made him aware of the stakes.

Then two weeks ago, on November 13, he had run away from Pickard's. Neil was now wanted by police for being "unlawfully at large." From the moment Pickard had reported his absence to the Saskatoon city police, officers on patrol were told to be on the lookout for Neil Christopher Stonechild, seventeen years old, aboriginal, 169 centimetres tall and weighing sixty-eight kilos. Since then Neil had cut school, playing hide-and-seek with cop cars that patrolled the largely native area where his family lived in low-income housing, on a crescent of bungalows off Confederation Drive, in Saskatoon's westernmost suburb.

Worried as she was, Stella couldn't find it in her heart to rat her son out, not to the police, or even to call Pickard and let her know Neil was sleeping at home. She felt guilty, but it just wasn't her way to try to *force* Neil, or any of her children, onto a better path. She believed that he had to arrive at the right choices on his own. He would be eighteen soon; surely he realized that run-ins with the justice system would soon mean facing time in adult prison.

Even as Stella avoided calling her, she clung to something Pickard had said, that she had seen many troubled teenagers like Neil in her career, and that by the age of twenty-five a lot of them had turned into Joe Citizen.

The back door banged open and two strong arms hugged her tightly. Neil's breath warmed her cheek as he kissed her. Boozy breath. Even without the booze, he was never shy about showing affection. He adored their big family gatherings, horsing with his nieces and nephews and his little brother Jake. Jake was another sore spot for Stella. He was only fourteen and was already serving his own stint in Kilburn Hall for petty theft.

"Hi, Mum, what're you up to?"

"Come sit with me. Have a cup of tea and make yourself some toast, Harry," she said. Stella's sister, Debbie Mason, had started calling him Harry when he was a baby, inspired by an obscure movie called *Harry in Your Pocket*, which had been released the year Neil was born; in it, James Coburn played a clever pickpocket with nerve and style. Debbie had quite a sense of humour, to Stella's chagrin: Harry was also Neil's birth father's name.

As her son sat down across from her, she said, "You've been drinking, Harry." Stella had house rules, one of which was no alcohol.

"Mum, how could you tell?" he joked, a grin wrapped across his face. "Just a little, I swear."

Stella reached across the table to take his hand, determined to get through to him.

"You gotta stop drinking."

"I know, I know," but he was looking down at the table, avoiding her eyes. "Pat's good to me. I just prefer to be home with you."

"You're spending your time running, watching your back. It's in and out. If it's not a B and E, you break the curfew and back you go. It's just a cycle. If you turn yourself in to Pat now, it won't be too hard on you. But if you get in trouble again, you'll never get out of this rut you're in."

"I've been thinking about it," he said, finally looking up. "You're right. I'll go back to Pat's."

Making the decision seemed to give Neil some relief. He was smiling at Stella, his big brown eyes lively. But just as she got up to hand him the phone so he could call Pickard, he stopped her.

"Let me have one last weekend," he said. "I'll go back, I promise." He leaned across the table to hug her, then stood up and went to bed.

Alone in her kitchen again, Stella picked up her mug and carried it to the counter. Everything had gone quiet around her, only the fridge humming in the background. One more weekend, Neil had said. Relief washed over her, too. Her boy didn't make promises unless he meant to keep them.

— — —

Stella Stonechild had moved to Saskatoon back in 1980 to save herself and her children from binge-drinking, poverty and despair.

She was born on February 23, 1941, about an hour's drive west of Dauphin, Manitoba. Throughout her life she was very attached to the history of her family. From her childhood, she remembered her father opposing government treaties he said were taking away the Saulteaux lands. And she loved the story of her parents' traditional marriage; her mother's dowry had been a gift of horses. Stella and her childhood friends had enjoyed a level of freedom unique to their aboriginal culture. Spending long hours with their grandparents, they were rarely reprimanded and were allowed to wander about even during sacred religious rites, such as the Sun Dance. According to one oft-told story, a child who disliked the food his parents provided would throw tantrums, falling onto his back. Instead of yelling at him or punishing him physically, his parents tied a bag filled with water to his back. When the boy threw his next tantrum, he got soaked and ended up joining everyone else in a good laugh at his own foolishness. This, in Stella's view, was the enlightened way to raise children.

Now, a year shy of her fiftieth birthday, Stella was just over five feet tall, with an infectious laugh and a generous heart. She'd given birth to five children. Dean, her eldest, had been adopted in the 1960s by a family in the United States. But Stella was proud that as a single mother she had been able to keep and raise Dean's four siblings. Her only girl, Erica, was born in 1969; like Neil, she had a family nickname, Gypsy. Then had come Marcel in 1971, Neil in 1973 and Jake in 1975.

In 1979, Stella was living in Thompson, Manitoba, when she met Norman Bignell, a quiet man with rugged good looks and thick black hair, which he wore in a style reminiscent of Elvis Presley. They moved in together, happily, but Stella was beginning to abhor many other things about her life. Whenever she faced a problem she turned to alcohol, and there didn't seem to be anyone around who didn't reinforce that pattern. She decided the only way to break free was to leave her friends in Thompson. If Norman wanted to come too, that was fine, but he'd also have to promise to give up drinking along with her.

She'd never been to Saskatoon, but she had relatives there. And so, as the cold weather was coming on in the fall of 1980, she packed their bags, stuffed her four kids into their snowsuits and bundled them all onto a bus headed for a new life in Saskatchewan. She still remembers how they climbed out of the bus at the downtown terminal in Saskatoon into weather so balmy they practically boiled in their winter clothes.

In many ways Stella's plan worked. She quit drinking and smoking and never started again. Norman had a bit of trouble. After one two-week binge when he disappeared to Manitoba, Stella followed him. She presented an ultimatum: come back with her and stop drinking or their relationship was finished. Norman returned and, over the years, with occasional lapses, he kept the word he had given Stella that day.

At first they lived in the North Park area of Saskatoon and then a little farther north in Lawson Heights, both stable working-class neighbourhoods. The principal at the public school

Clockwise from top left: Marcel, Neil, Erica, Norman, Jake and Stella, 1982.

took a benevolent interest in them, and after school and on weekends the kids played games in the bushes of Meewasin Park, which runs along the west bank of the South Saskatchewan River, downstream from the bridges of the business district. Stella began taking the family to the Lawson Heights Alliance Church and eventually hosted Bible-study meetings at their house.

But Saskatoon had a darker side, which her kids soon encountered. One day Marcel was out playing with a group of white kids when his little brothers showed up. The kids yelled, "You can't play with us—you're Indian." Marcel, a blue-eyed blond whose dad was white, stepped up. "I guess I can't play either. I'm Indian, too. These are my brothers."

The bus was the only mode of transportation the family

could afford. One time, riding with Stella and Norman, Erica noticed a group of white kids in their early teens pointing fingers and sniggering, "Look at the blackies,"referring to Norm's dark complexion. As the eldest of the siblings at home, Erica was not inclined to back down from anything. "Watch what you say about my parents, otherwise you'll be dealing with me," she hissed. The kids shut up. It was the first but not the last time she was prepared to fight for her parents and her brothers.

In 1986, Stella and Erica fell in love with a big white house on Avenue H, which ran north-south, crossing the major downtown roads, 20th, 22nd and 33rd streets. It was an older home, with a refined feel, and both Stella and Erica were thrilled at the thought of cooking family meals in the huge kitchen. The house, so different from the boxy, small, suburban places in which many of Saskatoon's native families lived, seduced them away from the relative quiet of the north end. The house struck Stella as somehow noble, and she managed to

ignore the reason it was so affordable. To any long-time resident of Saskatoon, the address provided an indelible code.

The South Saskatchewan River carves the city in half. On
the west side, the avenues are identified by the letters of the
alphabet, on the east side, by numbers. None of Saskatoon's
elite families lived on avenues A to Z; these alphabet streets
predominantly housed the working poor, with a high population of urban Indians. Numbered streets on the east bank of the
river conjured up the large, elegant homes of doctors, lawyers
and academics, sheltered beneath tall elm trees.

The house on Avenue H was also close to a notorious
stretch of downtown, 20th Street West, a strip of wretched
hotels, beer parlours and pool rooms, street punks, hustlers and
prostitutes. Stella focused instead on its proximity to jobs and
the downtown shopping core, but by moving her family to
Avenue H she brought her kids close to the seedy life she had
come to Saskatoon to escape. It didn't take them long to find it.

Erica and Marcel went off to high school. Neil and Jake
attended Westmount Community School, Neil in grade seven
and his little brother two grades behind him. Almost immediately a tough guy named Jeffrey Crowe challenged Neil to a
fight, and in the middle of the fray pulled a knife. Neil got the
better of him, took the knife away and threw it in a garbage
can. In the mysterious way of boys, Neil and Jeff became
inseparable.

Stella's kids initially stayed close to home and observed her
rules, including no alcohol in the house and certainly no drugs.
Neil even joined army cadets. But many of their peers roamed
the streets late into the evening, occasionally breaking into a car
or an unlocked house to search for a bottle of booze, or something to sell for the money to buy a bottle.

Stella caught Jake sniffing glue, and went from door to door
to find out who was giving him the stuff. Then she complained to
the police—something few native people in the city had the

courage to do. If Erica played truant, Stella would head to the downtown mall looking for her and drag her right back to school, heedless of her daughter's fierce objections. But their watchful mother couldn't be everywhere, and the boys soon became acquainted with justice at the hands of the Saskatoon Police Service. Twice during the summer they lived on Avenue H, young Jake, who was only eleven, came home exhausted and thirsty. When Stella asked him what had happened, he told her city cops had picked him up on the street and dropped him off out of town, leaving him no choice but to walk back. One of those times, he told her, the cops drove him to one of the bridges spanning the South Saskatchewan River and asked him if he wanted to swim home. Fearing they might single Jake out for even worse treatment, Stella didn't complain to the police.

The family left the big white house in 1987, because the owners were moving back in. Stella rented another place, still in the Westmount area. That's when Neil caught a break. He had begun hanging out with his friends at the nearby Cosmo Civic Centre. They would smoke outside the door to a gym where a group of young wrestlers from the Wolverine Wrestling Club practised; the gym door was usually propped open with a wooden block to let in fresh air. Occasionally Neil would poke his head into the brightly lit gym and aim a well-timed wisecrack at the athletes in their wrestling singlets, and then he and his buddies would have a good laugh.

While Neil was watching the wrestlers, one of the coaches was watching him—a tall, white-haired man named Geoff Wright, whose own sons were champion wrestlers. He was always on the lookout for new recruits; the kid with the bright eyes and the attitude looked like just the sort of boy who could get it done in the wrestling ring, if only he could get clear of the friends Wright thought were dragging him down.

One day, out in the snow for a cigarette break—he smoked to distract himself from chronic back pain—Wright went over to the kid. "Hey," he said, "I've heard you out here yakking at my guys. You seem pretty tough. They shouldn't be a problem for you, eh?"

Neil laughed good-naturedly.

Wright always moved gingerly. His back problem had forced him to take early retirement from his job at the correctional centre in the city's north end, and he was facing multiple surgeries, but nothing could keep him from coaching wrestling. And in a province that was mad for the sport, the Wolverines almost never lost a tournament.

"Well, what do you say? Why don't you join us? Show us how tough you are?"

"Yeah, right," Neil said, for the benefit of his pals, but Wright noticed him surreptitiously glancing inside, where the practice had begun.

A few days later, Neil approached him. "You know about the club, eh? I'd like to join but I can't afford it."

"Well, let's work on that," the coach said.

Within days the club had waived its fees and provided Neil with a slightly too small wrestling singlet and some shoes. Wright was so sure of Neil's potential, and so keen to get him involved, that he began picking the boy up for practice every Monday, Wednesday and Friday.

Two weeks after joining the Wolverines, fourteen-year-old Neil participated in his first tournament, in Prince Albert. Having barely learned the sport's basic moves, he found himself shaking hands before the match with a seasoned opponent. He was badly trounced in the first set, but Wright knew his new boy did not want to lose. Neil dug deep and won the match. All season long, he kept winning, turning into the Wolverines' top rookie. Even after the family moved again, to Richardson Road near the airport, Wright continued to drive Neil to and from practice.

But the "negative side," as Wright put it, still beckoned to Neil. For the whole two years Neil was wrestling, his friends kept hanging around outside the practices, drawing him out to the street. Increasingly, Wright would show up at Stella's house and Neil wouldn't be there. He urged Stella to intervene and to insist that Neil honour his commitment to the club. And he warned her that she needed to do more to counter the bad influence of Neil's friends. "Look, I'm not complaining about being involved in your son's life," he said one time, "but make sure he's here when I show up. And somebody be here when I drop him off. Or at least leave a light on for him." But insisting was not Stella's parenting style.

Neil quit the Wolverines, and soon the convictions for petty crimes began to add up. He and his friends spent their nights and weekends looking for booze and excitement. They cruised the sidewalks up and down 33rd Street close to home, trying car doors to see if they opened. A spark plug wrapped tightly with string could be easily concealed and would crack a car window with barely a sound. Car radios were simple to steal and easy to sell. By the time he turned seventeen, Neil had spent time at two youth detention centres in the city, Yarrow Farm and Kilburn Hall.

For a few years, moving to Saskatoon had looked like the best idea Stella ever had. Erica had been lured by the same temptations as her brother, but she had come through. Marcel had seemed as if he were headed for trouble, too, but luckily he'd found a construction job. He soon discovered that the thrill of a steady paycheque beat waking up with a hangover. Stella kept hoping Marcel's example would rub off on Neil and Jake. But ten years after Stella's break from Thompson, her youngest boys were plunging headlong into the life she'd travelled so far to escape.

— — —

Neil knew that once he called Pat Pickard and was picked up by the police, the courts would order him back into her care, or worse, Kilburn Hall. He was determined to have a good time on his last weekend of freedom.

Early on the afternoon of Saturday, November 24, a few days after making the promise to his mother, he headed downtown to the bus terminal, which on weekends resembled a bustling, if strange, youth centre. Teenagers, mostly natives, talked and smoked in small groups, leaning against the walls. The racket of announcements garbled over loudspeakers was constant, diesel fumes wafted through the waiting area, and there was absolutely nothing to do except scrounge together enough change to buy a cup of coffee. Regardless, local kids could always count on meeting someone they knew.

Sixteen-year-old Jason Roy, whom Neil knew from Kilburn Hall, was sipping coffee, smoking and listening to some white guy bragging about all the fights he had been in. Neil walked up and stood at the edge of their conversation. He wanted to party tonight, but had no money to buy booze, and his best friend, Jeff Crowe, was stuck in a residential alcohol rehab program as a result of his latest B and E.

Neil missed Jeff a lot. Other people couldn't understand the boys' connection, because Jeff could be a terrifying guy. Abandoned by his mother as a baby, Jeff had a harelip he tried to hide by always looking down when he spoke, and he was already a desperate alcoholic, prone to alternating rages and depressions. Only Neil seemed to know that there was much more to Jeff than his problems. Jeff dreamed of becoming an artist and drew constantly. While Neil's other friends filled their heads with AC/DC or Guns N' Roses, Jeff listened to the blues. And strangely, given his temperament, Jeff could see the humour in almost any situation. Just before he had been sent away to the rehab centre, a stray dog had chased them up Idylwyld Drive near 33rd Street as they walked home one night. They had to jump onto a huge bronze cannon to escape, and then they sat straddling it, laughing until the tears ran down their faces. Most of all, Neil valued Jeff's loyalty.

When the white guy went to the washroom, Neil and Jason started talking. They shared the same circle of friends, but they weren't close. Neil was muscular, and carried himself with the easy grace of a natural athlete. Jason perpetually slouched and was so skinny he looked like he had been smoking cigarettes and drinking coffee since birth. Playing hockey at Kilburn Hall, he chose goal so he wouldn't have to move around. Despite the trouble he was in, Neil met the eyes of the world with a confident gaze. Jason's gaze was constantly shifting, as if he always expected the worst.

They soon realized that they shared a quasi-desperado status, with Neil "unlawfully at large" and Jason in breach of his probation. They joked about being on the run, eyes roving the waiting area looking for "five-os," as they called the Saskatoon police. Playing cat and mouse with the cops entertained the boys, as much as anything. For now, Neil would keep his promise to return to Pickard's group home to himself.

They quickly decided on a party plan for Saturday night. They would have a few drinks at their friends the Binnings' house and play cards. Jason's girlfriend, Cheryl Antoine, was staying there, and it was only a two-minute walk from Neil's. Unlike at Stella's house, alcohol was overlooked at the Binnings'.

Money, however, was a different story. The boys had maybe twenty dollars between them. Holding his jacket out to hide his movements, Jason showed Neil a new pair of leather gloves, probably stolen. Neil figured he could persuade his brother, Marcel, who at nineteen was legal drinking age, to give them some cash for the gloves and maybe even go to the liquor store for them. Problem solved.

Neither boy was dressed for going outside on what was turning into one of the coldest days so far that year; Jason didn't have a hat and refused to wear the gloves, saving them for bartering. Neil was wearing the white baseball cap he was rarely seen without, but no gloves. He wore white Asics Tiger running shoes, striped blue jeans, a white T-shirt under a red-and-black-checkered flannel lumberjack shirt, and an unbuttoned and oversized blue and white jacket with a "Boys Town Cowboys" logo on the back and "Chris" stitched on the front. The jacket was a gift from his oldest brother, Dean, whose adoptive family had renamed him Chris. Now twenty-four, Dean had found his way back to Stella only in the last year. He had spent time in the U.S. Marines, and had become a hero to Neil.

The boys hopped on a bus at about quarter to three, heading for the east end to visit a buddy, Trevor Nowaselski, trading stories about girls and custody time along the way.

Jason had a way of talking that made people think he wasn't being straight with them. His speech was a stuttering, circular affair filled with false starts, long pauses and dead ends. Neil knew Jason's history from their time together at Kilburn. He was a "bingo baby" whose alcoholic parents abandoned him for days at a time to play at local halls like the Lucky Horseshoe on 20th Street. "I was an alcoholic before I was born," Jason would say. Sick of being left alone with nothing to eat, he took to the late-night streets and soon hooked up with older punks. They got the skinny little kid to crawl through narrow spaces, such as building heating ducts, to open doors for them from the inside. In dives like the Barry Hotel, they hid him under the bench seats whenever the cops showed up.

Despite his mother's role in his story, Jason brooked no criticism of Marleen. His mother, he would explain, had had an exceptionally rough life. "When she was just a teenager, she watched her aunt and her cousin get murdered. My mum was there and she was only nineteen at the time and pregnant. She got away, but she never recovered from the shock." Jason would point out that Don Worme, a native lawyer in the city, was his uncle, and had been present as a child at the murders back in the sixties. He'd avoid mentioning how much his Uncle Don seemed to dislike his mother, which puzzled Jason, and how little use Don had for the boy he regarded as his nephew— although they were in fact second cousins—and the trouble he got himself into. Jason's rap sheet already ran to several pages and included a substantial number of serious B and E's and thefts.

Though he liked hanging out with Jason and Trevor, talking about his time in Kilburn Hall depressed Neil. He was almost surely headed back there once he turned himself in to Pickard. He vividly remembered his three-metre-square room, furnished with a metal bed and a small wooden desk for school work. The walls were covered with graffiti and the badly scratched Plexiglas in the single window clouded his view of the outside world.

Unlike Jeff, whose anger exploded into manic fits of head-banging, Neil had never acted out enough to be dumped into one of the more spartan cells: only a metal toilet in one corner and a concrete bed with a thin plastic mattress. He never got strapped into the restraining devices or locked in the small room the authorities kept under constant video surveillance. Still, he hated the place.

To Neil's relief, after an hour or so they left Trevor and caught a bus back across the bridge to the west side. They got off at the "Sev" (7-Eleven) near Pendygrasse Road. By now it was close to five, and with the winter darkness and temperature falling they were both freezing. They quickly caught another bus.

The boys shared in some common rites. They never wore winter boots, no matter the temperature, nor how deep the snow, and they always rode in groups at the back of the bus—and Neil and Jason found themselves taking a seat beside Gary Horse. In the last few months, Gary had begun seeing Neil's former girl-friend, Lucille Neetz. Gary was as handsome and athletic-looking as Neil, but he had stopped drinking, and had sworn off the petty thefts everyone else resorted to in order to buy their booze.

A couple of stops further, at Confederation Mall, Lucille got on.

Neil had been fifteen and Lucille only thirteen when they went out; their parents had put an end to it because the two were second cousins. Neil still carried her picture in his wallet, even though the inscription on the back was not romantic. "To Neil," she had written, "from Cousin Lucille Neetz." Only Jeff Crowe knew that Neil was still hung up on Lucille.

Jason began trying to recruit Gary and Lucille to the party. "Can't," said Gary.

"Why not? What's up?" Jason asked.

"Babysitting."

Jason thought Gary was joking, but Neil asked, "Where?"

Gary and Lucille did not want these two showing up at their door. But finally they admitted they were going to be at the apartment of Lucille's sister, Claudine. Jason and Neil both knew Claudine lived with a white guy named Trent Ewart at the Snowberry Downs apartment complex, about a ten-minute walk north of the Binnings'. The complex was built roughly in the shape of a cross, on the northwest corner of Confederation Drive and 33rd Street, directly across from another Sev.

The bus pulled up at the stop a few metres from the Binnings' front door, just around the corner from Neil's home at 38 Confederation Crescent. Neil and Jason jumped off and watched the bus disappear up Confederation Drive into the night, with Gary and Lucille lit up in the window against the darkening sky. Brooding about Lucille, Neil headed home to see if Marcel would help them buy a bottle.

— — —

As Neil let himself into the kitchen that evening, Stella was at the kitchen table drinking tea with her sister, Debbie. The two were close; a few years after Stella moved, Debbie and her husband, Jerry Mason, had followed her to Saskatoon, where they now lived. Stella and Debbie talked on the phone every day and visited at least twice a week. Jerry and the kids were in the living room with Norman and Marcel. At the big family gatherings, Christmas, Easter, Thanksgiving, Neil's job was to keep his little cousins entertained, which he did with ease.

With so many people in the house, he couldn't approach Marcel about the gloves. But when Neil found out that his mother would be leaving soon to play bingo, he decided not to go far.

Stella fussed when she heard Neil was planning to go out again. "It's going to storm tonight."

"I won't be far away, Mum. C'mon, I'm just up the street. We're gonna play cards and listen to some tunes."

His Aunt Debbie got on his case, too, and Neil teased them for worrying about him, but Stella grew serious. "Don't go out, Neil," she said again.

"Mum, I just want to be out one last night, but I'll be home." Then he leaned toward her and said, softly, so no one but she could hear. "I've made peace with myself. I'm ready to move on now."

With that, he grabbed his blue and white jacket, brushed his black shoulder-length hair back off his face, and pulled on his white ball cap. He hugged his aunt and gave his mum a good squeeze, and was out the door.

A short time later, when Stella had left for bingo and the coast was clear, the boys returned. Leaving Jason at the door, Neil offered Marcel the few dollars they had managed to pool. Marcel balked. "You're short, bro."

So Neil tried to score twenty bucks from his stepfather. A bear of a man, Norman was actually a soft touch, and the Stonechild boys loved him.

Going into the bedroom, he reached up to a Christmas stocking pinned above the bed. He'd hidden a hundred dollars in it to buy gifts for the family. When he pulled the stocking down, it was completely empty. Norman laughed. Stella had found his secret stash and emptied it for her night at bingo.

Neil still had the leather gloves and he held them out to Marcel. His brother knew at a glance that they weren't cheap. He offered to get them a bottle of Silent Sam vodka. He'd even walk to the liquor store and drop it off at the Binnings'. The boys were set for the night.

— — —

That Saturday night, nothing seemed more perfect to Neil Stonechild than playing cards with his friends, with a bottle of Silent Sam. But the promise he'd made his mum was on his mind, and he knew he couldn't relax until he called Pat Pickard. If he didn't call her now, he might lose his nerve. Around seven-thirty, he finally dialled her number.

"I know I should have called you sooner," he said when she

picked up. "But I am calling to sort things out, Pat. I wanna turn myself in."

Pickard offered to pick him up immediately.

He hesitated, breathing into the receiver, mulling it over. He wasn't ready yet. And he couldn't go to the police station that night because he'd already been drinking.

Pickard assured him that he wouldn't spend a day in jail if he turned himself in to her right away. If he stayed out and got blitzed instead, he would likely get himself into a lot more trouble.

"I promised my mother I would turn myself in to you tomorrow," Neil said, "and I will. I'll phone you when I get up and you can pick me up. Then we'll go down to see the cops."

He hung up. He had promised his mum, he had promised Pat.

— — —

By ten-thirty that night Neil and Jason had drunk most of their Silent Sam. Neil stood in his T-shirt, jeans and sock feet in the washroom, leaning on the sink. In the mirror he could see the muscles in his arms and the blue-ink tattoo of his initials crudely drawn between his right thumb and forefinger. He had given himself that tattoo in Kilburn.

The Binnings' place was an oasis for Neil and the others, Eddie Rushton, Julie "Jo" Binning and her sisters, and Jason's girlfriend, Cheryl. Mrs. Binning never minded that her kitchen was like a social club for teens, with people coming and going and always a card game at the table. The living room overflowed with plants, and people often crashed in the partially finished basement, creating makeshift bedrooms with blanket walls.

Suddenly the volume of the stereo got cranked up, and the Guns N' Roses anthem "Sweet Child of Mine" blasted through the place. The song had been on an endless loop as the kids played cards and drank vodka coloured now and then with a splash of Tang. Axel Rose's plaintive lyrics about "childhood memories" and the "special place" a woman's smile can take you to always reminded Neil of Lucille.

The volume dropped, just as Neil opened the bathroom door. Flora, one of the Binning girls, had convinced them to turn the music down so they wouldn't wake her two-month-old baby, who was sleeping in her arms as she watched TV in the living room.

In the bathroom, Neil had decided to go find Lucille. But he wanted someone to go with him, and so he headed down the basement stairs to get Jason. Jason wasn't keen to go looking for Lucille, but he agreed to tag along—maybe they'd get a chance to do a B and E for more booze.

As they stood for a moment, hunched in the dark on the front steps, gloveless hands plunged in their pockets, and breathing in sharp, short gasps of brutally cold air, someone closed the door behind them, saying, "Don't forget to get some munchies."

— — —

Soft-spoken and perpetually red-faced, Constable Brad Senger had worked as a mechanic and as a psychiatric nurse for adolescents before joining the Saskatoon Police Service. Now he was a rookie cop, newly graduated from the police academy in Regina and still in his probationary period, working as the duty desk's dogsbody. He filled in for officers in communications and detention, did lunch and coffee relief at the front desk, went wherever he was needed.

About ten o'clock on the night of November 24, 1990, Senger was riding as a passenger in Cruiser 38 with Constable Larry Hartwig, patrolling District 8, Saskatoon's rough-and-tumble west end. Hartwig was without a partner at the moment. His regular riding buddy, Ken Munson, had just been seconded to Project Combo, a major investigation into B and E's across the city.

Only three years on the force himself, Hartwig was a lean and swaggering five feet seven inches and 140 pounds, and he had a way of constantly getting in people's faces. His slight stature seemed to give him something to prove. Hartwig's feisty temperament was married to deeply held Christian beliefs, and he could come across as fierce as a Baptist preacher.

District 8 ran from 22nd Street North to the edge of town, and from Circle Drive west to the city limits. On Saturday nights, the cops rounded up men, women and children involved in beatings, stabbings, domestic disputes, prostitution, theft, drugs, liquor law violations and illegal guns until the city jails were filled to standing room only. Most of the people they charged were aboriginal. Policing the west end was mind-numbingly repetitive. A cop would pick a drunk out of a back alley and throw him into the drunk tank, only to return the next week to find the same drunk sprawled in the same alley.

In the face of such work, morale among the 350 or so rank-and-file members of the Saskatoon police wasn't much to speak of, and had kept dropping like a stone since Joseph Penkala became chief in 1982. A thin, distinguished-looking officer with ramrod-straight posture, Penkala was a protégé of former chief James Kettles, who, despite notoriously poor people skills and a penchant for not looking others in the eye, had run the force with an iron hand from 1953 until 1977. Penkala had been an investigator at the crime scene after the murder of nurse's aide Gail Miller in the winter of 1969. As the chief of police he was now facing increasing pressure and questions about his handling of crime scene samples that had led to the conviction of David Milgaard for the murder a year later.

By 1990, members of the force had been raging publicly for years about excessive workloads and Penkala's fetish for paper-work and for spit and polish. Working cops complained that their bosses were more worried about the press of a uniform or the shine on their officers' shoes than about their performance in a frequently dangerous job. Officers could be called on the carpet for something as trivial as not wearing their hats while responding to the most urgent and horrifying of traffic accidents.

Nobody had come to him about a morale problem, Penkala insisted to the media, and if one existed, then the officers involved should just suck it up. "When you look at the people who cry about stress, they're in debt, they have spousal problems, they're separated, divorced or they're up to their ears in alimony. You can't have a wife and a girlfriend and expect things to go smoothly," he declared.

Penkala spoke with the officiousness of a born bureaucrat, and that was how he led. He prided himself on never having a deficit budget. And while city police elsewhere were confronting racism and diversity in their own ranks, policing remained status quo in Saskatoon.

— — —

Jason began swearing about the cold as soon as the Binnings' front door slammed behind them. Both boys slurred their words and swayed on their feet as they walked north up Confederation Drive, chins tucked to chests, hands jammed in pockets. The wind made tears run down their cheeks.

They went into the 7-Eleven on the southwest corner of Confederation and 33rd Street, right across the road from Neil's destination, the Snowberry Downs apartments, so Jason would shut up about being cold. Open twenty-four hours a day, seven days a week, 7-Elevens across the city served native teens with a buck or two in their pockets a diet of subs, slushies, Joe Louis and coffee they could doctor with unlimited sugar and cream.

Jason and Neil had no money. But there were lots of other kids in the store that night, so the boys tried to make themselves inconspicuous as they hovered near one of the potato chip racks at the back of the store, stuffing their faces and sneaking sips from a pop can. They might have escaped notice, but they started horsing around and shoving each other, knocking some things off the shelves.

Alerted by the commotion, the clerk shouted from the front cash for them to quiet down. Drunk, the boys shouted back. When the clerk threatened to call the cops, Neil and Jason took off.

They sprinted across 33rd, deserted that night because of the cold, and into the parking lot of Snowberry Downs, where they crouched in the shadow of a truck, every quick breath roaring in their ears.

Jason stayed crouched, worried that the clerk had recognized them. Ignoring him, Neil got up and headed toward the entrance to one of the apartment buildings. He was going to find Lucille. Reluctantly, Jason followed.

Inside the front foyer they looked for the names Neetz or Ewart on the residents' list, and when they didn't find either one, they pressed buttons at random, hoping someone would buzz them in. They tried the same tactic in a second foyer and then a third, but no one opened the doors.

Frustrated, they stood in the parking lot, wondering what to do next. Jason wanted to go back to the Binnings'. He was tired and his buzz was wearing off and this wasn't much fun. But Neil refused to give up.

"Fuck it," Jason said. "I'm fuckin' freezing. My fuckin' feet."

"Screw you then. I don't need you to find her anyway."

"Okay, fine."

As Jason turned to leave, he looked over his shoulder. Neil was crossing the tennis court between two of the buildings to try the apartment buzzers again. Jason changed his mind, in part because he didn't want to abandon his friend, but also because he really did not want to walk back alone.

"Hey, wait up," Jason yelled. "I'll come with you."

"Fuck you," said Neil, continuing to walk.

"It's okay, I'm coming, too." Neil broke into a run and Jason tried to do the same, but tripped on a snow-covered cement curb and fell face first. When he sat up, Neil was gone.

— — —

Neil's cousin, Bruce Genaille, also lived in Snowberry Downs. Sometime before eleven that night, after his wife had returned home from the first evening bingo session, he seized the opportunity to go out. He wanted to have a few drinks, maybe play some cards at a friend's place a short walk down the street.

Just after he passed the 7-Eleven, Hartwig and Senger's police cruiser pulled to a stop beside him. He had been walking for about five minutes.

He kept walking.

Behind him he heard one of the cops shout, "Neil, come here. Neil Stonechild?"

This had happened to him before. Though he was a few years older than his cousin, he and Neil looked so much alike that even friends sometimes got them confused.

Genaille stopped and turned, avoiding making eye contact with the two cops. His eyes settled on the empty back seat of the cruiser.

Neil was his cousin, he explained. "I call him Harry."

Hartwig and Senger insisted on seeing some ID, and Genaille handed over his driver's licence. They grilled him for several minutes more to make sure he wasn't Neil. Genaille became so flustered he couldn't tell whether or not they punched his name into the cruiser's mobile computer terminal.

He summoned enough courage to ask why they were looking for his cousin. They would only say that Neil was wanted for a disturbance at the 7-Eleven.

Finally they let him go. When he arrived at his friend's place, he cracked open a beer and wondered, "What's Harry got into this time?"

— — —

Trent Ewart was in a foul mood when he got back to his apartment, around eleven-thirty. He and Claudine had fought at the bar, and she'd gone off to drink with someone else. If recent history was any indication, she probably wouldn't be home that night. Ewart didn't feel much like partying after their argument, and had decided to come home, even though Claudine's little sister Lucille and her boyfriend were there minding Claudine's kids.

No sooner had he let himself into apartment 306 than the buzzer sounded behind him. He pushed the button to find out who was there and heard a male voice, thick with alcohol, asking to be buzzed up. Trent told the guy he had the wrong place.

He had taken off his coat and was untying his shoes, when someone opened the apartment door behind him. Trent bolted upright and saw a native teenager, about seventeen or so, gently swaying in his doorway. The kid was drunk and not any kind of a threat, but Ewart still laid on his heavy voice to ask the boy what in hell did he think he was doing. The kid mumbled something about a party.

Ewart said firmly, "There's no party here, buddy, get lost." He grabbed the boy's shoulder, spun him around and pushed him out the door. The stranger did not resist; in fact, he apologized.

"Sorry, dude."

"Get out of here, before I call the cops," Ewart said.

As Ewart was locking the door, Lucille and Gary came up behind him, curious about the noise. For a moment the three of them listened as the drunk pounded loudly on nearby doors. He was soon knocking on theirs again.

Lucille had a feeling it was Neil. He was the last thing she needed. She asked Gary to check through the peephole. Yes, he said, it was Neil.

"I don't understand how he found us. We didn't give him the apartment number," Lucille said. He must have been wandering from floor to floor knocking on everyone's door. Lucille peeked at Neil and backed up. His eyes were red-rimmed and seemed smaller than usual. He kept knocking.

Ewart pushed his way to the peephole. "Shit, man, that's the same guy who was just here."

"Call the cops before he does something," Lucille whispered, so Neil wouldn't hear her voice. "I know he's wanted. They'll pick him up and stop him from getting into real trouble."

Trent Ewart, a white guy, had no fear of calling the police. Lucille, on the other hand, was mildly panicked that he was actually going to do what she had suggested.

"I don't want Neil to know that I told you guys to call the cops," she said. "Promise me you won't tell the cops it was me."

— — —

At 11:51 p.m. a dispatch order flashed on the mobile terminal screen in Hartwig and Senger's cruiser. The terminals had been installed within the last year, and allowed cops to perform computer-assisted criminal-record checks in the field.

As Hartwig drove, Senger relayed the information to his partner. They had a 10–25, cop code for a drunk who needed to be removed, at number 306–3308 33rd. The caller said it was Neil Stonechild, the same kid they were looking for when they stopped Bruce Genaille. Senger pressed the "en route" button.

He punched "at scene" into the terminal, meaning they had reached Snowberry Downs. He indicated the time was 11:56.

— — —

On his way back to the Binnings', a very cold Jason Roy shuffled along, watching his feet, his slowly sobering mind a blank. The wind was at his back, but it felt even colder than before.

He was on the west side of the street about halfway back to the Binnings'. An apartment complex called Twin Gables was just ahead of him. Out of nowhere, a sound like breaking branches startled him. He looked up. A police cruiser rolled forward out of a darkened lane, one in a maze of driveways leading to houses behind the 7-Eleven.

The cruiser stopped, straddling the sidewalk and blocking his path. Neil was in the back seat, leaning awkwardly to one side, his face pressed against the closed window. He must have his hands cuffed, Jason thought. Neil's face was bloody, and he was shouting something that Jason couldn't hear.

Jason's mind raced. The cops had Neil and they would be carting him off to Kilburn Hall now. If Jason wasn't careful, he would be going along for the ride.

The driver's side window lowered. Jason heard Neil shout "Jay" and then scream that the cops were going to kill him. He begged Jason to identify himself.

"Do you know this guy?" one of the cops asked as Neil continued to yell.

Jason denied it. When they asked, he gave the officers a false name.

"Tracy Horse," he said, without missing a beat, and added a birth date. Tracy Horse was Jason's cousin, and he wasn't in trouble with the police. Jason had memorized Tracy's personal information in case of a fix just like this. The cop in the passenger seat punched the name into the terminal. 11:56. It was the same time Senger had earlier indicated they arrived at the scene of the Snowberry Downs disturbance.

Neil had stopped yelling.

Not to be tricked, the cops asked Jason for a middle name.

"Lee," he said. "Tracy Lee Horse." The cops punched the information into their computers a second time. When nothing came up, they let him go.

The cruiser pulled out onto Confederation Drive. Looking scared and angry, Neil twisted around to stare at Jason out the back window as it headed south.

By the time Jason made it back to the Binnings' house, everyone seemed to have gone to sleep. He knocked and finally Flora, barely awake, opened the door. Exhausted, he went downstairs to where his girlfriend was sleeping. He felt like he was going to pass out. He didn't turn on the light, just sat on the edge of the bed taking off his clothes. Sleepily, Cheryl asked why he had been gone so long.

"Neil and me got separated," he said. "He got picked up by the cops." He said nothing about seeing Neil handcuffed, his face bloodied, screaming that the police were going to kill him. Jason just wanted to sleep.

Cheryl soon dropped off again, too. Hearing that a friend had been picked up by the police was a fact of life. Nothing more than that.

— — —

Neil woke up lying on his stomach, his head cradled in his arms. When he lifted his hands, snow as fine as dust sifted through his ungloved fingers. He did not know where he was, how he got there or how long he had been unconscious. He had fallen into some kind of ditch.

His breathing slowed, becoming shallower with each passing minute. His muscles seemed to have lost their connection to his will. Trying to get to his feet, he finally managed to turn over.

The clouds from earlier in the evening had vanished. Thousands of stars pierced the night sky. Although the wind was light, the temperature had dropped to minus twenty-eight degrees Celsius. Neil did not feel the cold; he'd stopped shivering a while ago. He was drunk, the front of his face hurt and he was outside.

He staggered to his feet. He walked only two metres or so, stumbling along the footprints he'd left when he'd come out here. He swayed where he stood for a few seconds and then collapsed, pitching forward in the snow on his right side. A short time passed. He drew his left knee up slightly, and then was still.

THE INVESTIGATION

PAT PICKARD PRIDED HERSELF ON KNOWING "her boys," especially Neil. She'd developed a strong connection with him in the few months he'd been at the group home. He'd made a promise to her—and more importantly, to his mother—and Pat believed he would keep it. So why hadn't he called?

She waited through lunch, sitting at her kitchen table, smoking one cigarette after another and making excuses for him. He'd said he'd have one last party, and so he was probably sleeping it off. Maybe he was having a late lunch with his family. If he really wanted to remain AWOL, then surely he'd never have phoned in the first place. She slipped another cigarette from her pack and lit it off the dying glow of the last one. As the day wore on, she could no longer distinguish between her irritation at herself for believing Neil's promise and her disappointment that she wouldn't have the bright young man back in the house.

Across town, Stella sat at her own kitchen table, becoming grumpier by the minute, and he hadn't yet shown up. Her son's bed had not been slept in Saturday night. Early in the afternoon she asked Marcel to walk over to the Binnings' place to fetch Neil. Marcel had been over there around ten-thirty the night before to check up on his younger brother, but had just missed him leaving with Jason Roy. Going back on Sunday afternoon, Marcel wasn't surprised to be told that Neil had been scooped by the cops.

When Stella checked with the police station, the woman who answered her call told Stella that a car had been sent to pick up Neil the night before. She patched Stella's call through to the holding cells, but the officer there told her they had no Neil Stonechild in custody. Just to be sure, Marcel called too, only to be told the same thing.

Stella thought that maybe Neil had gone out of town with his friend Regis Gamble to visit a reserve. Marcel was growing increasingly anxious. Something didn't feel right, but he couldn't bear to worry his mother further by saying so.

On Tuesday, Stella returned home in the late-afternoon darkness from her shift in the maintenance department at Eaton's. As she walked through the door, she hoped more than anything to see her Harry sitting at the white kitchen table. But Neil wasn't there, and the disappointment hit her hard.

To stay busy, Stella made a pot of tea and sorted through Neil's wrestling medals, which she piled on the tabletop. Since he'd disappeared she'd had trouble concentrating. Now, as she sat alone, her thoughts drifted back to her boy's triumphs as a wrestler, to when his coaches told her he could be a champion.

Stella could never afford to make the trips to the out-of-town matches, but she loved the stories. After Neil's first match, in Prince Albert, he had told her how he'd made mistake after mistake, falling behind 5–1 in the first three-minute half. At the break he returned to his corner inconsolable. He swore. Tears streamed down his face. His coach bent down inches from his face.

"It's there, Neil. If you want it, it's there. Just go out there and be yourself.

"Let's go. Let's wrestle. Let's get it done," Coach Wright yelled as the whistle went to start the second half, and Neil walked to the centre of the ring. He leaned into his opponent. Most young wrestlers flinch at the intimate contact, but Neil was willing to press fiercely into his opponent's body, fighting for control of the match. Freestyle wrestling demands the mental toughness to battle one on one, and the will to dominate your opponent no matter how much you are hurting. Neil clawed his way back in a few minutes to do exactly that. He celebrated by reaching his arms skyward in victory, comically having to reach down with one hand to pull his undersized singlet out from where it was wedged in his crotch. Coach Wright told Stella that when Neil won it was as though the whole club had won.

Another time he had arrived home from a tournament with his ribs heavily bandaged. Wright could not believe what had happened. On all fours in a defensive position against an older, more experienced opponent, Neil had been trapped in a move called a "gut wrench." The older boy leaned over Neil's back, fists locked around his chest, cranking tighter and tighter, trying to flip him on his back. Neil refused to be turned, but he lost on points. Later he had trouble breathing, so they brought him to the emergency room. X-rays showed breaks in two ribs.

Stella shook her head. How did a boy like that simply go missing?

She was at her wits' end. Neil had not been picked up by the cops this time. Maybe he had gotten into some kind of other trouble. Usually he was too smart for that, but only a few months ago, he had been caught in a really bad scene.

Just after dawn on the morning of August 10, Stella awoke to find Neil standing beside her bed dressed in someone else's clothes, an oversized T-shirt and jeans so big around the waist he had to hold them up with one hand. His entire body trembled and he had a bruise over one eye.

For the next half hour a bizarre, disjointed story poured out of him. Half-crying, he told his mother how he and some friends had done a B and E in the neighbourhood a few days earlier, looking for booze. By accident, they came across a cache of automatic weapons, including some rifles with high-powered scopes, among them a Lee-Enfield, a Ruger semi-automatic and a Winchester. Unable to resist, they took the guns, fantasizing about selling them for large amounts of cash. Neil told her how he had stupidly refused to listen to Jeff Crowe, who had warned him to stay away from anything to do with stolen guns. The boys stored the rifles in Eddie Rushton's basement, and they made the mistake of showing them to Gary Pratt while they were drinking.

Stella knew Eddie Rushton. He was older than Neil, one of Marcel's friends. Eddie was always being arrested for one petty crime or another. As for Gary Pratt, he and his brothers were notorious in the neighbourhood; rumours linked them to everything from prostitution to weapons to drugs.

Gary wanted the guns, but he didn't want to pay. He and Neil argued. Gary left but came back later with his brothers. Neil came out of the bedroom where he was sleeping and walked into the middle of a fight. The Pratts beat Eddie up and threw him down the stairs. In the chaos, Neil got knocked out by a hard whack to the head with the butt end of a shotgun. When he came to he didn't stick around. Wearing only his underwear, he wrapped a sleeping bag around his shoulders and ran to his sister Erica's house, where he grabbed some clothes and came home.

Stella had hugged Neil tightly. He talked about turning his life around. He said he was going to join wrestling again when he went to high school in the fall. Stella had used her deeply held Christian faith to beat back her own demons years before. On that August morning, she encouraged Neil to trust in the Lord along with her, the way he used to. Gradually, he calmed down.

Stella's tea was now cold.

"Where are you, Harry?" she asked herself for the thousandth time since Saturday night. She stared at the old-fashioned wooden clock on the wall, but she was too distracted to notice the time.

Stella ran her fingertips along a gold medal Neil had won wrestling. She waited. Any minute now the kitchen door could fly open behind her, and Neil would race forward and wrap her in his arms.

— — —

Jason Roy was keeping a low profile. He and Cheryl had left the Binnings' after the weekend party. If Neil was in custody, most likely at Kilburn Hall, the cops would be searching for Jason, too. Cheryl was renting a basement suite from her friend Dinah Sunshine at a house on Avenue P. He hung out there and stayed off the streets.

Marcel asked around the neighbourhood for Jason, wanting to talk to him about Neil getting scooped, but couldn't find him. Marcel phoned other friends about his brother. Nobody had seen Neil, and no one had a clue about what had happened to him.

— — —

At nine in the morning on Thursday, November 29, two labourers in a gravel parking lot on the northern outskirts of Saskatoon were getting their tractor ready for a job. This remote industrial section of the city was home to little more than a few warehouses scattered across snow-covered prairie fields.

Richard Harms and his partner Bruce Meyers were there to dig post holes for a new chain-link fence behind a partially finished ambulance garage. The only other structures nearby were the Good Host Foods building, to the west of where they were setting up their guide lines, and the Hitachi warehouse across the field to the north.

Grey clouds filled the sky, but the cold snap of the last week had broken. Harms clambered high up into the tractor's cab, and felt the mild air brush his weather-beaten face. Looking over his shoulder, he backed up to begin levelling the area. A dark object in the field about forty metres to the north captured his attention. It seemed both ordinary and entirely out of place.

At one point, the two had convinced themselves they were looking at a discarded snowmobile cover. Despite their curiosity, they didn't approach the object for several hours.

"Go have a look," Harms finally said to Meyers after lunch.

The November sun pushed Meyers's long shadow toward the dark shape as he approached. When he was just a few metres away, he stopped.

— — —

Constable Brad Senger, working the dispatch desk, picked up Harms's call about the body in the field, and sent Constable René Lagimodiere to the scene. Lagimodiere, a sixteen-year veteran with the force, talked briefly to Harms and Meyers. Several fresh footprints led almost up to where the victim lay, contaminating the scene. Slightly embarrassed, they explained that other men in the neighbouring building had taken a look. Then Lagimodiere walked into the field directly toward the body.

He reached down and touched the figure. It was frozen solid. He stood up and took some notes.

The body was lying face down on its right side with the left arm bent and tucked underneath, and the left knee slightly bent. He was wearing faded striped jeans and a blue jacket with a "Boys Town Cowboys" crest on the back and two white chevrons on the left upper arm. Under that was a red-and-black-checked lumberjack shirt. A running shoe remained on the left foot, but the other shoe was missing and the right foot was covered by only a white sock.

A single set of footprints that seemed to be several days old came from the south and went past the body, ending in a ditch several metres to the north. It looked as though whoever it was had stumbled and rolled about in the snow there, and then retraced his steps to where he fell a final time. The constable guessed he was looking at the body of a male native who had been there for a while.

Lagimodiere's primary job, as far as he was concerned, was to secure the scene. The older footprints began at the edge of the parking lot, but he didn't follow them to determine where they originated and he did not look for the missing shoe—he would leave the investigating to others. But he did wonder how a person could have ended up in such a remote area of the city missing one shoe, without either hat or gloves.

Six minutes after arriving at the scene, Lagimodiere called dispatch to send out the coroner and the Identification team.

— — —

Although he often boasted about his efficiency as a coroner, Dr. Brian Fern had a habit, when taking a call about a new case, of scribbling notes on whatever paper was at hand, even a prescription pad. So when the Saskatoon police phoned his east-end office at 1 p.m. on November 29 to inform him of a sudden death in the north end, he grabbed a loose sheet of white paper and began writing.

A thin man with bird-like mannerisms, Fern first became a coroner in 1967, five years after immigrating to Canada from Manchester, England, with a medical degree. He started in a small Saskatchewan community that was in desperate need of a coroner following an accident, and then moved to Saskatoon. During the next twenty years, he received no special training as a coroner.

Fern's note from the call consisted of eleven lines. After the date, he noted the source of the call, the time and the address—57th Street in Saskatoon's north end, and then he wrote "NAI"—North American Indian.

Fern continued to capitalize his words as he wrote the next lines:

Face Down in Field behind new construction.
Body Frozen
About 30
Hands withdrawn in jacket.
Boystown. Craig. [Fern wrote the wrong name in his note; it should have read "Chris."]
Rt. Shoe Missing. Snow in Rt Shoe and Up Pant Leg.
Had Prob Fallen in Ditch.
No other injury—or ID.

The Identification team—Sergeant Bob Morton and Constable John Middleton—got there about ten minutes ahead of the coroner and began videotaping the scene.

Morton began, as usual, with a long establishing shot of the snow-covered field, with the body in the distance. His shot pans slowly from left to right and his long shadow intrudes on the frame. A low-rise lime-green building with large red letters spelling "Hitachi" bounds the field to the north, along with a few power lines. Here and there, brown earth shows through where the snow has melted. By the time Morton began taking his video the temperature had risen to nearly three degrees Celsius. Richard Harms had gone back to digging fence-post holes, busily driving his red and white forklift back and forth.

The shadows of two men—perhaps Lagimodiere and patrol officer Michael Petty, who joined the group—move across the whiteness of the snow. Tufts of prairie grass poke through, and the afternoon sky has by now turned a brilliant blue.

At 1:54 Morton moved in for a close-up of the dead body sprawled face down in the snow.

Like Lagimodiere, he noticed the blue jeans, the red-and-black lumberjack shirt and the blue jacket. Morton took special notice of the feet, including their condition, in his report.

On his left foot was a running shoe by the make of Asics Tiger. The running shoe was on the foot, the laces were undone and there was a white sport sock with a red trim on it on the foot. The right running shoe was completely missing. The only thing on the foot was a white sport sock with red stripes on the top. The sock was pulled down and bunched at the toe in a fashion that would indicate he had been walking with just his sock foot. The heel area of the sock was completely worn out and visible on the actual heel of the body was what appeared to be dirt etc, which left me to believe that he had been walking for some time without a running shoe on that foot.

By this point Dr. Fern was waiting to examine the body, so Morton shut off his camera.

From the frozen state of the body, and from the way the tracks were slightly blown over with crystallized snow, Fern believed that the man had been there for several days.

As Fern considered the missing shoe, he could hear the officers talking about the identity of the body. He thought he

OFFICE PHONE   RES PHONE
374-6904/374-8465   374-8465
BRIAN J. FERN, M.B., Ch.B., D.R.C.O.G.
PHYSICIAN AND SURGEON
3333 - 8TH ST. EAST   CKOM BLDG.   SASKATOON, Sask. S7H 0W3

For ...... *NEAL CHRISTOPHER STONE ECHILD*

Date ...... *24 Aug 1973*

℞   *Age 17.*
     Arrested 3 am late October.
     Young offender AWOL
     Kilburn Hall, missing

heard one of the officers say he knew him. The words "young offender" stuck in his mind, but the rest of the conversation barely registered, occupied as he was with his examination.

The officers looked briefly for the running shoe in the deeper snow where the boy had collapsed his second and final time, and they scanned the immediate vicinity. Seeing nothing, they gave up. Petty suggested bringing in the canine unit to have a dog work the area, and Lagimodiere made the call.

"Let's get some help here," said the coroner, indicating he wanted the body turned over. As they moved forward Morton and Lagimodiere had no idea that television crews, which by now had set up at a distance, had focused their high-power camera lenses closely on the body. The men rolled it over. It looked as though they were flipping the frozen carcass of a dead animal.

Fern checked for obvious wounds, but found nothing. The person's arms were collapsed together against his chest, hands tucked into his sleeves as if he were trying to keep them warm.

Morton called Fern's attention to two scratches across the bridge of the nose and a cut to the lower lip. Fern felt the marks were not serious. He said they could not have caused the death and could easily have come from falling face down.

Despite the cuts on the face, no one called the crime lab for an analysis. And despite the fact that somehow the young person had got to a remote location with no apparent means of transport, poorly dressed for the weather and wearing only one shoe, the men concluded there were no signs of foul play.

As they trampled the snow that surrounded the body, no one suggested that they might be handling a crime scene. Nor did anyone at the station, to whom they spoke by telephone, raise this possibility.

A half hour after arriving, Fern left. He arranged for an ambulance to transport the body to St. Paul's Hospital on 20th Street West.

After the coroner's departure, Morton turned on his camera again. It was 15:03, according to the camera's time code, and the area around the body was now a sea of tracks. He zooms in on the right foot, the one missing the shoe. Like a bad joke, or an indictment of the desultory investigation, the camera stares intently at the white sock with the gaping hole in the heel and the soiled skin where the fabric has worn away. The camera zooms in so close that the foot takes up the entire frame. At 15:05 the camera is switched off.

The tracking dog, Bear, arrived shortly after the ambulance took the body away. Following his handler's hand signals, Bear searched into the wind. He was trained to look for large articles with a human scent, or with a scent that seemed out of place, but the only fresh human scent belonged to the police and to witnesses who had approached the body. There was no hope that the dog could follow the footprints to their source. Still, Bear searched with enthusiasm for the next fifteen minutes, then returned to his master. The dog had found nothing. None of the police officers at the scene searched any further for the missing shoe.

— — —

Eyes shut as if against the glare from the bright lights above, the frozen body lay on its back on the long stainless steel autopsy table, the dark-haired head supported by a rubber prop. The gleaming table dominated the centre of the room. Above it hung a mechanical hoist and a metal scale for weighing organs. Large plastic vats of formaldehyde and small jars of miscellaneous organs lined the green-tiled walls. The room smelled as clean as a freshly scrubbed kitchen.

With Morton and Middleton looking on, pathologist Dr. Jack Adolph noted two parallel abrasions running horizontally across the middle of the subject's nose. To Adolph, with the experience of several thousand autopsies behind him, they appeared superficial, nothing that would cause death. He did his best to straighten the body's flexed arm, but couldn't. It was too frozen. The autopsy would have to wait until the next day.

But first Morton insisted on seizing the clothes and searching them for ID, so Adolph jotted down an inventory for his autopsy report. He had difficulty removing the blue jacket, the lumberjack shirt and the T-shirt. Morton looked through the pockets of both jackets as they were removed. In the padded lumberjack shirt he found a small vial of Hero cologne.

When they took off the left shoe and the two white socks, they saw a single small stone frozen to the outside of the left sock. Adolph wrote, "When the shoe was removed there was a flat stone in it exterior to the sock and this was causing an indentation in the sole of the foot, which remained because of the freezing."

The body lay on the cold steel, naked now from the waist up.

The men saw tattoos on the back of the right shoulder and on the left forearm, but they were too blurry to be easily read. Unlike the other tattoos, the initials N.S., drawn in blue ink at the base of the right thumb, were clearly visible.

They struggled trying to remove the jeans. The young man's knees had frozen in a bent position, making it impossible to pull them off.

Morton pushed his hand into the right rear pocket of the pants, and came up with some papers and several colour photographs. On the back of a photo of a beautiful teenage native girl Morton noted the inscription, "To Neil from Cousin Lucille Neetz."

The papers had phone numbers on them. In his report Morton noted two numbers, 382-0239 and 382-3665.

By four-thirty in the afternoon, Morton had sent Middleton back to the police station. Once there, he searched the identification card system using the initials from the tattoos and the photograph and quickly came up with the name Neil Christopher Stonechild.

By the late afternoon of November 29, 1990, the Saskatoon police had a good idea they were looking into the death of a seventeen-year-old native boy, not a thirty-year-old man. All that remained was to confirm the identity with fingerprints.

— — —

After he came on shift at three in the afternoon, Sergeant Keith Jarvis of the Morality Section of the Saskatoon Police Service was assigned to investigate the freezing death in the city's north end.

A tall, thin, slightly greying man, with a vaguely prudish demeanour, Jarvis was only three years from retirement. After twenty-four years in the Saskatoon Police Service, he had lost his British accent, which had softened to a slightly Bostonian pitch. After beginning as a beat cop in 1966, Jarvis was promoted to corporal in 1980 and spent two years working in Youth Division. A sergeant since 1984, he had worked on Break and Enter detail for two years before moving to Morality in 1986.

Morality got the case because the call from the scene described it as a "sudden death." Under Chief Penkala's reorganization of the SPS, Major Crimes dealt only with obvious homicides. Morality was the kitchen sink of departments, dealing with all offences against people—liquor-licensing laws, prostitution, family disputes, accidental deaths, suicides and sudden deaths.

According to his notes, Jarvis spent the first four and a half hours of his twelve-hour shift doing not much of anything, not even visiting the site where the body had been found.

Jarvis's first notes on Neil Stonechild's death are cryptic and contain no indication of when they were taken or to whom he was speaking. Jarvis once instructed new recruits at the police college in the art of note taking, but there was little sign of such expertise in his own record of the investigation.

He wrote down three phone numbers: 382-0239, 382-3665, 382-5838. Next to that he scribbled the words, "sister" and "mother," and below them he wrote "Lucille Neetz, found on person of the deceased Confed. Dr" There is no sign of the source of the information or what it meant to Jarvis.

— — —

"Mum, they found someone," said Marcel, watching the local six o'clock news on Thursday, November 29. Stella walked into the living room and caught the beginning of the report.

The television image showed the camera's long view of a desolate field. Small patches of brown, dead grass lay where the snow had melted during the recent thaw, and stringy tufts of ochre and dark brown prairie grass poked out of the remaining snow. She watched the camera zoom in as police rolled the frozen figure over, so stiff, the legs slightly drawn up, arms and hands folded almost as if in prayer.

If she had watched a little longer she might have caught the distinctive thin white stripes of the blue jeans and the blue jacket. But Stella returned to the kitchen as soon as the newscaster said police had found the body of a thirty- to thirty-five-year-old man in an industrial area north of Saskatoon.

The report had filled Marcel with a primal, indescribable fear. He tried to shake it off as he joined his mother in the kitchen.

— — —

The first written reports by Identification officers René Lagimodiere and Bob Morton would not be typed up until later in the evening, but Jarvis's notes show that by 7:20 p.m. he was pretty sure who he was dealing with: "The deceased, possibly Neil Stonechild, NFA [no fixed address]. 17 yrs, 73–8–24.

Unlawfully at large, Kilburn Hall as of the 90–11–14. Body located field behind 57th Street East, Hitachi plant. Body frozen solid. No apparent signs of foul play. Missing running shoe from right foot. Appears he had fallen in the ditch, pulled himself on to the level area where he was found." The entry again fails to indicate where Jarvis got the information.

Jarvis needed confirmation before notifying the family, so he got into Car 53 to make the short drive to the St. Paul's Hospital morgue to meet Morton. A nursing administrator unlocked the morgue for them shortly after eight that night. As Morton took fingerprints, Jarvis barely glanced at the body.

At 8:10, Morton identified Neil Stonechild from his right thumbprint, leaving the nursing administrator to lock and secure the morgue so that the body could continue to thaw.

— — —

Marcel heard the doorbell ring. That was odd in itself; most people who visited Stella's house never rang the bell but walked right into her kitchen through the back door.

He heard a man's voice, oddly formal, asking his mother whether he could talk to her about Neil. Neil must have been arrested after all, he thought.

Stella seemed almost jovial as she asked the police officer whether they'd caught Neil and what he'd done now. She told him she'd last seen him on Saturday night when he headed out to party with Jason Roy. Then Marcel heard her wail. He raced into the kitchen and managed to grab her just before she collapsed. He held her up as the officer repeated the news.

"Neil is dead."

Stella looked up at Marcel. "What happened?" she cried.

Marcel held her tightly as the officer's words began to sink in. Neil was found in a field, up in the north industrial area by the Hitachi plant, frozen. The body on TV, it was Neil.

Marcel felt the small kitchen spinning. An urge to get the hell out of the house threatened to overwhelm him. He was nineteen, only two years older than Neil, but he knew he had to be strong for Stella, at least until he got some help. Instinctively, he dialled his Uncle Jerry and Aunt Debbie's number. Jerry answered.

"Jer, you have to get Debbie to come right away, Mum needs her."

"What's going on?"

"Just get over here quick, he's gone," he said, voice trailing off as he hung up.

Jerry and Debbie soon arrived to help calm Stella and to start making phone calls to family members. Everybody in the house was going through automatic motions, listening to alien words about Neil. Stunned by the brutal facts. Neil. Frozen. Way out there. All by himself.

— — —

Following up on information Stella had given him, Keith Jarvis drove to Pat Pickard's group home in southeast Saskatoon that night at ten-thirty. Shocked, Pickard told Jarvis that she had last spoken to Neil when he had phoned her five days earlier, on the night of November 24. He had told her he wanted to turn himself in, but needed time to think. Before Jarvis left, Pickard gave him the names and addresses of five kids Neil hung around with. The list included one of the last people to see him alive, Jason Roy.

Jarvis returned to the station, where he compiled a brief report from his notes, at midnight. Most officers dictated their reports, to be typed up by the secretaries in Central Records, but Jarvis typed his own. Doing so eliminated any delay before the report would be ready. He used a large font and double-spaced his work. "Further follow up is required by the day shift in order that the person mentioned may be interviewed as soon as possible to determine what information they can give regarding their activities over the past 7 days," he typed.

The final paragraph of his report says that "an autopsy would likely not be performed till approx Sunday December 2/90 after the body has thawed out." Then Jarvis tried to have the file given to someone else. By December 2 Jarvis would be on a four-day break. He concluded his report of November 29 by typing the time: 2400.

Dr. Jack Adolph actually performed the autopsy on Neil the next day, November 30, at twelve-thirty. Jarvis missed it. Morton, the identification officer, was present, however, and took a series of still photos as Adolph dictated his findings. He measured the abrasions on Neil's face: "There were two parallel superficial abrasions across the mid point of the nose directed obliquely downward to the right. The upper was 2.0 cm and the lower was 2.5 cm in length." Adolph also took note of a

ST. PAUL'S HOSPITAL
(Grey Nuns') of Saskatoon

Γ49

AUTOPSY REPORT

SERIAL NO. ML 280-90

NAME: STONECHILD, Leo Christopher   AGE: 17   SEX: Male

PATHOLOGIST: Dr. J. Adolph   ATTENDING PHYSICIAN:

This man was found in a frozen state in the north end of the city. The autopsy findings were not specific but were compatible with death due to hypothermia. There are no specific findings when death is due to hypothermia and freezing.

The police have indicated that the blood alcohol level was 150 mgm/100 ml of blood. This may have been a contributing factor but is generally not associated with marked incapacitation or coma. No other explanation for an altered mental state was found

JA:sm:mbs

J. Adolph, M.D.
30 January 1991

crescent-shaped scratch just over five centimetres long on the upper part of Neil's left cheek.

While the scratches were recent and might have bled a bit, in Adolph's opinion they could not have caused death and were consistent with someone falling face down into the snow. He gave Morton some blood samples to be sent to the toxicology lab.

"Unremarkable" Adolph comments repeatedly in his two-page autopsy report in which he mistakenly calls Neil "Leo." He determined that Neil's death was due to hypothermia and freezing.

— — —

Marcel sat with Stella, trying to console her. She had cried all night. But Marcel's own tears stayed deep inside, leaving him veering between flat denial and a growing anger.

"Mum, from what they're saying, he just walked out there and froze to death."

Stella just looked at him, without a word, nodding.

"That night there was no way he would have walked out there, no way, sober or not."

"I don't know, Marcel, I don't know anything anymore," Stella whispered.

"A sober person wouldn't have been able to walk that far in that night in that cold," Marcel insisted.

"And the way they explained it, with him having one shoe and his baseball hat missing," Stella said, gazing at him.

"Yeah, I know, Mum. Neil never went anywhere without his baseball cap."

Marcel couldn't imagine Neil without his cap. Even when he passed out, it would still be on his head.

"I'm going out, Mum, just heading out for a walk, I gotta go for a walk."

He headed down Confederation Drive, where he figured Neil and Jason would have walked. He walked through all the alleys in the neighbourhood, watching the ground for Neil's missing runner and ball cap. It took him hours.

When he gave up, the guilt came right back. Maybe if he hadn't bought that bottle Neil wouldn't have gone to that party, he wouldn't have been drinking, he wouldn't . . . ? Now Marcel was the one who needed a drink. He'd been working since he was fourteen; alcohol's allure had never been that great for him. But right now all he wanted was to get plastered, completely, just forget it all.

— — —

When Keith Jarvis reported for work on the afternoon of November 30, the autopsy was over, and he had no choice but to continue with the Stonechild file. He started working through the names Pat Pickard had given him.

At four in the afternoon, he spoke on the telephone to Trevor Nowaselski, who said that Neil had dropped by with Jason about three on the afternoon of November 24 and then left to catch a bus.

By now local media were reporting that the frozen body found in the north end was not that of a man in his thirties, but rather seventeen-year-old Neil Stonechild. At 4:42 a Crime Stoppers tip came into the station that Neil had been beaten up and dumped in the north end by Gary and Danny Pratt. According to the caller, Neil had been fooling around with Gary's girlfriend.

That same afternoon, having heard about Neil's death, Sergeant Douglas Wylie visited Jarvis. He told him about the Pratts' assault on Eddie Rushton in August over some guns Neil had stolen. Neil had never had to testify, but Wylie said the word on the street was that the Pratts had it in for him.

Jarvis dismissed the information. His report states, "None of this information can be verified at this time, and it is felt that this info is the result of persons trying to get back at the Pratts."

Jason Roy watched the supper-hour news in disbelief. His friend was dead. He was so upset that even the thought of being sent back to Kilburn did not stop him from calling the cops. He got put through immediately to Jarvis and told him he had been with Neil most of the night. After negotiating that he would not be sent back to Kilburn Hall in return for information, Jason agreed to meet Jarvis.

Jarvis did not mention in his notes that Jason told him Neil had been picked up by the cops. Around the time he talked to Jason on the phone, Jarvis went to the Communication Section and searched the dispatch cards for the night of November 24.

In his looping hand, he wrote what he learned from the dispatch cards: "On November 24th. 2351 hours. 306–3308–33rd Street West, deceased at party. Comp. Trent Ewart. Wanted deceased removed due to intoxicated. Constable Hartwig and Senger attended at 2356 and cleared at 0017 hours on November 25th, '90." In his notes, Jarvis did not include a time, nor did he mention that the details came from the dispatch cards.

He wrote the time of Jason's call as 18:30 and then wrote over it to change it to 18:52. The times of the next entries jumped all over the place. Jarvis double-underlined "2030 Meet Roy for statement @ 1121 P So." Further down the page he wrote "1940 Spoke to Claudine Neetz." Then he recorded "2200 Meet Trent Ewart at station re: statement," followed by "2045 Attended Ave P So for witness statement from Jason Roy."

Police are taught to put the time of the actual occurrence of an event, such as talking to a witness, in the left-hand column of the notebook page. Jarvis, however, freely interspersed times at which he set up appointments with his notes from attending the meetings later in the evening. He wrote over previously re-

On Nov 24/90 2351 hrs
Deceased @ Party
306 - 330 + 53 ♂ W.
Comp: Twin & Everett
38? - 45 88

Wanted Deceased removed.
[?] & Intoxicated.
Cst. Hartwig & [Senger]
attended @ 2356
and cleared 0017 hrs
on Nov 25/90.

Cst. McLean advised
deceased in a fight
1822 Jason Roy Called
advised he was
[?] Deceased most

corded times and generally ignored any imperative to maintain his notes in chronological order.

Nowhere in his notes did Jarvis mention speaking to Constable Larry Hartwig. Yet the fact that Hartwig was "unable to locate the deceased" turned up in Jarvis's final report, suggesting that the two officers had had some kind of contact that should have been recorded.

— — —

At about 8:45 p.m., Jason Roy opened the door and invited Jarvis into the bungalow on Avenue P where he and Cheryl Antoine had been lying low since November 24. To mask his anxiety, Jason flashed his best street smile at the skinny cop in the suit and motioned with his arm toward the living room. He noticed Jarvis was carrying a silver briefcase, the gleaming metal kind he had seen in movies about secret agents.

Jason wanted to make sure he had witnesses in case Jarvis reneged on their deal, so his friend Dinah Sunshine joined him and Cheryl while Jarvis took the statement.

For the next fifty-five minutes, Jason went through what had happened on the night of November 24. He described how he and Neil had spent the afternoon with a friend in the east end, how after drinking some vodka they had walked to the Sev, then rung the buzzers at Snowberry Downs trying to find Lucille, and how they'd argued and gotten separated when Jason wanted to give up.

He told Jarvis that he was walking south on Confederation Drive about halfway back to the Binnings' when a police car with two officers in the front seat drove out of an alley. He said he saw Neil leaning to one side in the back seat as if he were handcuffed and yelling, "Jay, Jay, tell them who you are."

According to Jason, the driver had asked him, "Do you know this guy in the back?" Jason said he denied knowing Neil because he didn't want to join him in the back seat, heading to Kilburn Hall. He'd expected to have some explaining to do to Neil in a few days, not to hear that his friend had turned up dead.

Jason said the driver then wanted to know who he was, so Jason had given them the name of a cousin with no warrants and they'd let him go. Jason's obvious satisfaction at having deceived the police irritated Jarvis.

His last image of Neil, angry and scared, looking at him out the back window as the cruiser headed south down Confederation, was never far from Jason's mind as he talked with Jarvis. Like most natives living in Saskatoon, Jason had heard about "starlight tours," stories about Saskatoon police driving natives out of town and forcing them to walk back. He wondered if that's how Neil had gotten to the industrial area where he'd died.

Jarvis did not take notes or use a tape recorder while Jason was talking. When they had almost finished the interview, he had Jason write out a statement. The shaky, childish scrawl and grammatically flawed sentences filled only a page and a half. Because he had told Jarvis the whole story already, or because he could not put his thoughts on paper, Jason left out where he had last seen Neil. When he described where they split up, at Snowberry Downs, he wrote, "We stood there and argued, for what I don't, and he turned around and said fucking Jay." The statement then jumped to when Jason blacked out and woke up at the Binnings'.

After Jason finished, Jarvis wrote down a few questions with Jason's answers:

What time approx. did you last see Neil Stonechild alive on November 24th, 1990?
Could be about 1130 p.m.
When you say the name Trevor is that Trevor Nowaselski?
Yes.
What condition was Neil in when you last saw him?
Pretty drunk. Well totally out of it.
Is there anything else you wish to tell me?
No, that's all I can think of.
Is this a true statement?
Yes.

Despite what he knew from the dispatch cards and from what Jason had told him during the conversation, Jarvis did not write down that Jason had last seen Neil in the custody of the police.

As Jarvis stood to leave, Jason asked what the officer would do with the information he had provided. Jarvis said he would look into it and get back to him.

He never did.

— — —

After his meeting with Jason, Jarvis returned quickly to the station. He had agreed to meet Trent Ewart there around ten.

Back at his desk, he phoned Lucille Neetz to ask her about the night of November 24, but never asked her to give a statement.

Trent Ewart showed up early. Jarvis took a look at the jumpy eighteen-year-old white kid: he was clearly uncomfortable at being in the station and wanted to get this over with.

Jarvis began with generic questions for a bit of background, but Ewart launched right into his encounter with Neil.

"Did the police come?" Jarvis asked.

"Yeah, the police came and me and Gary lied to the police because Lucille Neetz didn't want them to give Neil her name. We told them we thought it was Neil Stonechild."

It took Ewart less than ten minutes to scribble out the fifteen lines of his statement. He had confirmed for Jarvis that he saw only Neil, not Jason, and that the police had been called; however, none of the relevant details made it into Jarvis's notes.

As he prepared his report, Jarvis failed to record that Jason told him about seeing Neil in the custody of Saskatoon police around midnight.

As for tips from Sergeant Wylie and Crime Stoppers about the Pratts' possible vendetta against Neil, the report at one point dismissed them. But two pages later, Jarvis typed, "At this time there is no evidence to support foul play but the information about Pratts cannot be ruled out."

He then offered his own theory about what had happened: "It is possible that the deceased was in fact going to turn himself in as indicated by the witnesses and was possibly heading for the Correctional Centre on 60th Street to do so when due to his alledged [sic] intoxicated state he stumbled, fell asleep and froze to death. More investigation required." Pat Pickard had not said anything about the correctional centre to Jarvis. Neil

SASKATOO(POLICE DEPARTMENT
WITNESS STATEMENT

CASE NUMBER 97411-90
DATE OF STATEMENT 90 11 30
TIME STARTED 2145
TIME FINISHED 2155

EWART TRENT   SEX M DATE OF BIRTH 72 11 08

336 AVE K. So.   HOME PHONE 244-7422   BUSINESS PHONE 664 2004

DEATH OF NEIL STONECHILD.

I was drinking with lucille neets 870 confederation drive and gary konrse. the buzzer rang and the person apologized for ringing the wrong buzzer and then their was a knock on the door lucille neets said it was neil stonechild she was scared an paranoid I asked what he wanted he said he wanted a party" I said their is "no party here" he mumbled some things I said "get out of here or me I called the cops" he said "sorry dude" and left he came back and lucille neets said that I should call the police because he was wanted then the police came and me and garry lied to the police because lucille neets didn't want them to give neil her name we told them we thought it was neil stonechild.

had planned to turn himself in to her. He was seventeen years old and the Saskatoon Correctional Centre was an adult facility. Jarvis doesn't identify the witnesses who inspired his theory.

At the conclusion of the report, he wrote, "Sgt Jarvis is on weekly leave for the next 4 days. It is suggested with the possibility of foul play, that this file be turned over to Major Crimes for immediate follow up."

— — —

Stella was now spending most of her time lying on the couch, her mind racing. Debbie and Jerry had not left her side. They called Kilburn Hall to notify Jake. At fourteen, Jake had already

SASKAT ⟩N POLICE DEPARTMENT	CASE NUMBER 97411/90
CONTINUATION REPORT	PAGE NUMBER 2

YPE OF OCCURRENCE SUDDEN DEATH	TIME OF REPORT 24 HR. 2245.	DATE OF REPORT 90 11 30

cont: 1940 hrs I spoke to Claudine Neetz who stated that she was out
on the evening of November 24/90 and her former common law was babysitting
along with her sister LUCILLE NEETZ 870 Confederation Drive 384 6218, and
TRENT EWART 336 AVE K SOUTH 244 7422, and GARY HORSE 428 Ave H South.

On checking the calls dispatched I learned that Cst Hartwig had
attended at this residence at approx 2356 hrs and cleared at 0017 hrs on
November 25/90 being unable to locate the deceased.

1852 hrs JASON ROY called and advised he was with the deceased for
most of the day and evening of Nov 24/90.

2045 hrs attended at 1121 Ave P South where I met with JASON ROY
who provided a witness statement and indicates that he and the deceased were
{ ether that date . Roy and the deceased went to JULIE BINNINGS at
3269 Milton Street where they sat around from approx 1400 hrs at which time
they left and went to TREVOR NOWASELSKI home arriving at approx 1445 hrs.
They then went to Circle Park Mall till approx 1830 hrs then to Stella
Stonechilds. They allegedly consumed a bottle of alcoholt at Binnings then
decided to look for Lucille Neetz. Roy states they tried several buzzers
at Snowberry Downs but couldnt get in and finally whent their seperate ways.
Roy claims he blacked out and woke up at Binnings Later.

Trent Ewart confirmed that the deceased was at Snowberry Downs but
he did not see Roy with him.

been in and out of Kilburn several times for stealing. He was in
his room just around lock-up when one of his counsellors came
to his door. He took Jake to the visitors' room and told him
about Neil, gave him a pass and got someone to drive him home.
He found his mother on the living room couch crying, surrounded by his family and cousins. Jake sat hugging her for a
long while, thinking about Neil.

Around the time Neil had disappeared from Pickard's
group home, he had phoned Jake at Kilburn, and Jake had fanta-
sized about escaping so they could be together. Jake knew just

how to climb Kilburn's walls. Using toothbrushes stuck in strategic places, boys could pull themselves up and get over the fence. But Neil had told him to stay put—their mother was worried enough as it was. She couldn't take two of them on the run. Jake now regretted listening to his brother.

Erica arrived from Valley River, Manitoba, where she lived with her two daughters. In the spring, Neil had begged to go stay with her and she had insisted he remain in Saskatoon to sort himself out.

Dean had gone to Ontario, where he had just bought a car and was driving home. He called to say he'd hit some black ice on the Trans-Canada Highway and totalled the car. A lady at a nearby farm was letting him use her phone. He was devastated when they told him about Neil. The woman prayed with him and called the highway patrol, who took him to the nearest bus stop so he could get home immediately.

Like Erica, Dean had also refused to take Neil away from Saskatoon. Neil had wanted to go with him on the trip to Ontario, but Dean had said no, that running away would not solve his troubles.

The house was filling up with people. They were sleeping on couches and in the basement. Everyone brought food and they sat around talking and drinking tea, trying to keep Stella from falling apart. Debbie took her to the doctor, who prescribed sedatives so Stella could rest.

Jerry was not aboriginal and was not intimidated by Saskatoon's bureaucracy. He was the one who went to the hospital morgue to identify Neil. He made several phone calls to the city police for Stella, trying to recover Neil's belongings, and was told the clothes were still at the hospital.

Jerry started making arrangements with the Westwood Funeral Chapel. Stella's sister, Marcie, and her husband, Archie McKay, were working at a Bible college in Caronport, Saskatchewan, and they came immediately. Archie would perform the service for Neil.

Erica went with Jerry and Debbie and some of her cousins to the chapel, a simple dark-brown brick building on 20th Street West, to see her brother. Stella could not face it yet.

Erica was shocked when she saw the coffin. The body was unrecognizable as her brother. She studied Neil's swollen face. If not for the initials tattooed on his right hand, she would never have believed this was her brother. She reached into her pocket. She had brought a ring that Neil had often admired. She slipped the small parting gift onto his finger.

"Do you think we should have an open or shut casket?" Debbie asked.

"I don't think we should have a closed casket." Erica's eyes were focused on Neil. Two deep, ugly gashes ran like railway tracks across his nose. "Look at all the bruising and those cuts. If it's a closed casket nobody will see what he looks like." The makeup couldn't hide the damage to Neil.

She continued to study him. His beautiful black hair had been cut unevenly. Whether it was done at the hospital or at the funeral home, someone had been in a hurry with blunt scissors.

"Why would they cut his hair, Auntie Deb?"

"Erica, I don't—I have no idea."

As Debbie faltered, Erica ran her hand through Neil's hair. She felt compelled to touch him, to confirm what had been done to him, and within seconds she was running her hands all over his head. There were numerous large bumps on the skull, along with a strange ridge. She parted his hair to see it properly.

"Is this from freezing, all these cuts and bruises?" she asked Debbie. She reached for the buttons of Neil's shirt. She wanted to strip him and investigate every single mark.

Debbie urged her to stop, not to disturb Neil any further; and Erica struggled to pull her hands away.

"What happened to him? What happened?" Erica repeated as she and Debbie walked away.

— — —

Erica and Debbie each took one of Stella's arms, propping her up as she walked into the chapel the next day. At the coffin, Stella leaned down and hugged Neil as best she could. She kissed his cheek and very lightly touched his hair. She wanted to look at him, talk to him, say goodbye properly, but faced with this battered boy lying in a cheap grey plywood box, the standard-issue social services casket, she couldn't find the words.

Pat Pickard and her husband, Gary, brought their teenage daughter to the visitation. She was the same age as Neil, and they had chummed around when he was living at their house. All three of them were struck by the condition of Neil's face.

"Mum, look, Neil's nose is broken," Pat's daughter said. Pickard was shocked at what she saw.

Marcel was also taken aback by the two cuts on Neil's nose. They ran in parallel lines, one deeper than the other. Jerry drew Marcel's attention to the base of Neil's right hand. There was skin missing, and there were scrapes about two centimetres long.

Marcel was caught completely off guard. The skin had been chafed raw just at the tattoo. Nearer the wrist he could see a curving indentation in the skin. He'd been arrested himself, and immediately thought it looked like the mark caused by someone pulling at handcuffs. He knew the sensation of having his wrists handcuffed behind his body, of being hauled backwards by the cuffs, and how the cuffs hurt so bad they left bruises.

— — —

On the afternoon of December 3, 1990, about four hundred people tried to fit into the simple wooden pews for Neil's funeral service. The louvred doors at the back of the chapel had to be opened to let the crowd fill the entrance area. An electronic bell over the door, designed to dissuade thieves, was triggered so often it had to be turned off. Teachers, counsellors from Kilburn Hall, but mostly teenagers from the neighbourhoods and schools where Neil had grown up showed up out of respect for the family.

Light flooded the room from the right, through a row of long, slim brightly coloured windows. The greyish-blue open casket was placed at the front of the chapel for the service, flanked by the Canadian and Saskatchewan flags.

Archie McKay had a hard time uttering the familiar words meant to comfort mourners at funerals. They seemed of scant value when burying a nephew of his own. He would never want to conduct another funeral service after this one.

Jeff Crowe arrived under guard. He had been taken from the treatment centre to Kilburn Hall following the news of Neil's death. At first he had been refused permission to attend, but fearing threats he might hurt himself, administrators relented. He never showed much emotion, even upon seeing Neil's body. Nobody would see him grieve. It was Jeff's first experience with death, but even he sensed something more was wrong. He vowed to never forget that suspicion.

Jason Roy had never been to a funeral before. He had no clue how to behave. Terrified, he moved through the crowd self-consciously, afraid of saying or doing anything inappropriate. The memory of Neil's face in the police cruiser's rear window plagued him. The guilt made him shake.

— — —

After the service a small group of the closest family and friends accompanied Neil to Woodlawn Cemetery on the west side of the river, near the North Park neighbourhood where Stella and the kids had first lived in Saskatoon. The sky was very grey. The recent thaw left the air thick with mist.

Memorial Avenue ran through the middle of the cemetery, bordered on both sides by trees, each one planted in honour of a

Saskatoon citizen who had died in the world wars. There were now more than a thousand trees, giving the cemetery an air reminiscent of dignified European burial grounds.

Neil, however, was to be buried far away from Memorial Avenue. He would lie in lot 53 in the 77 A block of the cemetery, its most northern tip, close to the storage sheds and the sprawling industrial area from 42nd Street East up to 57th Street East.

Stella had just buried her father in the spring, at Waywaysecapo, her home reserve in Manitoba. She ached to bury Neil alongside his grandfather, but social services was paying for the funeral and Neil would have to stay in Saskatoon. He would be the only Stonechild listed in the cemetery registry.

After the interment, the mourners, mainly family, met back at 38 Confederation Crescent for a simple reception. The guards accompanying Jeff Crowe allowed him to go back to the house. Jason didn't join them.

Stella was with relatives in the kitchen, where she felt most comfortable. Friends were down the hallway and in the living room. People stood in small groups speculating about Neil's death. The consensus built: there was no way he could get out there on his own. Teenagers don't walk that far in sub-zero weather, especially missing a shoe.

— — —

On patrol Constable Ernie Louttit had developed the habit of parking his car and walking his beat along 20th Street. In the late afternoon of December 4, 1990, Louttit opened the door of an arcade on Avenue G just off 20th. Noise from the video and pinball machines washed over him. When his eyes adjusted to the dim light, he saw a young man beckoning him from the corner. Jake Stonechild, Neil's younger brother, wanted to talk.

Louttit was one of the few native police officers in the Saskatoon Police Service when he joined from the Canadian military in 1987, and he quickly developed unmatched credibility among the native youth in the downtown core. He stood just over six feet tall, with an easy confidence and a disarming smile. The handsome cop talked to whoever would talk to him, and worked his sources for information and rumours about B and E's, weapons, thefts, drugs and prostitution. Some of the native teens gave him a wide berth, saying he was a hard-ass who cut nobody any slack and didn't hesitate to get rough when making an arrest. Other kids felt "Indian Ernie," as they called him, was the only cop who understood what they were going through, a sort of guidance counsellor with a badge.

Louttit acknowledged Jake with a subtle gesture and edged through the crowd of bodies toward him. As he did with several other native families, Louttit enjoyed a fairly close relationship with the Stonechild boys. He even called Stella "Mum." He was still a cop though, so Jake was taking a surprising risk talking to him around his friends.

It was the day after Neil's funeral. Jake's temporary absence from Kilburn Hall had been extended so he could be with his family. Louttit had heard and read the media reports about Neil freezing to death. He was curious about the circumstances and had asked around, but no one was talking.

Jake and Louttit huddled in the middle of the arcade, their heads together. As conspicuous as they were, the din camouflaged their conversation. After a few minutes, Louttit nodded at Jake and left.

When he got back to his cruiser, he opened his notebook and began writing in a hurried hand. Jake had heard rumours on the street connecting Neil and Gary Pratt. During his eight years in the military, Louttit had trained at the Canadian Forces School of Intelligence and Security in Wainwright, Alberta. Despite being a uniformed military cop, he managed to play a major role in investigations of sexual assault and theft of military munitions. He decided to pass the information on to Major Crimes and would poke around a little on his own.

— — —

Keith Jarvis came back to work on Wednesday, December 5, to find that no one had lifted a finger on the Stonechild file. Before his four-day break, Jarvis had urged that the case be dealt with by Major Crimes, but finding the file unopened, he complained to no one.

He was working the early shift on this rotation, eight in the morning to eight at night.

By mid-morning he had telephoned one of the names on the list Pat Pickard had given him, a fellow named Shawn Draper. But Draper hadn't seen Neil since mid-November. Jarvis also began dealing with unrelated matters. At 10:35, he handled a domestic dispute about unpaid support payments, noting that the woman "rambled on about anything and everything."

About one-thirty, Jarvis drove by the Binnings'. He stopped in and was able to interview one of the teens who had been there on November 24. Sharon Night said that Jason and Neil had been drinking vodka and had left later for the 7-Eleven at 33rd Street and Confederation Drive.

From there, Jarvis drove to Gary Pratt's residence at 104–28 Saskatchewan Crescent East, but he wasn't there. Jarvis couldn't find Eddie Rushton either. When he arrived at Rushton's house at 1106 Avenue K North, he could tell from the unmarked snow that no one had been around for days.

Back at his desk, he phoned Dr. Adolph at about 3:35. Adolph told him that the autopsy revealed no signs of trauma sufficient to cause death. Jarvis wrote his own interpretation in his notebook: "There was no evidence of any trauma to the body whatsoever."

Furthermore, the pathologist, who had initially thought Neil had been dead for a minimum of forty-eight hours, now told Jarvis that Neil could have died as early as November 25.

At four-thirty, less than an hour after hearing that Neil might have died around the time that police were looking for him, Jarvis concluded his investigation and filed his final report on the boy's death.

In all, his investigation took less than three full shifts. He obtained written statements from Trent Ewart and Jason Roy, and did not record in his notes and reports what Jason had told him about seeing Neil in the police car. Jarvis made no mention of discussing with either Hartwig or Senger their having been dispatched to remove Neil from Snowberry Downs. He did not visit the site where Neil died, missed the autopsy and inspected neither the body nor the still photographs Morton had taken. He didn't look at Neil's clothing or send it to be analyzed. His notes show he made a single attempt to locate the only suspect named in the investigation reports, Gary Pratt.

He wrote in his report, "It is felt that unless something concrete by way of evidence to the contrary is obtained the deceased died from exposure and froze to death. There is nothing to indicate why he was in the area other than possibilities he was going to turn himself in to the correctional centre or was attempting to follow the tracks back to Pickard's group home, or simply wandered around drunk until he passed out from the cold and alcohol and froze. Concluded at this time."

Approval of his report by a supervisor was a formality. Jarvis was finished with the investigation, except for one thing. He had to inform the mother.

The following day, Thursday, December 6, he phoned Stella. Having just buried her son, she didn't initially remember Jarvis. He told her that the investigation had determined that Neil had simply wandered about in the north end after drinking, and had fallen down and died from the cold. He shared his theory that Neil might have been trying to turn himself in to the correctional centre.

Anger temporarily washed away Stella's grief. She told Jarvis that his story was simply not like her boy. He never went to the north end. And what about the fact that he had only one shoe?

Jarvis said they would have to see if any new evidence came forward, and thereby avoided telling Stella that the case was closed.

CASE CLOSED

THE DAY AFTER HE MET JAKE STONECHILD IN the arcade and shortly after Sergeant Keith Jarvis filed his final report, Constable Ernie Louttit asked one of the clerks behind the counter in Central Records for the Stonechild file. She asked no questions and returned quickly with the thin file, no more than twenty pages. Louttit did not want to risk being seen by other officers reading the file, so he told the secretary he was going to photocopy it. When he finished he put the copies on the clipboard he carried with him everywhere, handed back the original and left.

Later that night he read his copy of Neil's file, case number 97411–90. When he got to the last sentence, "Case concluded at this time," he sat back, stunned. How had Jarvis finished the investigation in less than a week with so many unanswered questions?

Even before talking to Jake Stonechild, Louttit had heard speculation around the station that Neil had been in the north end to turn himself in at the correctional centre. That made no sense to him. And now he'd read that it was Jarvis himself who had come up with the theory. The two officers had never worked together, but Louttit had watched Jarvis interact with other cops and had found him to be arrogant.

As for Gary and Danny Pratt, he knew the kind of street justice they dealt in. Jarvis, though, had barely tried to locate the brothers.

Having read the file, and armed with the tip from Jake, Louttit arrived at Major Crimes on December 6 in an inspired mood. Facing the detectives at their cluster of desks on the third floor, he told them what he'd learned in the arcade. They dismissed him outright. They suggested that he was only a junior beat cop and this sort of thing was beyond him—he should stop meddling in other people's affairs. As he walked out into the corridor, Louttit's excitement had plummeted into cold anger.

— — —

On December 7, Stella was still fuming from Jarvis's call. Out of politeness more than a desire to see anyone, she answered a knock at her door and smiled warmly when she saw who it was.

"Mum," said Louttit, smiling back. He carried his clipboard under one arm.

Stella got Louttit settled at the kitchen table and brought him tea. He offered awkward sympathies for the loss of her son. Then he told her about talking to Jake and, pointing to the papers on his clipboard, said he had looked through the file and had serious concerns about how the case was being handled. Louttit was risking discipline under the Police Act by talking this way to Stella, but the detectives in Major Crimes had gotten under his skin. He wanted answers.

Stella told him that someone from the SPS had called the day before to tell her that Neil had just drunk too much and wandered until he froze to death. "You know Neil," Stella said, indignant. "He would never go way up there by himself. None of my boys would. And how could he walk with one shoe, for good-ness sake? It doesn't add up."

Louttit had to agree. Stella confessed that everything had been sort of a blur for her since Neil died. But Louttit had come forward and it gave Stella some measure of hope for the first time since Neil had been found. He clearly cared. They talked about the fight Neil had had with Gary Pratt in August over the stolen guns. Stella told him how Neil had taken a hit on the head and was scared enough to come running home.

"That's exactly the kind of information I need. If I'm going to look into this thing, I need you and the boys to try to remember everything that happened. That way I can follow up."

"Is that what you're going to do, then?" Stella asked.

"Yeah," said Louttit. "I can't believe how poorly they're treating you. It's not right."

Stella nodded, tears coming to her eyes. She knew her son had not died naturally, but she was afraid to believe someone would really look into it. It seemed too good to be true.

When he got back to his car, Louttit grabbed his notebook to record the details of his meeting with Stella, but stopped himself. If he was going to risk discipline, he would not be hanged by his own words. He put the notebook away.

— — —

Marcel was hitting the bars on 20th Street daily. After one or two pints, he sometimes allowed himself to feel his loss. Mostly, the booze just numbed him. Marcel had concocted a cruel new image of himself. He was a shit. He was the one who had bought Neil the Silent Sam in exchange for a fucking pair of gloves.

Marcel had already spent days looking everywhere for Jason Roy, but it was as if he'd been swallowed whole by the nether world of the 20th Street 'hood.

When he finally managed to track down Gary Pratt, whose nickname was "Charlie Brown," they met over a draft at the Elephant and Castle pub. Marcel had known him since grade school when they used to ride BMX bikes and jump the dirt hills in the Confederation area together, along with all the other kids who roamed the streets on their bikes well past dark.

"Marcel, how's it going, ain't seen you since the funeral."

"Just hangin' in, Charlie Brown, just hangin in," Marcel said, as Gary slumped into the chair opposite him. Gary never seemed to change. He was about nineteen now, a wiry, jumpy kid with the toned body of somebody who had wrestled on and off while he was still in high school. Like Marcel, he now worked construction. The Pratts were invariably associated with criminal activity, and Gary had had numerous convictions. He didn't talk much, but he was a no-bullshit kind of guy and Marcel got right to the point.

"Let's cut the crap, Chuck. The street says you had something to do with Neil."

"Fuck you, Marcel, I done a lot of shit in my life, but I never killed anyone."

Marcel knew from talking to Neil this past summer that Gary had given Eddie Rushton a beating. "What about that fight over those stolen guns. Maybe you threatened him?"

"Fuck no. Neil was in the bedroom with the girl. He woke up from all the commotion. I told 'em Neil had nothing to do with anything, and they pushed him back into the room. I told him to get the hell out of there, and he ran home, you know that."

The two men stared straight into one another's eyes.

"I never hurt Neil, I loved him like he was my little bro."

Two years older than Neil, Gary had taught him wrestling while at Bedford Road Collegiate. High school students were regularly enlisted to teach wrestling to the older grade school children, like Neil, from Westmount Community School.

Marcel believed him. That's all there was to it. If the Pratts were going to beat somebody up, they would not do it in half measures. Their target would end up in the hospital or have a broken arm or something.

Gary was no longer in the mood to stick around and drink. He cleared out fast, but Marcel, haggard looking and depressed, stayed at the pub. If he stayed out long enough he'd get home after his mother had gone to bed. Enough alcohol allowed his fatigue to trump the guilt, and sleep, albeit fitful, would come quickly.

— — —

Ernie Louttit kept his word through the month of December. He continued to work the streets for information, and met several times with Stella, Norman, Marcel, Jake and Erica. Marcel told him that he'd thought the marks on Neil's wrists looked as if they'd been caused by handcuffs. Louttit said he'd look into it.

Louttit never wavered from his certainty that the shabby investigation of Neil's death had everything to do with race. "It makes you wonder," he once said to Stella. "If Neil were the son of the mayor or commissioner, police would still be investigating."

Louttit's pursuit raised the whole family's expectations, but Erica was especially certain that something would finally give with Louttit now on their side. She was counting on him.

— — —

Around Christmas, Jason Roy was laying low at his mother's house, and feeling low too. He sat in the living room of the low-income-designated house Marleen rented, trying unsuccessfully to nurse a hangover with a coffee.

On December 20, two days before his seventeenth birthday, he had been charged with "theft under" for stealing six hundred dollars from a local Humpty's restaurant in late October. He had reached into the till when no one was looking and dashed out the door with two friends.

Someone knocked on the door and Marleen answered. It was Jason's uncle Don Worme, the lawyer. It was the weekend, and he was dressed casually but still impeccably, making Jason self-conscious in his worn T-shirt and sweatpants. He wanted to talk to his uncle about Neil, but he felt awkward and didn't know how to approach him.

Marleen asked if he wanted to come in, but Don said he couldn't stay. That was nothing new. He always seemed to be in a hurry.

Jason never completely understood how Don could treat Marleen so coldly. There was always tension between them. Don's mother, Margaret, had been Marleen's aunt. Marleen had been in the kitchen with Don when Margaret and her daughter, Pat, were murdered back in the sixties. Marleen had had a rough life after she witnessed the murders, so why couldn't he cut her some slack? But Marleen had never told Jason the whole story. She didn't tell him that she had bolted when the murderer attacked Margaret and Pat, leaving Don, Dale and Pat's little boy Kim to face the killer alone.

Jason was intimidated by his uncle. After graduating from the University of Saskatchewan law school in 1985, Don had become one of the first aboriginal criminal lawyers in the country. Word was that he was getting rich. In the city jail, among the natives who packed the place every Monday morning after a weekend of hard drinking, Don had a reputation as someone who could win your case. That also kept Jason from confronting Don about his treatment of Marleen: he needed his uncle to drag him out of the succession of charges—B and E's, thefts, breaches of probation—that he added to his juvenile criminal record every month. Though Jason frustrated him, Don would never turn away from the boy; Jason was family. But he had no patience for what he saw in Jason as a lack of warrior spirit.

By 1990, Don Worme was married with two children, Tara and Rhiannon. He had met his wife, a beautiful Cree woman named Helen Semaganis, when they were university students. Helen provided a steadying influence for Don. He'd had his own wild streak as a boy and quit school at the age of fourteen.

The young lawyer modelled himself in the image of his grandfather, Edward Worme, who had raised Don and his brothers after Margaret's murder. After dinner on the Kawacatoose reserve, south of Saskatoon, the old man used to tell stories of battling white bureaucrats. They would put up obstacle after obstacle so he couldn't sell his livestock and produce, and his farm eventually went bankrupt. This loss drove bitterness as sharp as a nail into him, but in the best warrior tradition he fought to the end, even with no prospect of winning. He repeatedly drilled into the boys the one lesson he'd learned about whites: "They won't stop until they kill us all."

Edward once held one of the Cree's most sacred ceremonies, the Sun Dance, *enpahkwaysimohk* in Cree, in open defiance of the federal Indian Act, which prevented natives from practising their religion. People from Kawacatoose still talked about it decades later. The spirit of such disobedience always made Don smile. Edward, whose Cree nickname was "Distant Rolling Thunder," died in his eighties in 1979. To Don, he embodied what it meant to be a great man.

Seeing that Don was about to leave, Jason got up from where he was sitting, determined to talk about Neil.

The conversation was a disaster. Don had an unspoken way of communicating his lack of interest in people he didn't want to be with. Jason's clumsy, backtracking manner of talking instantly raised his uncle's hackles and whatever Jason was trying to say barely registered. When Jason managed to spit out that he had seen a friend in the back of a cruiser on the night he died and that he thought the police might have had something to do with his death, he got his uncle's attention briefly, but only to receive a warning. Don warned Jason that saying such things was serious and he should be careful if he went forward with that kind of accusation against the police, and left.

— — —

By the end of December, Ernie Louttit was still bogged down on the same nagging questions.

On December 30, 1990, to help sort out his own thoughts, he wrote the questions down in his notebook. As usual, beneath the entry he drew two horizontal lines separated by a single quotation mark.

On January 7, he met with the head of Major Crimes, Staff Sergeant Bruce Bolton.

Once in Bolton's office, Louttit barely opened his mouth before the meeting was over. Bolton made it clear that he was not going to talk about the Stonechild investigation. He told Louttit that he would have to take it up with the investigator. If he wanted to talk to him, Jarvis was in his office.

Back in the corridor, Louttit took several deep breaths then stepped into Jarvis's office.

"Sir," said Louttit, showing Jarvis the respect due his rank.

"What is it?" Jarvis asked. His tone made Louttit suspect he was being dismissed before he could speak. Louttit told Jarvis he wanted them to go through the Stonechild file together, willing himself to speak calmly and deliberately, no matter Jarvis's reaction.

For the next forty minutes Louttit walked Jarvis through his report, point by point. Why would a seventeen-year-old try to turn himself in to an adult facility? Where was the ball cap Neil always wore? What about a story he'd heard about Jason and Neil being chased by the police after a B and E on the night Neil died? The supposed party in the north end? The Eddie Rushton connection?

Soon both men were nearly shouting. Jarvis repeatedly told Louttit to stop meddling, and Louttit accused Jarvis of not doing his job as an investigator—the file clearly showed Jarvis had wanted to rid himself of the Stonechild case as quickly as he could.

By the end of the meeting, Louttit could tell Jarvis had taken all he was going to from a native beat cop with three years' service. If he pushed it further, he'd be disciplined. The threat was real. He had seen it before, a cop reassigned to a desk job, or worse. No warning. No explanation. He thought about his family. His wife was expecting another baby in the spring. He had gone as far up the chain of command as he could go. As an ex-military guy he knew he would be punished for going any higher with his complaint.

Tomorrow he would have to tell Stella he was done with it. He took the elevator down to the basement. Sitting in the nearly deserted locker room he took out his notebook and jabbed his pen at the paper in anger and frustration. In bold, sharp strokes sharply angled to the right he wrote only:

1600

S/Sgt

Bolton

1605–1645

SGT Jarvis

Erica stayed with Stella for a few months. They met regularly for lunch at the Eaton's food court during Stella's break. One day in mid-January Erica came home excited and told Marcel that she had talked to Ernie Louttit and that the officer was coming by. The family looked forward to his visits. He was the only cop who had given Neil's case any serious consideration.

They waited into the night for Louttit, but he never showed up. Marcel had nothing but respect for Louttit, but his failure to show was as rude as it was puzzling, and it had upset Stella, terribly. Now, Indian Ernie had let her down too.

Marcel was nursing a pint of Canadian at the Red Rock Grill, brooding and frustrated, watching a group of teenagers shoot pool. Confronting Gary Pratt had provided no answers, and he had no idea where to look next. He needed to hear what the big cop had to say for himself.

He knew that if he walked up and down the 20th Street sidewalk long enough, he'd run into Louttit, patrolling on foot. At his height, Louttit was easy to spot, and unmistakable as a cop from a distance in his standard-issue flapped winter hat.

"What's going on, Ernie? We were waiting for you the other night. You never showed."

"Yeah, the plain truth is, I won't be coming back," Louttit replied.

Marcel was confused. He tried again, and put it plainly.

"Why aren't you coming back?"

"I don't have any answers for Stella," Louttit said. "I can't check into things for you no more; my superiors have asked me to drop the case because it's a closed case now."

"That's the point, Ernie, that's why we need you."

"They're threatening me with a reprimand." Louttit stared past Marcel.

"Did you find anything?" Marcel asked.

"No, I have to get going. I'll be seeing you."

Chasing down Louttit had landed him a few doors from the Barry. The bar had such a rough reputation that people joked it had a no-stabbing section. Marcel had rarely gone in there, but today he didn't give a shit—the Barry would do fine. If Indian Ernie couldn't get any answers, how in hell was a punk like him going to get anywhere?

— — —

Stella stepped empty-handed and dejected into the elevator from the second floor of the Saskatoon police station. Officers had just told her, again, that she could not have Neil's clothes back. She'd been through this several times before: "The case is still open, we can't release the clothes." It made no sense. Marcel had told her that Louttit had been scared off Neil's case precisely because it was closed.

"What's wrong with these people?" she thought. "I've lost Harry and no one wants to do anything, even though it stinks to high heaven."

Distracted, Stella didn't notice the short, bald officer pressed into a corner of the tiny elevator until he spoke to her.

"Excuse me," he said, clearing his throat.

Looking up, she recognized the officer, remembered his glasses and timid eyes. She saw the man regularly at church and knew him quite well. Neil used to play with his son. But, as names so often did for Stella, his escaped her. Stella did recall the boy's name, however: Dion. He was a native boy about Neil's age whom the man had adopted. When Stella's family had lived in Lawson Heights a couple of years back, Neil was at their house all the time.

"Eli, Eli Tarasoff," said the officer as the elevator door closed. "How are you doing? I was sorry to hear about Neil." Tarasoff had read the obituary in the Saskatoon *Star Phoenix*, then gone to Central Records, pulled Neil's file and read it. But he didn't mention that to Stella.

"Neil and Dion, you know . . ." Tarasoff's attempt at sympathy trailed off into an uncomfortable silence that lasted until the elevator reached the ground floor. The doors opened.

Finally Stella spoke. Grief lent bluntness to her words. "Not good. We're not doing very good, you know, Mr. Tarasoff."

"I can't imagine what you're going through. Umm, it's a terrible loss. Just terrible." Tarasoff looked as if he wanted to be anywhere but trapped in a conversation with Stella.

She refused to let him go.

"Yeah, well, the thing is—" she began.

Tarasoff nodded. His eyes blinked rapidly behind his glasses.

"The thing is, you know, you know Neil."

"Yeah," Tarasoff replied cautiously, wondering where Stella was going with this.

"He never would have gone out there by himself. You know that. Never."

"Yes, I know that," Tarasoff said. He paused to soften what he was going to say next. "But, Stella, there's nothing I can do. I'm at a desk now, I'm not . . . active, you see."

Stella simply gazed at him, her solemn persistence a more effective petition than any imploring overture.

"My hands are tied, but I believe Neil didn't go out there either," Tarasoff finally said.

He agonized after parting with Stella. Like Ernie Louttit, he did not think Neil's case had been properly investigated, nor did that surprise him. He knew Jarvis. The two men had joined the force about the same time, almost thirty years back. They had never worked together, but it was a small department. Tarasoff found Jarvis to be an Englishman with a colonial attitude, who didn't take matters related to natives very seriously. He might have made a good PR man, Tarasoff thought, but he was not a good investigator.

Tarasoff's own life was in shambles, his marriage disintegrating, but Stella had made him feel even worse. He decided to go see Jarvis.

Their conversation was not a long one. Jarvis made it clear the file on Neil's death was concluded. His attitude offended Tarasoff, but faced with the indifference of a senior investigator, the desk cop backed off. He tried to press Jarvis for his take on the file, but all Jarvis would say was that the kid went out, got drunk, went for a walk and froze to death.

Tarasoff phoned Stella and advised her to find a lawyer if she wanted the case reopened. His suggestion was of little help to a woman who was working as a cleaner at Eaton's. But what registered most with her was that one more person had admitted defeat.

— — —

Stella had started to give up, too. She had put all her faith in Ernie Louttit and now he was ignoring her calls and had stopped visiting the family. But he had put questions about Stonechild's death into play.

In 1991, Terry Craig was a reporter for the Saskatoon *Star Phoenix*. He'd been a journalist for ten years, and had spent half his career covering police and the courts. In early March he received a tip from a cop about a native mother who believed her seventeen-year-old son's death had not been properly investigated. The officer clearly agreed with her. Terry had good sources at the police department, and some of them, decent guys, felt this story had legs. When a cop goes out of his way to tell a reporter that an investigation is flawed, there's most likely good reason to begin snooping around, even if in any eventual story Craig could only attribute the tip to an anonymous source.

All he had to do now was talk to this woman, Stella Stone-child. Of course, most native women in Saskatoon wouldn't talk to the local media because they felt the paper gave natives a bum rap. Maybe she had run out of options.

Around seven o'clock one night that March Craig decided to try his luck and headed out to the west end. Stella answered the door. He introduced himself and without hesitation she invited him to sit at her kitchen table. Good, he thought, this is obviously where she feels most comfortable, the best place in the house to talk.

He began by offering his condolences. She was clearly suffering from the loss of her child. Her daughter and son sat supportively nearby. Stella spread pictures of Neil across the table.

"You know, Mr. Craig, Neil was just a boy, he didn't have to die like that," she said.

Stella didn't need much prompting and Craig gave her free rein to talk.

Stella picked up a school picture of a smiling Neil, at age ten or twelve, and pressed it into his hand.

"Call me Stella, that's what everybody calls me."

Craig did not tape-record the interview, making notes instead in his spiral-bound notepad.

"When they found Neil in November, frozen out there in

that field, way up in the north end, they said there was no foul play. But we don't believe that."

"What did the police do?"

"They never looked into it properly. Just a few days after his funeral, it was all over. I know something's wrong. There's no way he walked out there."

They sat around the table in Stella's kitchen for close to two hours. Both Stella and Erica were surprisingly relaxed and open. Stella talked about her appeals for help to the two police officers she knew, and how both had been shot down by their superiors with the same line about Neil going for a walk, drunk, and freezing to death. Neither would risk investigating on his own. One had told her to get a lawyer.

"Who are they kidding, I can't afford that," Stella said, as she looked at the reporter.

She told Craig that they'd dealt closely with a native officer who really cared about the community, but didn't want to name him. She didn't have to. Ernie Louttit was one of Craig's regular sources. He was a real cowboy, but he was out there sincerely trying to be a good cop. On ride-alongs, Craig had seen Louttit in action, running through back alleys, chasing guys down. He'd watched Louttit pick up a girl on the strip and order her into his cruiser. As authoritative as Louttit had been with her on the street, he showed a strong compassionate side as he spoke to the young woman inside the car.

As the conversation continued, Stella was the first to admit that Neil was no angel. When she told him about Neil's run-ins with the police, he didn't interject; there was little to be gained in questioning Neil's character. However, Stella insisted, Neil had begun to come to terms with his drinking and had been in counselling in the months before he died.

Craig found himself admiring Stella. She was keeping her emotions in check, only occasionally wiping a tear from her eyes. The investigation, she insisted, had been too short. Craig's source in the police department had guardedly agreed.

"Why was he found, way up in the north industrial area with only one shoe? What kid goes out with only one shoe?"

Erica jumped in. "I don't believe the theory they have that he was walking to the correctional centre to give himself up. No juvenile is ever going to walk up to an adult facility. That's just plain bullshit."

"I know my son very well," continued Stella. "He wouldn't go out there by himself. Even though he was on the run, he always called home."

"We think he was driven to that area and abandoned," Erica said.

Stella turned from theories and speculation and drove home the simple tragedy of her son's death. "Not a day goes by when I don't shed a tear for my boy. I can't let him rest in peace knowing he didn't die naturally. Whoever did it is still out there."

Craig wrote it all down. He already knew how to end his article.

As he drove away, the reporter replayed the facts in his mind. He was inclined to believe Stella. Here was a mother who had lost her son and was looking for answers. He realized he'd begun to worry about failing her, but quickly banished such thoughts. That was no way for a journalist to think.

Back at the office he typed up his handwritten notes and started making calls. A social services worker corroborated that Neil was taking substance abuse counselling and that he was a smart kid. Neil's old wrestling coaches agreed, calling him a "kid with more potential than ninety percent of the other kids."

Craig then headed to the police station for some word on this investigation from the brass. Craig prided himself on his relationship with Dave Scott, the media-relations officer. Blessed with blond good looks and an approachable manner,

Scott was a smooth character, a golden boy at the SPS. When Craig first met him, Scott was a corporal, but he'd quickly made sergeant, and was now the public face of the Saskatoon police.

Craig thought Scott might be good for the city. He was ambitious and, at this pace, might well be a future chief. He'd received good tips from Scott. He occasionally worried that Scott might be using him, but he ignored such suspicions, glad to have such a well-connected source. Craig himself had fans on the force. A few years earlier, he'd written a story that claimed morale among beat cops was incredibly low. Chief Penkala had phoned him at home and blasted him. His story might have angered the chief, but it had also gained him the respect of the uniformed officers, and consequently better access to them.

He strode confidently into Scott's office on the main floor and sat down. The men were used to each other and generally chatted easily. Craig told Scott what Stella had told him. Scott vehemently denied Stella's assessment.

"I don't agree. A tremendous amount of work went into that case," he said, pointing to a hefty folder. Craig assumed this must be the Stonechild file.

Scott assured Craig that investigators had pursued every avenue. "The profile we have at this time was death by hypothermia. It was an unfortunate incident."

So, the police felt they'd done all they had to do.

Craig had hoped Scott would allow him to flip through the file, but Scott didn't offer. The reporter was surprised by the abrupt way Scott dismissed Stella's allegations. Craig was left with the distinct impression that Scott wanted him to go away and stop bothering him.

Craig believed policing was based on common sense and intuition. His own intuition was telling him something was wrong, but to date he had never gone wrong trusting Scott.

Family suspects foul play

Police say every avenue investigated

By Terry Craig
of The Star-Phoenix

When Neil Stonechild's frozen body was found in a vacant field in north Saskatoon last November, family members immediately suspected foul play.

Three months later, they still subscribe to that theory, even though the police file on the case has been closed.

The official cause of death was listed as hypothermia. Aside from some scratches on his nose, there were no marks of physical abuse. His blood-alcohol level was .15, almost twice the legal limit for impaired driving.

Stonechild's mother, Stella, and sister, Erica, are the first to admit Neil had a problem with alcohol but they say in the months before his death, he was coming to terms with his problem.

They also say that, had Stonechild been white, police would have been more thorough in the investigation of his death.

"It makes me wonder. If Neil was the son of the mayor or commission-

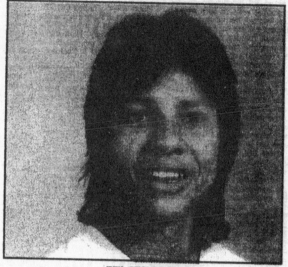

NEIL STONECHILD

er, police would still be investigating," Stella said.

A senior officer within the department guardedly agreed.

But department spokesman Sgt. Dave Scott vehemently denies Stel-

la's assessment of the investigation.

"I don't agree. A tremendous amount of work went into that case," he says.

MORE ON PAGE A2

— — —

Terry Craig's article dominated the March 4, 1991, edition of the *Star Phoenix*. Stella was sure that someone would finally take notice. The police would have to reopen the investigation. They couldn't ignore Neil's death after the headlines blasted his name into almost every household in Saskatoon.

But the SPS never called. Neither did any native leaders. Constitutional wrangling with the federal government was preoccupying the chiefs, and they failed to say a word about her son. The article had been on the front page but life went on as if no one read it. Canada and the world were preoccupied with the

Persian Gulf War. The death of Neil Stonechild seemed to matter only to his mother, and to a family that was falling apart.

Marcel kept drinking through the spring. Stella couldn't take much more. Night after night she'd hear him slamming on the brakes as he drove his car home early in the morning. He'd stumble around as he tried to put himself to bed. She blamed his behaviour on Neil's death. Marcel had never been a drinker.

Early one morning, Stella slipped on her robe and walked into the dark kitchen. Marcel opened the door and flicked on the light, surprised to see his mother there.

"Mum, didn't think I'd see you up this late, sorry I woke you."

"You can't keep doing this, you gotta stop drinking now." She'd worked herself up to this confrontation. Marcel could not escape; he sat down and stayed quiet. "You're gonna kill someone, or you're gonna kill yourself," his mother said. "I don't want another funeral."

The memory of Neil in that awful cheap box was enough for Marcel. He broke down. He looked up at his mother, his vision of her blurring through the alcohol-fuelled tears pouring down his face.

"Mum, there's something else."

"Did you do something?"

"Yeah," he said. "The night Neil died, I bought him that bottle."

Now she could understand why he was putting himself through hell. She was silent for a moment.

"You've told me now, but you've gotta stop, otherwise you'll drive us both crazy. Every day I'm worried I'm going to have to bury you, too."

He lurched forward to hug her. There was no other way to say he was sorry.

"You have to start working again. They're looking for somebody in maintenance at Eaton's, I'll talk to them." Marcel was exhausted, but coming clean with Stella relieved his pain somewhat. Together they'd find some way to get him out from under the weight of all that guilt.

Sleep had delivered only nightmares until one dream offered the release Marcel craved. He was in the bathroom of a bar when he saw Neil. Marcel was washing his face in the sink, splashing water on himself, trying to feel more conscious. Neil appeared behind him. Marcel turned.

"What are you doing here? You're dead."

"I know. I'm sitting with God; I want you to quit what you're doing. It's not your fault," answered Neil. "Don't worry about me. The Lord told me that we will get justice out of this."

Marcel woke up sobbing, pleading with his brother to stay, his brain seared with the remnants of the vision, lifelike reminders of a brother no amount of boozing could make him forget. After that the nightmares stopped.

— — —

About eight o'clock one spring evening in 1991, Jason Roy entered the cavernous, starkly lit Lucky Horseshoe bingo parlour. "The Shoe," as it was known locally, was the size of an Olympic swimming pool, a barn of a building on 20th Street, not far from St. Paul's Hospital. Reading Terry Craig's recent article about Neil in the *Star Phoenix* finally made Jason feel guilty enough to speak to Stella. When Neil had turned up frozen, Jason had told his friends, people like Cheryl, Eddie and Marcel, about seeing Neil cuffed in the cruiser, but he'd never had the courage to face Stella.

He figured he'd find her here.

For the last few months, Jason had gone back to his old pattern of B and E's and petty thefts. Always scared that he might be next, he stayed indoors a lot and drank heavily. Worst of all, he could not sleep. When he did, the nightmares came, usually the same one. Two cops were escorting him from the parking garage below the police station into an elevator. They crowded him into the narrow cell-like space. When the door opened he walked out behind them into a caged area. Suddenly the cops turned and pushed him, hard. The elevator had disappeared, and he fell backwards into black space.

Jason scanned the heads of the concentrating players seated at the long rows of cafeteria-style tables.

"Bingo," came a disembodied voice from one corner of the room. A collective groan went up. Still holding her fluorescent dabber, Stella looked at the twelve cards spread in front of her with disappointment. "Ah, well, what can you do," she said.

The call signaled the halftime break of the early-evening dabbing session at the Shoe. Norman wandered off to the snack counter across the room to get Stella some coffee and onion rings. Even beneath harsh fluorescent lights the big barn felt, and often functioned, a bit like a community centre. Stella was as relaxed during evening bingo here as she was watching TV at home.

"Excuse me," someone said. A teenage boy she recognized as a friend of Neil's stood beside her. His dark-brown eyes were sad and nervous and he stood with his shoulders slumped and his arms hanging limply at his side, as defeated as an old man.

"Jason Roy," the boy said as if sensing she did not immediately recognize him.

"M'hm, oh, yes. Hi," said Stella. She could tell he was shy so she smiled at him.

"Uhmm, you see," he said hesitating, his voice catching. "I mean, I was one of Neil's friends." He paused and gathered the strength to say why he had come. "I've been looking for you, 'cause I need to talk, you know . . ." His voice failed again.

"Let's go to a table over there," Stella said kindly, motioning to a kiosk a few tables away where volunteers sold extra cards. "The game won't start again for a bit. We can talk." Stella motioned to Norman, returning with the tray of food, to let him know that she would be back shortly.

When they sat down, Jason clasped his hands in front of him and looked down, unable to meet Stella's gaze. His words, when he began to speak, sounded like a confession. He described the events of the night Neil died, going to the Binnings', buying the bottle of Silent Sam, drinking, going to the 7-Eleven, walking to Snowberry Downs, coming back. Here he paused to get his breath.

"What is it?" Stella asked gently.

He looked up. He was starting to cry.

"Mrs. Stonechild," Jason said politely. "I'm sorry I didn't come before." He paused. "I didn't come because I didn't want you to hate me."

"Don't worry," she said. "I won't hate you. What is it?"

"Uhmm, the thing is I don't think Neil was—I don't think he—I don't think he walked to—to where he was found."

"M'hm."

"I saw Neil—in the back of a police car. A couple of cops stopped me on the way back. When they asked me my name I lied and gave them an alias. I didn't want to go with them. Neil—Neil was handcuffed in the back of the car. They didn't pick me up because I gave them a false name and . . ." He stopped, unable to continue. For a moment he looked as if he wanted to say something else, but then he pressed his face into his hands.

"Don't worry, Jason. I don't hate you. It's not in me to hate anybody. It's okay." Stella placed her hand on his arm. "Did you report it?"

"Yeah." Jason sniffled loudly and wiped his eyes with the palms of his hands. He thought about the cop in the suit, remembered giving his statement. "Yeah, I did."

"Well, that's okay then," Stella said. "Everything should be okay."

— — —

Jason's conversation with Stella at the Lucky Horseshoe didn't help his growing paranoia. Convinced the police were out to get him, he quit school, went back, then quit again. On one of the rare occasions he went out, he ran into Diana Fraser, a social worker. He knew Fraser from time he had spent at the Yarrow Youth Farm in the city's north end near the airport. They had always gotten along well. She had been the one to phone Crime Stoppers in early December, after hearing the rumour that the Pratts were responsible for dumping Neil in the north end field. She didn't tell Jason this.

Neil had been at Yarrow too, and his name soon came up. Jason quickly became upset and told Fraser about what he'd seen on the night Neil died, how Neil was screaming that the police were going to kill him.

Jason didn't ask for her help, so Fraser did not go to the police. Besides, who would believe a complaint against them from the likes of Jason Roy?

— — —

Jake Stonechild and Jeff Crowe were both sent back to Kilburn after Neil's funeral. Jake retreated entirely and never showed emotion about Neil's death. The facility's common rooms and classrooms, which would not be out of place at any community college, became a haven for him. The other kids at Kilburn had all come the same route he had. They had started by stealing bicycles and car radios under the influence of marijuana and booze and graduated to breaking into houses. They ended up in Kilburn, but as soon as they were out they would breach probation. As much as they might try to avoid getting caught and thrown back in, they would also arrange to get arrested at the same time so they could do their time together, like some bizarre extended family.

In a photograph taken inside Kilburn in the spring of 1991, Jake, who was known at the detention centre as "Jake the Brake," jostles a group of his buddies just as the photographer snaps the shutter. As thin as a stick, he wears a huge shit-kicking grin on his face. He looks like a kid enjoying summer camp.

Unlike Jake, Jeff Crowe raged, his pain morphing into suicidal despair. He couldn't understand why it was Neil who had died. Why not him? If only he'd been with Neil that night, he could have protected him. He felt useless, and wanted to die. He smashed furniture and punched and kicked the Kilburn staff. He cut himself with anything sharp. His desperate slashing left a ladder of scars on each arm, from elbow to wrist.

Later that spring, Jeff was in the gym with the other boys. The grey breeze-blocks along one wall caught his eye. He stood staring at the vast expanse of grey, ignoring all the boys around him. It had suddenly become a huge canvas. He wanted to fill this grey with colour.

He asked the staff for permission to paint a mural. Some argued he shouldn't be rewarded for acting out so violently. Others thought the project might be a way to keep him from killing himself. They gathered in the staff room, drinking coffee and discussing the tragic source of Jeff's despair. They had their own questions about Neil Stonechild's death.

Many of them had attended Neil's funeral service and had since read the article about him in the paper. They mocked outright the police theory that Neil was trying to find the correctional centre. They worked daily with these kids; young offenders typically knew the justice system better than most adults. Neil wouldn't go anywhere near the correctional centre. To most gathered in that staff room, Neil had clearly been taken out there and left to die.

Jeff got his permission. The staff bought him acrylic paints and soon he was standing on scaffolding, facing the wall and painting obsessively. Jeff brushed colour angrily across the rough cement. His hand moved without hesitation. He worked free-hand straight onto the wall, with no outlines or sketches. The staff usually had to force him to stop at the end of whatever time he had been allowed.

It took Jeff three months to paint the haunting mural. When he was finished, the painting was three metres high and over twelve metres wide. It filled one entire wall of the gym, dominating the room. Almost none of the boys who saw it for the first time could ignore it. Some dared only say, "What's up with that?" Others asked questions, without appearing to be interested, until gradually the story behind the unsettling panels came to be told.

In the first panel, a boy on the left leans forward. He is painted in stark white enclosed by thick black lines, head raised and arms stretched up and out toward the right. Trapped in the spirit world, he pleads without a sound. To his right, another boy looks back from the land of the living. Either he cannot understand what his friend is saying or there is nothing he can do to help him.

The images on the second panel have been distorted into a nightmare vision. The boy on the right crouches down, bent over from the waist, right arm extended. Deep-red slash marks rise like steps on a ladder from his wrist to his elbow. Demons in animal shapes beat down upon his head, swirling and spinning. The monsters appear to confuse and crush his soul.

The last two panels show characters representing Neil and his family gathering protectively around the boy, who is still alive and suffering. Gradually, with difficulty, he finds the strength to fight off the urge to kill himself. Jeff called the third panel "Brothers" and at the bottom of the fourth panel on the far right, he signed the name he had now taken as an artist: Jeffrey Bluesky Crowe. He dedicated the mural to the Stonechild family and marked it with a curious symbol, the image of the medicine wheel turning backwards, to the left, against nature.

When he finished the painting, Jeff vowed to continue signing his work with the same symbol until the questions about his friend's death were answered, no matter how long it might take.

GIVING UP AND GOING HOME

BY THE FALL OF 1991 JASON ROY LOOKED AND smelled like a street person. Within months of seeing Diana Fraser on the street, Jason was back in custody at Kilburn Hall, where she was assigned to be his caseworker. Jason's downward spiral troubled her enough that she referred him to a young teacher-therapist named Brenda Valiaho.

Valiaho had been teaching at Kilburn since 1986, but through the fall of 1991 she also did part-time, unpaid coun- selling there as part of her work toward a master's degree in educational psychology from the University of Saskatchewan.

Jason met with Valiaho a couple of times in Kilburn just before he was set to be released in November. On the first visit he revealed his difficulty sleeping because of what had hap- pened to Neil. From her work at school, Valiaho thought a visu- alization exercise to evoke the senses, sights and sounds of that night might help him work through the emotional trauma he was experiencing. Jason agreed, and the next time they met he lay on his back on a couch in a quiet room, closed his eyes, and went through a step-by-step description of what happened the night Neil and he went to Snowberry Downs. Occasionally as he talked he could hear Valiaho's voice: "Where are you now? What are you doing?"

When Jason got to the point of seeing Neil in the police car, he became extremely agitated. Valiaho thought he was half crying, half holding his breath. He choked out that Neil wanted help and was screaming, "Help me! Help me! They're going to kill me," but that he had denied knowing his friend.

Jason would not let her talk to anyone about what he had told her; he was too afraid to push things with the police. Valiaho thought that he should talk everything through with Neil's family. Having spoken only briefly to Stella, he agreed, and she began working with him on a plan to do so.

— — —

Stella and her family stayed in Saskatoon for two years after the March 4, 1991, article in the *Star Phoenix*. If anything, she became more and more preoccupied with Neil, to the point where she began to watch for him. She knew he was dead, but couldn't help thinking that she sometimes saw him on the street. One day she found herself looking up the escalator in the basement of Eaton's. She thought she saw him coming down toward her. She started to move forward, her heart raced. She stood staring for a few seconds longer at the metal stairs steadily disappearing into the floor, then realized that Neil was not there. She burst into tears. A few minutes later in the washroom, she made up her mind. She could not stay in Saskatoon any longer.

— — —

Constable Bob Morton, who had seized Neil's clothes in the St. Paul's Hospital morgue in 1990, threw them into the trash on January 12, 1993. In his report, Morton says he disposed of the clothing because Jarvis indicated the case was closed and the exhibits could be destroyed. The report shows no sign that Morton questioned Jarvis in any way about the strange request.

Stella had gone to the station several times, trying to get Neil's clothes back, but without success. The usual police policy was to return the clothes to the family once a case was over, but on that afternoon in January 1993, Morton simply did as Jarvis told him and threw the clothes away.

They were hauled to the Saskatoon landfill several miles south of the city. At that time of year icy fog crept over the banks of the nearby river and smoke billowed from the stacks of the power station. Lost and invisible amid the sea of refuse that flowed out when one of the trucks tipped its load into the dump were a boy's blue jacket, a checkered lumberjack shirt, a pair of blue jeans, a pair of underwear, a pair of spandex shorts, two socks and a single running shoe for the left foot.

Keith Jarvis retired from the Saskatoon Police Service in August 1993 after twenty-seven years of service.

— — —

On a morning of cold rain in October 1993, Norman finished tying the bright orange plastic tarp over his and Stella's belongings in the back of an ancient red pickup. Stella had tried to get rid of what she could, but the truck was crammed to the gunnels with chairs and tables, beds, clothing, living-room furniture, boxes of papers and two TVs.

"Looks good," Norman announced in a jaunty mumble as he opened the passenger door.

"Uhmm," said Stella doubtfully.

Sheets of rain driven by a blustery wind slashed against the windshield as Norman's brother Louis, who had offered to help them move, put the old truck in gear. Stella sat in the middle of the roomy cab leaning slightly against Norman. Just after five, they pulled away from the house on Confederation Crescent for the last time.

The truck headed north up Confederation Drive. A minute

or so later Louis turned right onto 33rd Street at the 7-Eleven convenience store where Neil and Jason had stopped to warm up. The ugly complex of Snowberry Downs stood on the northwest corner of the intersection. After a few more minutes they reached Circle Drive and turned north again.

Stella felt only relief at leaving Saskatoon behind. Their twenty-hour drive would take them to Prince Albert, east to The Pas, Manitoba, and then north again to the Cree reserve encircling the small Métis community of Cross Lake. As remote as it was, north of the farthest tip of Lake Winnipeg, Cross Lake was a natural destination for her and Norman. He came from Cross Lake, where he had inherited his father's trapline. Stella's older sister Marcie also lived in Cross Lake with her husband, Archie McKay, the pastor who had conducted Neil's funeral. The two women had talked on the phone several times before Stella made up her mind to move. The situation was complicated. Jake, now seventeen, was back in Kilburn Hall. Marcel was taking a bus to join them, but they would be leaving Jake behind. Still, Marcie encouraged her to make the move. Jake could be with them when he got out. The most important thing, she said, was for Stella to make a fresh start.

The decision seemed to be working out even before they got there. Shortly before they'd left that morning, Marcie called with the good news that she had found a neighbour willing to rent them a four-bedroom house. It barely mattered to Stella that the house had no heat, no electricity and no running water.

The occupants of the pickup truck grew silent as night fell. They had been on the road for fifteen hours. A wall of spruce trees lit by their high beams passed hypnotically on either side of the truck. Norman dozed and occasionally looked out the window. Exhausted, Stella watched large, wet snowflakes begin to flash out of the blackness and melt on the windshield as soon as they hit. Louis switched on the wipers.

"What's that?" Stella asked, hearing Norman mutter something.

"Think I saw something fly off," he said.

"Oh no," said Stella. "Louis, stop the truck. We better stop the truck and have a look."

Moments later the three tired travellers stood illuminated by the red tail lights. They stared in dismay at a sea of papers scattered across the asphalt. The tarp had come loose miles back. Each passing bump had sent another of their possessions careening off into the wilderness.

Hoping that nothing important had been lost, Stella found herself looking down at a TV lying on the ground, its screen intact but the back shattered.

"Uh-oh," she said beginning to chuckle under her breath, "Oh my." For whatever reason, the scene caused by Norman's poor knotsmanship suddenly struck her as comical.

Her chuckle turned into loud laughter. In a few hours she would be sleeping at her sister's home far away from Saskatoon. For now, for her, that was enough.

PART II

HIGHEST POWER

Prologue

On May 22, 1976, three aboriginal people, two men and a pregnant woman, walked slowly toward Saskatoon from beyond the city limits. The woman had no idea how long they had been walking or how far they had gone. The only way she could keep moving was to keep her eyes fixed on the four dusty shoes of her companions in front of her. They'd stayed with her, at least.

Her eyes stayed focused on those shoes, crunching gravel and kicking wisps of dust into the dry air. The weight of the baby made her pitch awkwardly forward with each step. She reached under her swollen belly and joined her hands in a sort of makeshift cradle, doing her best to support the baby's weight. But the shoulder of the road was uneven and too often she had to reach out for balance, or press one hand against her aching back. The baby, due in less than a month, reacted violently to the lurching and stumbling with repeated flurries of hard kicks.

The next thing the woman knew she was sitting on a boulder at the side of the road. Her two companions had not noticed that she was no longer behind them. They were nowhere in sight.

Her breathing slowly calmed and grew less ragged. The baby must have fallen asleep because its kicking had stopped. The strong spring scent of wildflowers in the ditch filled her nostrils like smelling salts. Sober now, and sitting still, she remembered how she'd gotten here.

The woman hadn't been afraid when the cop had appeared unexpectedly and accused them of drinking in public. She and her friends had most likely laughed when he'd demanded an explanation for their behaviour. Even when he forced the three of them into the back of the Saskatoon Police Services cruiser, he hadn't scared them. There were much worse places to sleep it off than the drunk tank.

No, the fear had started when she'd noticed they were going in the wrong direction, away from the police station and out of town. The three friends had stopped laughing. Where was the cop taking them? What he was going to do to them? They had heard the stories. Like a creature out of legend, fear stole their voices. They fell silent in the back of the police car, and watched as the outskirts of Saskatoon moved past in a steady blur.

The car had rolled slowly to a stop. The cop got out, opened the door and hauled them by their collars from the back seat. Then he simply climbed back behind the wheel, closed his door and drove off. Being dumped miles from the city came almost as a relief. The cop hadn't beaten anybody, he hadn't even taken their names. Then they had started to walk and realized how far it was to get home.

The woman pulled herself to her feet and looked down the road, toward where she figured the city must be. The short rest had settled her nerves and given her a chance to get angry. She forgot to be afraid that something might happen to her, that no one would believe her.

"I'm going to say something," she said to herself. "No matter what, I'm going to say something."

Resolved, she folded her hands under her unborn child and marshalled the strength and determination to start walking again. Maybe, if she walked quickly, she could catch up to her friends. Maybe they were waiting for her just ahead.

— — —

On October 18, 1976, Chief James Kettles posted a one-page memo to staff on the Saskatoon police station bulletin board.

P126
P.D. 10—M.P.
For Ident.

RG-031

OFFICE OF CHIEF OF POLICE

October 18, 19 76.

TO .... PERSONNEL

GENERAL ORDER

▇▇▇▇▇▇▇▇▇▇▇▇▇▇▇▇▇ was charged with Breaches of Discipline under the Saskatchewan Police Act, Part 3 of the Discipline Code, that on the 22nd day of May, 1976, he did commit:-

(1) Neglect of duty under Section 3.01(3) of the Discipline Code

and

(2) Discreditable conduct under Section 3.01(1), in that he failed to charge three people or any one of them, of having liquor in a place other than a dwelling under The Liquor Act and did further, in regard to the second charge, act in a manner prejudicial to discipline or likely to bring discredit upon the reputation of the Saskatoon Police Force by forcing the said persons into a Police vehicle and driving them to a remote area outside the City Limits and leaving said individuals to walk back to the City, particularly a female who was then eight months pregnant.

▇▇▇▇▇▇▇▇▇▇▇ appeared before me in my office on Thursday, June 24th and denied the charge. He appeared again on July 28th for Hearing, at which time the matter was adjourned to August 11th for Finding. On August 11th, he appeared in my Office, at which time I held that the charges as laid were proven and the matter was adjourned to Friday, October 15th, for submissions by Counsel and Punishment.

On Friday, October 15th, ▇▇▇▇▇▇▇▇▇▇ appeared before me, was reprimanded and under the provisions of Section 1.23(1)(d) was assessed a fine of $200.00, payable forthwith.

James G. Kettles,
Chief of Police.

JGK:sb

STARLIGHT TOUR

IT WAS FRIDAY, JANUARY 21, 2000, NEARLY TEN years after the death of Neil Stonechild. Jocelan Shandler, the owner of a government-approved group home in Saskatoon, stood in her bedroom smoking a cigarette and crying.

Shandler worked hard to run the facility like a real home, with a minimum of rules. But she kept prescription drugs for her five residents, everything from tranquilizers to morphine, in a locked cabinet in her bedroom. She had just come back from getting groceries, toward evening, and had gone up to her bedroom and found both the bedroom door and the cabinet locks jimmied and several doses of Clonazepam and Benztropine tablets missing. She was certain that thirty-year-old Lawrence Wegner, a Cree Indian from the Saulteaux reserve near North Battleford who had been living in her home for the last three years, had stolen the drugs.

He had pilfered the drug cabinet twice in the past few months. Realizing her only choice was to evict him upset Shandler terribly. She sat on her bed to think it through.

In frequent telephone conversations over the years with Wegner's mother, Mary, a social worker who also helped natives with drug and alcohol addictions, Shandler had often said she loved the young man like a son. He was achingly thin for his five-foot-nine-inch frame; his eyeglasses magnified the soft, startled look of his eyes. Wegner was always the first around the home to help out with anything that needed doing, and the other residents trusted and talked to him about their problems. Shandler described him as "a gentle, sweet, good person."

She dreaded the inevitable confrontation with Wegner. His thoughtfulness and kindness took even strangers by surprise, but he could not handle the slightest tension. Even if he was just a bystander, any conflict or argument paralyzed him with fear and anxiety. His muscles would go rigid and he'd stumble over his words. He'd shake and try to retreat, even flee outright. "I got to go. I got to go. We'll talk later," he'd say. If any of the other residents in the home took something away from him, he would not ask for it back. If the other residents were being pushy and overbearing, he would retreat to his room. She had long ago concluded that his bouts of panic were the biggest reason Wegner had begun using drugs in his late teens. He had developed a craving for marijuana and then morphine, which he would inject whenever alarm gripped his insides. Over the years, some hard-won and lengthy periods of abstinence had invariably given way to old dependencies.

In September 1997, Wegner reached a new low. His Aunt Celina brought him to the emergency room of Saskatoon's Royal University Hospital, where he screamed that his brain was draining out and that his kidneys itched madly. "I need my blood out of my body," he insisted, pouring salt and pepper into his coffee. Eight years ago, he'd shown up at another Saskatoon emergency room, ranting about non-existent music and the sound of ocean waves. In both cases, psychiatrists diagnosed a psychosis brought on by drug use.

After that low point, Wegner's fortunes started to turn around. Haloperidol and Benztropine, heavy tranquilizers the doctors had prescribed to prevent his psychosis, seemed to keep his anxieties at bay. This, in turn, kept him from resorting to drugs.

Most importantly, in December 1997, Lawrence Wegner moved into Shandler's group home.

Mary Wegner worried that doctors saw her son as nothing more than a set of symptoms. As a social worker, she understood how being labelled as "mentally ill" forever distorted the way people looked at you. Shandler agreed and shared Wegner's belief that her son was not schizophrenic, as some doctors suspected. At Shandler's home, he never once exhibited anything resembling a hallucination; he clearly suffered not from schizophrenia but from a drug problem, depression and panic disorder.

With Shandler's help, Wegner had been able to work at the Abilities Council sheltered workshop and even took a job for a few months soldering components for a company called WaveCom Electronics, until the shaking in his hands from his prescription drugs had forced him to quit.

By the fall of 1999, Wegner, apparently clean of street drugs, managed to enroll at his mother's alma mater, the Saskatchewan Indian Federated College, for courses in social work. He told his mother about his dream of becoming a voice for Saskatchewan native people. "I want to make you proud of me. I want to stand up for our band, our people. I love sitting listening to the elders with the stories. I love learning about what happened to my people. I love it."

Despite his enthusiasm, the pressures of homework and exams overwhelmed Wegner. Soon after classes started, he began smoking marijuana frequently, and being stoned drained him of energy. Shandler remembered him at dinner once, his fork frozen in space halfway to his mouth. Another time he fell asleep with his head lolling over the back of his chair. Another resident, who had tried to blow his own head off with a shotgun and now took morphine to dull the constant pain of reconstructive surgery to his face, had to carry Wegner to bed.

Shandler had caught Wegner saving up his meds in his dresser drawer. Twice in December he had broken into the locked bedroom and stolen money and morphine. The real problem, in Shandler's view, was a girlfriend Wegner had met at school. She was gorgeous, but she had been on the street since she was thirteen and she mainlined drugs. Shandler feared the girl had Wegner back at it.

Shandler took Wegner to visit Dr. David Keegan, his psychiatrist. At the session Wegner was unusually frank. He said he was depressed and admitted using pot and morphine again. Keegan, who had recently reduced the dosage of the drugs Wegner was taking to help him concentrate on his schoolwork, now increased the Haloperidol prescription to prevent the drug-induced psychosis from recurring.

Keegan had started treating Wegner in 1999, and agreed with Shandler that Wegner did not suffer from schizophrenia. His own diagnosis of the young man, whom he described as "a sincere, honest, dedicated, quiet, respectful individual," was that he suffered from a substance-abuse disorder, combined with a mood disorder that included clinical depression. Now, in addition to the Clonazepam he prescribed to help with the anxiety symptoms, Keegan prescribed one of the newer antidepressants, Venlafaxine.

Doing everything she could to help Lawrence turn himself around, Shandler got him to write out a note, taking responsibility for the thefts. His hand shook as he wrote the short note on a sheet of lined writing paper, dated December 8, 1999. The simply but neatly written letters tilted to the right and the left like buildings about to fall. He tried to correct the spelling errors by writing over them.

After Christmas, Wegner returned to the group home from a family visit to the reserve with new winter clothes, including a sweater and boots. He loved to dress well and the visit also gave him a new resolve to keep the promises he had made in his note.

Dec 8/99

I Laurence K Wegner 170$ without permission to do so. I took money from the drawer in two incidents. The first time was 60$ the second time was 20$. I am going to pay them back at the end of the month. I plan on staying off the drugs, and go to addiction services today.

Signed Lawrence WEGNER.

In the first few weeks of 2000, he began lifting weights in the school gym, hoping to pack some muscle onto his skinny frame. He and Shandler spent hours at the kitchen table chain-smoking and discussing his latest school project—an essay on the Cree *ehmaykwanowake*—a tradition whose name has been translated as "a passing of something to each other," or the Give-Away ceremony. Held normally in the fall or late winter, it was dedicated to a spirit power known as *pa-kakkus,* or the Bony Spectre. After an initial feast, dancing followed for four nights. Even children took part, and as they danced they gave one another gifts. Like many native religious ceremonies, the Give-Away dance was banned once and had long been practised discreetly. The belief that generosity in gift giving would bring status and blessings from the spirit world fascinated Wegner. As did its inverse: anyone who gave poor gifts in exchange for good ones would not enjoy them and would experience bad luck.

But no matter how hard he tried, Wegner could not keep his demons at bay. In the third week of January 2000, sitting on her bed looking at the pried-open cabinet door, Shandler knew that his depression had returned, and so had his drug use. She wiped the tears off her face and went downstairs to find him.

Telling Wegner he would have to leave was one of the most painful things Shandler had ever done. Surprisingly, he didn't panic. Sitting at the kitchen table, he tried to make the case that he was only taking his own drugs, and that he would do better. But the two of them had agreed that there could be no more chances after last December. He seemed to understand. They stood and hugged each other and both of them cried.

Unable to find a place to stay, Wegner remained at the group home for a few more days. At some point Shandler called Mary Wegner, who called Lawrence's brother, Wayne. But neither knew what to do. Lawrence had smoked dope in front of Wayne's one-year-old son, Bailey, when visiting. He had stopped when Wayne asked him to, but Wayne didn't want anyone smoking dope around his child.

On Sunday, January 23, Wegner gathered up a box of winter clothes and a few personal effects, including a photo of Bailey, and headed out. Shandler had been shocked to see the address on Avenue P South he was moving to. It was the home of one of Wegner's drug-using friends, Brent Ahenakew. Shandler embraced Wegner at the door as he left and they cried again.

Ahenakew lived in the kind of apartment building that didn't ask for references and where you could expect to have your door kicked in at all hours. Most of the arrests in the city were made just a block away, on 20th Street West, and a steady procession of ambulances raced by each night toward St. Paul's, Saskatoon's oldest hospital. Nearby, on the Stroll, native girls as young as eleven and twelve sold themselves to farm boys in town for a good time, or to lawyers, doctors and university professors discreetly visiting from across the river.

Shandler had only met Ahenakew once, a few weeks earlier when Wegner had brought him to the home. Coming through the door with grocery bags cradled in both arms, Shandler heard Ahenakew bumming cigarettes from a resident. His willingness to prey on people not strong enough to say no infuriated her. She told Wegner never to bring Ahenakew back, but he didn't listen. Some of the other residents told her that Ahenakew had come back and pushed Wegner to steal drugs, prodding him, "Get me some, get me some."

Wegner came back to Shandler's only once after he left. He showed up on Wednesday, January 26, to pick up some laundry she had done for him, and to promise to pay back at the beginning of the month the money he'd taken from her. Shandler cried again as he left, but Wegner reassured her. "Jocelan, Jocelan," he said. "I should be okay. I should be okay."

— — —

Some time after midnight on the morning of January 28, 2000, Constable Dan Hatchen partnered up with Constable Ken Munson in marked police cruiser number 27. Both men were husky, but Munson had a way of carrying himself, a sort of game-on walk that signalled he meant business. With sixteen years' experience in the service, much more than his partner, Hatchen took a laid-back approach. However, Munson had the higher profile. He had arrived in September 1982 from England, where he'd worked as a police officer for six years, receiving a commendation for rescuing a man from a burning house. After starting with the SPS in January of 1984, he received a decoration for talking a native man out of jumping from a third-floor balcony window holding his three-month-old baby.

Especially while on the graveyard shift, patrolling the Stroll, with its young hookers and druggies, the partners could talk about their families. Munson was an avid soccer coach who had three children ages thirteen, sixteen and eighteen. Hatchen had five children, between the ages of eleven and sixteen.

Despite their differing styles, Hatchen and Munson got along well; they'd been partners for the last six years.

— — —

At roughly three in the morning, Darrell Night walked out of a popular native nightclub in downtown Saskatoon called C-Weeds. His thick eyeglasses fogged over in the minus twenty-two-degree wind chill. As he took them off to wipe them with his shirt, he opened his right eye and immediately started to lose his balance. The dizziness had nothing to do with the alcohol he had drunk; it was a complication from a bout of tuberculosis and meningitis almost six years earlier that had nearly cost him his life. "I like living," he used to tell friends to explain how he had recovered. Since then, he had to keep his right eye shut or risk staggering and falling over. When people Night met for the first time asked him about it, he said he had been told the problem could be fixed for ten thousand dollars in an American hospital, and he'd shrug. He was an unemployed native man living in Saskatoon, with a grade eleven education and a drinking problem. Ten grand was a sum he was unlikely ever to see, much less spend.

Night was dressed for a night spent taxiing between bars or taking short walks to visit friends: a blue jean jacket with a fleece collar, light blue denim shirt hanging loosely over a pair of jeans, white running shoes, no hat, no gloves. Staying warm was no concern. He blew on his hands to warm them up, while he and his friends decided what to do next.

Over the years, Night had been in his share of brawls at two of the city's worst hotels, the Albany and the Barry. Well over six feet tall and weighing 260 pounds, the big man could take care of himself. He had accrued the majority of his twenty-two convictions for drunken scuffles.

But tonight he was in a good mood and ready to party. He'd started out around nine at a neighbourhood bar called the

Red Rock Tavern at Avenue W and 22nd Street. He'd downed a couple of beers and watched some pool with his cousin Harry and Harry's wife, Donna. Night could be good company. He'd tell jokes in a drawl so slow and innocent his friends wouldn't realize they'd been had until his mischievous grin gave him away. The threesome then joined a couple of friends and taxied down to C-Weeds, where they'd stayed until closing.

Starting to feel the cold as he lingered in the nightclub doorway, Night suggested they all jump in another cab and grab some more booze. He knew of a house party at an apartment in the west end between Avenue T and Avenue U, not far from his sister Sharon's place. He'd get to party for a few hours longer and not be far from a bed for the night.

They first tried the "off sales"—a bar that also sold takeout cases of beer—but it had closed at three. Their only choice was a bootlegger. Night got the cab to take them to a house at the corner of Avenue G and 18th Street, a few blocks away. When the door opened, a bald white pensioner looked out at the group suspiciously. The grumpy old man had been selling booze illegally since Night had first met his son in grade seven. They put down sixty dollars for two twenty-sixers of vodka.

When the cab dropped them off at the building with the house party, they simply followed the music and loud voices to the right door. Night had paid for the vodka, and was determined to get his share.

As he sat the two bottles on the kitchen table, he kept a huge hand securely wrapped around one of them, reaching with the other hand for a coffee mug. He filled the mug at least half full and then flavoured the vodka with a splash of orange soda. Three or four ounces of alcohol would give him a nice buzz, which was fine to finish out the night. He wandered into the living room to settle down and enjoy himself.

A fight broke out as he was contemplating the bottom of his empty mug. It was just after five in the morning. Night tried to ignore the quarrel at first. Two women were cursing and kicking a man. "The usual," thought Night. "Asshole is probably sleeping with both of them and got caught." Out of the corner of his eye, he saw another man cross the room with his head lowered, shoving people aside as he approached.

"Ah, come on, man. No," Night muttered. This was trouble. Within seconds the two men were whaling on each other on the floor, the women were tearing at each other's clothes and the fight was spreading like a brushfire through the room.

Night made for the door. No way was he getting caught up in this. He waited a minute to see if things might die down. He wasn't ready to face Sharon. His sister had already read him the riot act about drinking and coming in too late if he expected to stay with her—and he'd promised to help her move the next day. A woman grabbed the phone to call the police. "Fucking assholes," he thought. The party was over. Without looking back, he headed for the stairs.

— — —

Dispatch called in a weapons disturbance at 136 Avenue Q South between 22nd and 21st at 5:20 a.m., not far from where Hatchen and Munson were in the west end of the city. A man had reportedly gone berserk in the house with a knife and was threatening the other occupants. They heard over the radio that the man had fled on foot and that a tracking dog had been brought in. About ten cars responded, and Hatchen and Munson were among the last to arrive at 136 Avenue Q South. Hatchen punched their time into the computer at 5:23:36. But there was nothing for them to do. The first two cars stayed at the house, and another officer stayed with the canine unit to start the track. Other cars called over the radio that they were setting up a perimeter to contain the suspect. Car 27 continued past the house toward the intersection of 21st Street. Hatchen didn't punch in the fact that they were leaving the scene.

"Nothing for us here," Munson said.

— — —

At least he didn't have far to go, Night thought, as he emerged from the apartment building. The temperature with the wind chill was still minus twenty-two, but his sister lived just across a small park from where he was standing, and he could get there in three minutes if he cut through.

A police car drove by him. As it passed, it slowed slightly. Seeing the police triggered all of Night's latent anger. He lunged off the sidewalk toward the cruiser and raised his right hand with the middle finger extended. Normally the Stroll was full of activity, day or night. But at five-thirty on the morning of January 28, Night and the two police officers were the only people on the street.

All Hatchen could hear through the rolled-up windows of the cruiser was "fucking bastards." As the car continued to move past, Night pounded two or three times on either the trunk or the side panels.

Munson looked at his partner as if to say, "That's not on." He stopped the car and, without hurrying, backed up until he was even with Night. He rolled down his window and, looking directly at him, asked, "What's your problem?"

Night stood his ground and looked back at the officer with disgust. "About fucking time you guys showed up. Do I have to tell you how to do your jobs? Get up there and fucking stop those fights." Something in the way Munson looked back at him made Night cover the last few steps to the cruiser. Leaning toward Munson until their faces were only twenty centimetres apart, he said, "What's *your* fucking problem?"

Hatchen had had enough. He got out quickly and walked around the back of the car to the driver's side. Night turned away from the driver to face Hatchen and started shouting, "What's your problem? I didn't start the fuckin' fight. Do your jobs. Get up there and stop those guys." When Night stepped back to face Hatchen, Munson jumped out of the car as well.

Now Night stood between the two police officers. He grew quiet; no matter what he said now he was going to the drunk tank. It wasn't the first time, and he was even somewhat relieved that he wouldn't have to face Sharon. Hatchen said, "You're under arrest," and reached for Night's right hand and started to pull it behind him to put on the cuffs. Night clenched his fist and obstructed Hatchen's attempt by raising his arm to shoulder level. Hatchen managed to attach one of the cuffs to Night's outstretched arm. For a moment it looked as if the situation might escalate into a fight, but suddenly Night relaxed, unclenched his fist, dropped his arm and let Hatchen cuff his other wrist.

The street was deserted, and the windows of nearby houses were obscured by blinds pulled down against the cold. No one but Night, Hatchen and Munson seemed to be awake, but the reason the officers later gave for the arrest was "causing a disturbance." The Criminal Code describes few infractions more minor, but Night was going for a ride. As far as the dispatchers back at the police station knew, Hatchen and Munson were still involved in the dispute at 136 Avenue Q South. They had never indicated on their computer that they'd left.

They shoved him roughly onto the hard back seat of the cruiser. Hatchen had had trouble securing the cuffs, and to Night it felt as if the handcuffs were tightening further. He grunted in pain. "You racist bastards. You're only doing this 'cause I'm an Indian." He leaned as far as he could to one side, trying to take his full weight off his hands. He'd been in the same fix enough times to realize he should never have opened his mouth.

The car made a U-turn, headed east toward the police station. "C'mon, guys," Night begged, "you don't have to do this. I wasn't doin' anything. Just let me go." Munson and Hatchen ignored him.

Riding as the passenger, Hatchen was responsible for making entries in the mobile terminal. Although they had arrested Night, neither of the police officers had asked him his name. Nor did Hatchen punch anything into the computer to record that they had someone in their back seat.

The cruiser turned south from 20th onto Avenue H, away from the police station. Night didn't give the turn much thought, at first. Having lived in Saskatoon all his life, he knew they were in the Riversdale section of town. The light industrial sheds that buzzed with delivery trucks by day were silent now.

When they passed the intersection of Avenue H and 11th Street and carried on along the South Saskatchewan River, Night realized something was wrong. As it dawned on him they were leaving town, heading toward the power station, he remembered the rumours he'd heard. "I'm done for," he thought. "These guys are going to beat the shit out of me, maybe even kill me. What the hell am I supposed to do?"

Scared for his life, he began pleading to be let go. His mind raced for something that would make them listen to him. He remembered the name of a beat cop he knew.

"Guys, let me out. Y'know Marv Hanson? You can talk to him. I know him. You gotta let me outta here."

He got no reply.

"What are ya goin' to do? Take me out to the landfill and shoot me?"

This time Hatchen did answer. "No, you just have a little walk."

Near the city limits, the car passed a one-storey building flooded with light. Darrell recognized the Queen Elizabeth power station. He remembered this place from almost a quarter century earlier. He and his older brother, Merv, used to ride their BMX bikes past the power station all the time when they were eleven or twelve years old. It seemed like the greatest adventure in the world. They'd leave their house near 11th Street and Avenue P, and ride sometimes from morning until dinner time. They used to pedal like maniacs down Spadina Crescent, along the same route the cops were taking him now.

A few minutes later the car stopped. They were now more than two kilometres past the power plant and very near the entrance to Leisureland trailer park. It was five-thirty in the morning. All of the trailer windows were dark. Darrell Night sat perfectly still, expecting the worst.

Hatchen got out of the passenger side and opened the door to the back seat. Munson stayed behind the wheel.

"Get out of the car," Hatchen said.

Night did not move. It was so cold that Hatchen's boots made a cracking sound as he stepped toward him.

"I said, get out of the car."

When Night still refused to get out, Hatchen grabbed his arm and started to pull him out. The sudden pain made him yield, and he bashed his head into the top of the door frame on the way out of the back seat.

On the small roadway near an expanse of desolate, dark fields and a sleeping trailer park, the only light came from the stars, which flashed like shards of ice set in the blackness overhead.

Hatchen had no worries about their prisoner freezing to death. He obviously knew the area. Why else would he mention the landfill? He didn't know the guy's name, but he'd seen him countless times wandering 20th Street in the same kind of cold wearing the same clothes. In fact, Hatchen couldn't remember ever seeing him dressed differently, winter or summer.

Hatchen shoved Night a few steps toward the back of the cruiser and spun him around so he could remove the cuffs. Somehow the man's denim shirt had gotten stuck in the mechanism. Hatchen cursed under his breath.

Through the rear-view mirror, Munson could see his partner was having trouble. This was taking too long. He got out of the car to help.

Night fell awkwardly forward over the car's trunk and the cold of the metal burned his cheek. Hatchen pressed down on the cuffs' locking mechanism. With his good eye, Night made out the numbers stencilled on the cruiser's rear window. He thought he saw a 5 and a 7.

Once the cuffs were off, the two officers got back in the car and slammed their doors. Night shouted: "I know your car number. It's 57." The car began to pull away. "I know Marv Hanson."

The brittle snow crunched beneath the cruiser's tires. "You can't leave me here, I'll freeze to death," he screamed.

The cruiser crawled forward a hundred metres or so and pulled a U-turn. As it approached Night, it slowed and stopped. The silence and the cold magnified the sound of the electric window on the driver's side being lowered. It seemed like the only sound in the world. Munson eyeballed him again, almost exactly as he had in the beginning.

"That's your fucking problem," he said.

Night watched in a daze as the red tail lights receded into the darkness and then disappeared entirely. As soon as Hatchen and Munson got onto Valley Road heading back to Saskatoon, Hatchen keyed "Available" into the car's mobile data terminal. Immediately, the dispatcher back at the station requested they go to a parking dispute on Clancy Drive in the west end. Hatchen and Munson wrote nothing about the big native guy in their notebooks.

"It'll be your fuckin' problem, if I get back," Night said out loud. He took a few seconds to get his bearings as the alcohol and the adrenaline kept the cold briefly at bay. No use going straight north, he knew. Nothing there but the CN railway yards and the city dump, a giant mound that obscured the lights of Saskatoon. He didn't even consider trying the trailers directly behind him, figuring no one would open the door for him. His best bet was the power station. They'd let him in and he could call a cab.

He turned up the collar of his jean jacket and hunched his shoulders, trying to protect his ears. He stuffed his hands in his jeans pockets and started walking eastward along Spadina, bordering the river, toward the lights of the power station. With his chin tucked into his jacket he watched his running shoes hitting the snow with a kind of hypnotic rhythm. He looked up after a few minutes. The power station seemed as far away as when he began. He despaired at his lack of progress. But the only thing he could do was to put his head down against the bitter wind and keep walking. When he looked up a second time and the lights seemed to be as far away as before, fear knotted his gut. "I'm not going to freeze to death out here," he told himself over and over to ward off the other thoughts preying on the edges of his determination.

— — —

As Darrell Night was beginning his walk toward the power station, Mark Evoy was finishing his twelve-hour shift. With twenty years' experience at SaskPower, Evoy was one of six shift workers responsible for the twenty-four-hour-a-day operation of the plant.

Shortly after six, Evoy went to the second-floor control room to listen to the radio and finish off his paperwork, as he did at the end of every shift. As he sorted through the mail, he heard the announcer report that the cold weather was going to continue. When he finished, he gathered the inter-office mail to take to the front office, which faced Spadina Crescent.

— — —

Darrell Night's breath froze as it blew back in his face, slowly turning his eyebrows and hairline pure white. He wasn't thinking clearly and each step was becoming increasingly difficult. He only realized he had reached the front door of the power station when light surrounded him on all sides. Strangely, he no longer felt the full bite of the cold. But he had been walking for twenty minutes and knew better than his deteriorating senses were telling him.

He stared at the shovelled sidewalk and the front door. For the briefest of moments he wondered if he shouldn't continue walking the remaining five kilometres into town.

"No, I need a cab. I'm not going to freeze to death," he told himself for the thousandth time. He hammered with his bare hands on the glass doors. Only a night light illuminated the front office, but Darrell didn't care. He was so focused on getting someone to let him in he failed to notice an entrance buzzer at shoulder level to his right. After a few minutes he gave up and walked around to the back where he knocked on every door he could find. Nobody answered. As he came back around to the front, he knew he was going to freeze if he didn't get inside soon.

"If I have to I'll break in," he thought. But if the same cops who had dumped him out here came back and caught him, they might dump him even farther away. When one hand got too cold he put it in his jeans and slammed the door with soft underside of his other fist. He soon began to feel creeping warmth. He hammered on the glass for fifteen to twenty minutes. Surely someone had to hear him, eventually.

When Evoy walked into the front office with the mail shortly after six, he was startled to see a giant native man wearing only a jean jacket banging on the other side of the glass.

Evoy did not let Night in at first, figuring he was drunk. Night was so preoccupied with banging on the window and not succumbing to the cold that he didn't see Evoy. For a minute or so, the charge engineer watched him swaying slightly, struggling to keep his balance. Evoy took a step backwards into the darkened office. He hesitated, not wanting to open the door.

Night must have noticed the movement in the shadows because he looked up and then made eye contact. He began miming like a street performer, hunching over and bringing both arms in front of his chest to show he was freezing. Several times in rapid succession he brought his right hand up to his ear as though he were using a phone.

"They're going to find this guy on the front lawn in the morning if I don't let him in," Evoy said to himself, thinking of how cold it was outside. SaskPower wouldn't be too pleased with him for allowing that to happen. So, despite his misgivings, he unlocked the door. He smelled alcohol and felt a blast of frigid air as Night's bulk moved past him.

In his anxiety, Evoy started speaking before the man had even turned around. "What the hell are you doing out here at six o'clock in the morning?"

Night squinted back at Evoy with his one good eye. With his whitened hair and eyebrows, and ice-encrusted eyeglasses, he cut a sorry figure. The engineer took in the flimsy jean jacket, jeans, denim shirt and running shoes and could only shake his head in disbelief.

"What, do you think I want to be out here?" said Night in his booming, slow drawl. "The police. Those fuckin' bastards. Excuse my language. The police just dumped me out here."

Evoy could smell the alcohol on the large man's breath, but he didn't seem overly drunk. He was, however, clearly agitated.

"I don't understand. You're saying the police did this to you?"

"I'm telling you those bastards picked me up downtown, drove me out here and said 'Get out, you fucking Indian.' Then they left me to walk home."

"It doesn't make any sense," said Evoy, afraid to say too directly that he didn't believe him. He decided to change the subject. "What do you want to do now?" he said.

"I need a cab. All I want to do now is go to my sister's and go to bed. Could you call me a cab?"

"Do you have any money on you?" Night nodded, so Evoy searched one of the desks for a phone book. Not finding one, he turned back and asked, "Do you have a number?"

Night smiled. For him, taxis were the city's transit system. The number rolled off his tongue: "652-2222."

— — —

Evoy motioned for Night to sit down on the long wooden bench in the reception area. As incredible as this guy's story was, Evoy could not figure out how else Night could have gotten out here dressed so lightly. Sensing Evoy's skepticism, Night rolled up the sleeves of his jean jacket and extended his arms in front of Evoy's face. "There. Look at these. What do you think they are?" Red marks circled Night's wrists. After that Evoy said nothing else and just sat down to wait for the cab beside the man he had let in from the cold.

Minutes later, United Cab driver John Friesen was having troubling finding his fare. He didn't see anybody when he passed the glass front doors, so he drove around back. Having seen the headlights go by, Evoy led Night outside and said, "Stand here and I'll go to the back of the building and send the cab around." The cabbie had finished trying all of the doors at the rear of the building when the plant supervisor opened the door and told him he could find his rider around front. Evoy didn't return to the front to make sure that Night found his ride.

As he started back into the city along the river, Friesen glanced into the back seat. The cold that had entered the car with Night magnified the stink of alcohol on his breath. His passenger was silent, but John could tell he wasn't happy.

"Drinkin'?" asked Friesen.

"M'hm."

"Not a bad job if you can get it, my friend. You got it good if you can do that. Wouldn't work too well drinkin' and drivin' cab."

"Nah," said Night in disgust. "I don't work out there, you know. Guy just let me in. Couple of cops dumped me near the

trailer park on the far side of the power plant and I walked back."
Friesen did a double take in the mirror: the fellow was only wearing jeans, a denim shirt, and a jean jacket.

"Fuckin' bastards, excuse my language, I'm just pissed. I shouldn't swear like that. They'll regret this if I report them, you know." Night so doubted that anyone would believe his story he didn't even sound convincing to himself. Complaining was a waste of time, Night decided, and might even make things worse, so he shut up.

"Take these," Night said to Friesen when they pulled up to Sharon's place. He handed over his jean jacket and his health card for collateral and went into the apartment building to get some cash.

He was back at the cab quickly, with a twenty-dollar bill. Friesen took Night's money and gave him back a ten, along with his jacket and identification.

His sister was fully awake when Night got back.

"I told you not to do this. You promised you wouldn't. Do you even know what time it is?" Sharon barely took a breath before continuing. "I told you, you're not drinking and staying here. You can get out. That's all there is to it. I can't take this anymore, you know that."

Night tried a few times to explain that the cops had taken him out to the outskirts of town and left him there, but his sister only glared at him for a few seconds before starting in again.

As he closed the bedroom door she was still talking to his back. "I don't care how hung over you are. You're still helping me move today."

— — —

A pale sun rose above the horizon and cast long shadows behind even the tiniest pebbles on the road. In the weak morning light, something on the floor of his cab caught John Friesen's eye. He picked up a plastic card—the health card belonging to the man he had driven to the west end from the power station. Thinking the guy might come back for it, Friesen reached over his head and stuck it in the sun visor.

— — —

The day after the cab dropped Night at his sister's place, local politician Pat Lorje was jogging with her dog on Schuyler Street, a light industrial area in the south end of Saskatoon. As she passed Shamrock Feeds around eleven o'clock on Saturday, January 29, she thought she heard someone calling. She turned her head and saw a man gesturing wildly for her to come over. When she did, Sam Jamison, who owned Shamrock Feeds, got her to walk with him to the corner of the building. The frozen body of a young native man lay sprawled on the snow near a metal fence, his half-open eyes staring sightlessly toward the brilliant blue sky. She waited with the body while Jamison called 911.

The dead man was wearing running shoes and a pair of black sweat pants, and nothing else. Legs extended with his toes pointed up, he held his bare left arm folded across the left side of his naked chest and had flung out his right arm to the side, palm facing up. When the police arrived, they pulled the native man's sales-tax exemption card out of his sweat pants and identified him as twenty-five-year-old Rodney Naistus of the Onion Lake reserve. They were not surprised to find his T-shirt and camouflage army jacket nearby. Victims of hypothermia are often found undressed; it looked as if Naistus had succumbed to hallucinations that made him think he was warm enough to start taking off his clothes.

The officers called to the scene had no way of knowing that Dan Hatchen and Ken Munson had dropped off Darrell Night a day earlier only about a kilometre south of where Naistus had finally collapsed on his back and died alone in the snow.

FROZEN BODIES

LYING ON HIS MATTRESS ON THE SHABBY BED-
room floor, around eight on the morning of Sunday, January 30,
Lawrence Wegner listened to Brent Ahenakew and his girlfriend, Jennifer, yelling and hitting each other. His bedroom
door was closed, but their row filled the whole apartment. The
couple fought a lot, about money, about drugs, about anything.
Except for the mattress, a cardboard box with his belongings
and the handful of pictures he had brought from the group
home, Wegner's bedroom was empty.

He lay quietly, retracing the regrets that had landed him in
this miserable place. If he hadn't stolen from Jocelan Shandler,
he wouldn't be here. He had reassured her he would be okay, but
he was not okay. He was scared and living with Ahenakew was a
disaster.

Wegner got up and peeked out his door. Beer bottles lay
scattered all over the floor. Brent and Jennifer were clawing at
each other viciously. Without warning she grabbed Brent and bit
his lip until she drew blood.

Terrified that he had to stop the fight before his friends
killed each other, Wegner phoned the police. He thought they
would come and just settle everyone down, but as soon as they
arrived, the big cop, Indian Ernie, said he wanted to talk to
Wegner in the hallway. Wegner refused to be separated from the
others. Calling the cops was nothing out of the ordinary, but

making an actual complaint would infuriate Ahenakew. Wegner had nowhere else to live and couldn't afford to make Ahenakew angry at him.

The cops only stayed for a few minutes. After they left, Wegner went out to buy drugs with what was left of the money he had stolen from Shandler the week before. He returned and the bitter smell of hash burning on hot knives soon filled the grimy apartment. Jennifer and Brent calmed down.

At some point that Sunday, Wegner called one of his closest friends, Alvin Baptiste, to see if he'd pick him up in his car. Maybe they could play darts or something. Baptiste had always encouraged Wegner to stay off drugs. Occasionally he even hired Wegner to help with his small household-repairs business.

But Wegner's laconic speech soon betrayed his condition. Alvin didn't want to deal with his stoned friend, so he said he couldn't come by. Besides, they both had a school project due on Tuesday. "What about you, Lawrence? You should be working on it too, shouldn't you?" Wegner confessed that he hadn't even started.

With nowhere to go, Wegner stayed at the apartment smoking hash off the stove. As the day wore on, a friend named Dwaine Moccasin showed up. By evening, Brent, Jennifer and Dwaine were trashed. Another friend, Howard Moosomin, arrived. He was sober when he showed up, a welcome relief for Wegner, who wasn't so far gone as the others.

He and Howard chatted comfortably for a while at the kitchen table. Dwaine, meanwhile, was deeply out of it. Wegner and Howard watched him pour an entire mug of hot coffee on his lap and sit there for several seconds with no response. Finally, with a delayed reaction straight out of a cartoon, he jumped up and started cursing and running madly around the apartment.

Howard suggested they all play a game of kaiser, a card game like euchre, to pass the time. Lawrence was clear-headed enough to shuffle a deck of cards without difficulty. He then found a pencil and paper and offered to keep score. But it was hopeless. Dwaine passed out again, and Brent and Jennifer kept falling out of their chairs.

Wegner patted his pockets looking for his cigarette tobacco. Not finding it, he accused Howard, completely without warning, of stealing it. Howard patiently helped him look for the tobacco in his bedroom. No luck. He suggested Wegner try his wallet. Sure enough, it had been there all along.

Later in the evening, Dwaine managed to stagger to his feet and out the door, followed a short time afterwards by Howard. Brent and Jennifer had passed out on the living-room couch. Lawrence stood crying, but couldn't remember why. He had lost his cigarette tobacco again, and his remorse for accusing Moosomin earlier for stealing it was blowing itself out of proportion.

He went to his bedroom. Although he hadn't injected anything, he had probably never smoked so much hash in his life. The effects of the drug washed over him in successive waves, each stronger than the last.

In his white T-shirt, jeans and white socks, he stood frozen in place, looking exactly the way Jocelan Shandler had always said he looked when stoned. In a slow tide, his thoughts tumbled over each other. He had let everyone down. What would become of him? He had nowhere else to live. Tears flowed down his face. The room closed in on him.

Numb and terrified, Wegner bolted from the apartment without his winter clothes or his shoes, trying to outrun his own panic. He walked quickly, focused on shedding the fear that clung to him like a second skin, not even feeling the cold at first. He covered the few hundred metres to 20th Street in about a minute and headed in the general direction of the nearby home of a cousin of his mother's, Eliza Whitecap.

— — —

Eliza Whitecap was watching TV that evening around midnight. A heavy curtain hung closed across her front picture window overlooking 20th Street. Her daughter, Jennifer, was in the bathroom getting ready for bed. Aside from the TV, the small house was quiet. Her two sons had gone out for the evening.

For the past seven years the Cree woman had lived in the same house, with its front door facing the south side of 20th Street and the side door facing St. Paul's Hospital. Four or five times a year she had to call the police to report a disturbance of some kind, usually a fight or a break-in. As often as not, the police never showed up.

A sharp knock at the side door startled her. As she stood up to open the door, Jennifer came out of the bath with a towel wrapped like a turban around her wet hair.

"Don't, Mum," she said, putting her hand on her mother's arm, and she walked down the first few basement steps to reach the side door instead. She lifted the curtain covering its small rectangular window. Her mother had seen Lawrence Wegner before, at a dance once and during visits to her cousin, Mary Wegner. But Jennifer did not recognize the thin native man with metal-framed glasses standing outside her mother's door.

While he waited, the man bounced up and down trying to stay warm. He looked panicked. "No wonder," she thought. "It's freezing out and the guy's only wearing a T-shirt and blue jeans. He doesn't even have any shoes on." She thought he looked high or drunk.

"Who is it?" she said, to get his attention. With his dishevelled hair and eyes that seemed to bulge from their sockets, he scared her.

"Pizza, pizza," he said when he finally looked up and saw her.

"No, I didn't order pizza," Jennifer said firmly. There was no way she would let this guy in, no matter how he was dressed, especially with her brothers out of the house. Without another word she let the curtain fall back into place and went back up to the kitchen.

All Whitecap could see of the man her daughter had talked to was the top of his head and his short hair sticking up in all directions as though it were gelled. She and her daughter watched out the kitchen window to see what he'd do next.

His back to them, Wegner cut across the snow-covered front yard. He looked slim, childlike even, Whitecap thought. Within a few seconds he broke into a kind of shuffling run across 20th and headed westward in the direction of St. Paul's. She did not recognize him as her cousin's son, but she could see he was wearing only a T-shirt and jeans and was out in the snow in his socks. Despite her misgivings about the police, she knew she had to do something.

"Quick, Jennifer," she said. "Call 911. That guy's going to freeze to death dressed like that." Her old frustration rose to the surface. "Just in case. They never come anyway." It was 12:20 in the morning.

As Jennifer dialled, they watched Wegner trot along the far sidewalk toward the hospital. An ambulance came from the direction of downtown, its emergency lights off. The vehicle slowed as it went by Wegner, and Whitecap was relieved, certain the driver would stop. But instead it sped up and continued on its way. She couldn't believe it. "They should have—they should have stopped," she said to Jennifer. "They see that guy's got only a T-shirt on, you know. They could save his life."

Her daughter was explaining to the 911 dispatcher what had happened, saying that they had last seen the man running up the street toward the hospital. When she hung up, she said to her mother, "He told me they already had a complaint about the guy and that they'll look into it."

What she didn't point out to her mother, who was already looking outside again, was that the police officer on the other end of the line hadn't bothered to ask for her address.

— — —

Almost every night for the past six years, winter or summer, pensioner Albert Chatsis walked the exact same five kilometres. He drove to Diefenbaker Park on the east side of the South Saskatchewan River and parked his late-model Oldsmobile near the CN Rail trestle, then hiked the trails that followed the river-bank. Several hundred yards across the river, the Queen Elizabeth power station and the city dump served him as landmarks to gauge how far he had walked. That last Sunday night of January 2000 was particularly cold, so Chatsis laid out his heavy parka, sheepskin boots and an extra pair of warm pants. Feeling drowsy, he lay down on his bed and fell asleep for almost three hours, not waking until eleven-thirty. It was late, but nothing would keep Chatsis from his walk. He warmed up the car and fifteen minutes later was on his way.

He drove slowly eastward on 20th Street toward St. Paul's; he was not in a rush. As he crested a small hill he saw a police cruiser parked to his left, near the main hospital entrance, straddling the curb between two parking meters.

The car's emergency lights were off but someone was standing outside the passenger window. "What do we have here?" Chatsis said to himself. "Some kind of trouble. A boxing match or something. Maybe I'll get a free show." He tapped the brakes until his big car crawled forward at just a few kilometres an hour.

— — —

At about the same time that Sunday night, Benita Moccasin and Darlene Katcheech approached the hospital from the other direction in Moccasin's wine-coloured Chevy Caprice. They were driving back from retrieving a backpack forgotten at a friend's on Avenue G. The bag contained her notes for a school project due on Tuesday, which she hadn't started. With another paper due tomorrow, she had a late night ahead of her. Like Wegner, the two friends studied at the Saskatchewan Indian Federated College.

Moccasin was Wegner's cousin. Katcheech had known him while growing up on the Saulteaux reserve in the early nineties. But since moving to Saskatoon, both women's acquaintance with Wegner had dwindled to little more than the occasional hello between classes. Still, they knew each other well enough that Wegner had stopped to talk to Moccasin in the hallway, on Thursday morning, just before her Indian Studies class. Determined to pay back the money he had stolen, he'd asked if the monthly student assistance cheques from the government had arrived yet.

As they cruised slowly westward up 20th, a small car came up quickly behind them and darted past. Otherwise, the street was empty.

"No one's out. Strange, eh?" said Moccasin, stopping in the right lane for a red light at Avenue P.

"It's freezing out. Everyone's inside," Katcheech replied, putting her cigarettes on the dash while she rummaged through her purse for her lighter. The light turned green and Moccasin hit the gas, sending the pack flying to the floor. Her friend bent forward and groped in the darkness for her cigarettes.

"Darlene, check this out."

"What? What?" Katcheech said, sitting up quickly and searching the darkness outside.

— — —

Albert Chatsis rolled down his window, hoping to catch some of the conversation when he passed the cruiser. The thin man standing between the car and the sidewalk, and pointing toward downtown, was wearing just a T-shirt and jeans. As Chatsis neared, his headlights reflected off the man's glasses. "Probably just came out of the hospital to talk to the cops," he thought as he rolled by. Still, he continued looking into his rear-view mirror, pumping his brakes so as to stop as the light just ahead turned red.

— — —

The two women gawked at the scene as they approached. Moccasin had to steer wide, out toward the centre of the street to avoid the idling SPS cruiser parked with its rear end angled into the curb lane. None of its lights were flashing; only the rear parking lights were lit. A tall police officer wearing a fur hat and parka was manhandling a slim native man toward the passenger side of the car. Despite the cold the man was wearing only a white T-shirt and jeans, no shoes even. A shorter, pot-bellied cop whose parka reached his knees had already opened the back passenger door. He came around to help his partner. The native man seemed to be handcuffed, given the way his arms were pulled behind his back. He wasn't resisting as the officers manoeuvred him around the car; their roughness surprised the women. As the police pressed down on the crown of the man's head and pushed him backwards into the car, he briefly faced the oncoming Caprice, now only seven or eight metres away.

"Hey, that's Wegner. That's Wegner!" Darlene cried.

Before the traffic light turned green, Albert Chatsis had seen, in his rear-view mirror, the police get out of the cruiser and put the man in the back seat. As he drove eastbound from the intersection, he thought he could see the cop car pull away in the opposite direction. But he had already lost interest. After all, Chatsis told himself, an Indian being arrested on 20th Street in Saskatoon is an everyday occurrence.

— — —

At the moment that Darlene Katcheech had recognized Law-rence Wegner, he fell into the police car. She and Moccasin watched as his shoeless right foot in a light-coloured sock shot up as he tumbled back.

Stunned, the women continued west, past the cruiser.

"Hey, Benita? Benita, that really was Wagonburner," said Katcheech, using Wegner's nickname.

"Yep," her friend agreed. "I thought it looked like him too. That was Lawrence."

Katcheech laughed nervously. "Well, I'm going to ask him tomorrow what the hell he was doing on 20th getting roughed up and picked up by the cops. It's not like him, you know."

Squinting into the mirror, she did not see the cruiser's headlights or brake lights come on. By the time they reached Avenue U, she had lost sight of the car completely.

— — —

A couple of hours later, at about two in the morning, Mary Wegner awoke from a dream that contained no sounds, no words, no images. A suffocating presence pressed in on her as she slept in the tidy wooden bungalow at the extreme north end of the Saulteaux reserve, well away from the other houses. Like a snake, the sensation tightened its coils around her heart. She woke up crying and gasping for breath and reached across the bed to touch her husband.

She had met and married Gary Wegner, a retired railway worker of German descent, almost thirty years ago. Marrying a white man had made her something of an outsider within the band, and people had been not so much hostile as cool toward her ever since. She often felt as if she were joining a gathering at the end of a conversation.

"What is it?" Gary asked her.

"I don't know," she finally said. Her body trembled with the memory of the dream, but she couldn't describe what it had been about.

So they lay back and Gary held her while she gazed out the window, hoping to fall asleep again. Pale moonlight reflecting off the snow etched the small trees and undulating hills behind their house in shades of silver and black.

Mary's mind wandered amongst the fading echoes of her nightmare. She thought about a wooden chest Lawrence had crafted for her a year or so ago at a woodworking workshop in Saskatoon. She loved it, the way he had taken the time to fit the joints with glue instead of using nails. He'd always had a way of making and fixing things. Mary had the sudden and unmistakable sense that her bad dream had been about her son.

— — —

About eight the following Thursday morning, February 3, Robert Leschyshyn emerged with a few other workers from one of the two ATCO trailers that served as offices at the CN rail yard. Leschyshyn was always the first to arrive at work. He spent the majority of his days as a railcar technician for General Electric Railcar Services down here, where the rail yard, dump and power plant marked the outside edge of Saskatoon and the beginning of the bleak, frozen prairie. The arctic wind blasted him in the face. From the top of a small berm, he could see where snow had drifted and packed into rigid gullies across the surrounding field. He noticed something odd about a hundred metres out. Debris from the dump blew around all the time, though, so he dismissed it.

Around three, Leschyshyn was back on the berm, helping co-worker Monty Wilkins tow a railway car with a five-tonne truck. He hooked a chain to the rail car and hopped on for the ride. From his high perch he could see criss-crossing telephone poles and power lines stretching all the way across the field and, in a small gully, a human body.

The Queen Elizabeth power station.

He yelled at Wilkins to put the brakes on, then jumped down and the two walked into the field. They stopped eight metres from a man lying face down in the crusted, hard-packed snow. Leschyshyn estimated the frozen body to be about a half a kilometre south of the dump and about the same distance from the power station. Dundonald Avenue, a major road that headed back into Saskatoon, was no more than a kilometre west.

Leschyshyn stopped Wilkins from going any closer. This could very well be a crime scene and they'd surely catch hell for disturbing it. A small group of workers had gathered at the berm to see what was going on. Leschyshyn yelled over the wind for them to call the police.

The matter was out of his hands now. The winter sun reflected off the snowy field, which spread far into the distance. Out here, bitter winds burned exposed skin, but Leschyshyn could see that no snow had accumulated on or around the body. The field's icy crust kept the snow packed tight to the ground. Consequently, the dead man's clothes were plainly visible: jeans, a white T-shirt and no shoes. Just socks. Leschyshyn turned and walked back over the berm to finish his shift.

Less than ten minutes later, Victor Hargraves, Leschyshyn's boss, sat in the heated cab of the company's four-by-four looking at the scene through powerful binoculars. He was an avid hunter and never left them behind. Hargraves had seen enough TV to know how important it was not to contaminate the scene, so he stopped the truck in the deep snow seven to ten metres from the body. The cellphone he had used to notify the police lay where he had tossed it on the passenger seat.

Hargraves took a long look at the body. Pale blue jeans, a white short-sleeved T-shirt and light-grey socks.

When he had come to work that morning, the temperature had been minus eight degrees Celsius, and the wind chill had made it feel like minus sixteen. He focused on the man's feet again. Not only was he without shoes, his socks were in good condition. Five kilometres from downtown in the middle of a wide-open field in the dead of winter, dressed like that. Hargraves shook his head in disbelief.

As a hunter, Hargraves had a trained eye for tracks, and he panned his binoculars over the single set that came from the north-northeast and ended where the body lay. He re-created the dead man's last steps. First he had walked, then he had lengthened his stride and begun to run. From what? Toward what? Shortly after starting to run, he had stumbled and fallen in the snow. He'd rolled about, then stood, walked, run and stumbled again, his body making a wide impression in the snow where he'd fallen. On the third and final time that he had risen to his feet, he'd staggered back to the northeast, leaving a zigzag track until he'd fallen again. This time, he hadn't gotten up.

While Hargraves was visually tracing the man's last steps, a marked SPS cruiser showed up with three officers in it: rookie Constable Bruce Hagel, Constable Bruce Gordon and the man in charge until someone from Major Crimes arrived, Sergeant Bob Eder.

Afraid of getting the cruiser stuck in the snow, Eder conscripted Hargraves to ferry them to the scene in the four-by-four. Figuring the police knew what they were doing, Hargraves kept his analysis to himself.

He stopped, as he had before, about ten metres away from the body. Eder jumped out the passenger side and walked the remaining distance. From the truck, the men could see Eder bend over, reach into the right back pocket of the man's blue jeans and pull out a wallet. After looking briefly at its contents, Eder motioned to Hargraves to get out of the truck. When he did, Eder casually flipped him the wallet. Hargraves caught it without difficulty, but it struck him as an odd thing for an officer to do.

Eder was having trouble with the body. When the man fell his body heat had melted the snow, and frozen him against the ground. No matter how hard Eder pulled, he couldn't turn the body over. After a few tries he walked back to the truck.

"Lawrence Wegner," he said, answering the question the other three men hadn't yet asked. "At least that's what it says in his wallet."

Hargraves's informal taxi service for the Saskatoon police did brisk business as the afternoon wore on. Somehow the media had caught wind of the body's discovery. They were kept behind a police blockade at the entrance of the small roadway that led from Dundonald into the field, at least a kilometre away.

The canine unit arrived at 3:54 p.m., and the identification team shortly after that. Constable Robin Wintermute and Constable Doug Marianchuk had been training their dogs just north of the dump on the Holiday Park golf course. Eder led the two men to within a few feet of the body. No one took any heed of where they stepped.

One look at the greyness of the man's skin and the way the snow had refrozen around him, and the handlers decided to leave the dogs in the car. Any human scent would be long gone.

Eder insisted that someone needed to follow the tracks before darkness fell: there might be clothing or other evidence along the dead man's route. Only the canine constables were wearing warm winter boots. Eder seemed not to realize that sending men along the trail would likely destroy the tracks themselves, a key piece of evidence.

Already chilled from working with the dogs throughout the afternoon, Wintermute and Marianchuk could not have been pleased with the idea. But until someone from Major Crimes arrived, it was Eder's scene and his call.

They walked northeast in the direction the tracks came from, the rookie Hagel following several paces behind. The going was tough. In some spots the snow's crust supported their body weight, and they walked on top of it without difficulty. Elsewhere it gave way without warning and they plunged up to their knees. The dead man had clearly broken through the icy crust too, several times. He had then rolled around, staggered to his feet and begun to walk again. Where this had happened, the tracks were easy to follow, only to disappear on the icy, wind-polished surface. They continued following the tracks north-ward for the next hour and a half, as it grew dark.

Major Crimes investigator Bob Peters did not show up until just after four-thirty. He was not happy; the area was as trampled as a fairground.

Peters put the Identification officers to work making a video and photographic summary of the scene. He motioned to Eder to join him out of hearing of the others, and the two men had a brief, heated discussion. In an age when microscopic evidence could make a difference, Eder had allowed his men to contaminate the scene with hundreds of tracks and to disturb the body, something even the civilian railway workers had been smart enough to avoid.

By this time the Identification team had finished taking close-up photos of the body. Peters approached to see for himself. The man lay face down, more or less naturally, but he held his right hand clutched beneath him. He was so solidly frozen to the ground that he seemed sculpted out of stone. Peters realized Wegner was actually wearing two pairs of socks. He wore the light grey wool socks over a pair of white socks. The outer socks, bunched toward the toes, did not seem worn or dirty. Peters saw some scratches on the left knuckles and fingers, which could have been caused by falling in the snow. A blood smear on the back of the T-shirt caught Peters's eye for a moment, but when he managed to lift the shirt slightly to look at the man's back, there was no sign of a wound. He did see, however, some red marks and bruising in the upper shoulder area.

When the searchers returned, cold and exhausted, they showed Peters the only item they'd found: a pair of silver-rimmed eyeglasses with both lenses intact. They had spotted the glasses on the hard surface of the snow where Wegner had stumbled, seventy-five metres from where he had died.

Peters realized that the scene had been hopelessly contaminated, so he ordered Marianchuk and Wintermute to do a hand-drawing, back at the station, of the tracks as they remembered them when they had arrived at the scene. Peters had been around long enough to know the drawing would be better than nothing, should the police ever be taken to task for the condition of the scene.

According to the sketch marked "not to any scale," Wegner's tracks began at the eastern edge of a spot labelled "Parking Area" near the chain-link fence around the perimeter of the dump. The area was a popular partying spot for local kids. Enough cars had driven through and turned around that the snow was packed as hard as concrete. A lane linked the parking area with Dundonald Avenue, the major road leading out of Saskatoon to the city dump.

From the parking area, Wegner's tracks headed south for just over a hundred metres, in the shape of a backward S. Then Wegner had doubled back on his own tracks before continuing southwest where he'd fallen and frozen to death.

— — —

Darrell Night's uncle, Randy Desjarlais, could not wait to use his new driver's licence. Drinking had cost him his driving privileges a while back. As soon as his new licence arrived in the mail on February 3, Desjarlais and Night decided to celebrate by going for a ride.

Desjarlais strapped his four-year-old son in the back seat. They dropped his wife at the Shoe just before the evening's first bingo session began at six-thirty, and hit the streets of Saskatoon. Bingo wouldn't get out until nine-thirty, so they were in no rush to get back. Desjarlais drove slowly, turning right off 20th on to Avenue I, savouring the joys of being behind the wheel again.

"Feels good, Darrell," he said to the big man lounging beside him. Desjarlais made a left, westbound on 21st Street. "Feels good."

Constable Bruce Eholt was a little more than three hours into his shift, and had been tucked in traffic behind Night and Desjarlais since they'd left the Lucky Horseshoe parking lot. After a few blocks, a small head popped up in their rear window. A little boy smiled back at the cop and bounced around, clearly without a seatbelt. Cute, but Eholt had been a cop for twenty-two years; he knew when it was ticket time.

On 21st near Avenue M, Desjarlais pointed at his rear-view mirror. "Ah, man, look at that." Night looked over his shoulder and saw flashing lights in the window of an unmarked police cruiser. "Yep, looks like the cops, Randy," he said. He grinned and squinted at his uncle with his good eye. Although he had almost frozen to death a few days earlier, Night still had his dark sense of humour. "Look at the bright side, at least you have a licence to show him. Could be worse, right?"

Desjarlais laughed despite himself.

After Night's cab ride home from the power station, he'd told his uncle and sisters what had happened, how he'd nearly frozen to death. There was outrage and some talk of going to the media, but no one had complained to the police. The feeling among natives was that complaining about police only meant that next time you'd have farther to walk.

Desjarlais pulled over to the curb. In his side mirror, he watched Eholt approach. Stocky, with wide, powerful shoulders, the cop moved like an athlete.

Eholt had once been scouted as a centre for the Edmonton Oilers of the old World Hockey Association. That dream died when he blew out his knee in a soccer game. He met his future wife, Val, at a local bible school. Marrying her after graduation, he decided to get serious and pursue his other lifelong ambition, policing. In October 1978, Eholt joined the Saskatoon Police Service. He'd since worked mostly on patrol, but was especially proud of his undercover work and aspired to make detective.

Morale at the station had continued to plummet through the nineties, after Chief Penkala retired. By 1996, Dave Scott had finally won the big job, but he had inherited a troubled force. Front-line cops grumbled constantly in the locker room about being taxed to their limits. Budget cutbacks and a lack of new recruits meant that there were never enough officers to fill the cars. Another call always seemed to be waiting before they finished the last one—another fight, another drunk, another domestic dispute, the same scenario repeated at an exhausting pace. Eholt's transfer to traffic in 1998 came as a relief. It meant he mostly worked alone and was not constantly on call.

When he reached the driver's-side window, which was open, Desjarlais handed over his licence with pride. He was polite and seemed surprised to hear that the boy in the back seat was not strapped in. He said the child must have undone the belt when they weren't looking. Eholt told them to sit tight while he went back to his car to write up a ticket.

While they waited, Desjarlais turned on the car radio to catch the news. The two friends stared in astonishment at the radio as the announcer began to read the lead story.

ABOUT THREE P.M. TODAY, RAILWAY WORKERS DISCOVERED THE BODY OF A THIRTY-YEAR-OLD NATIVE MAN FROZEN IN THE SNOW NEAR THE QUEEN ELIZABETH POWER STATION SOUTH OF TOWN. POLICE ARE ON THE SCENE. THE NAME OF THE MAN HAS NOT BEEN RELEASED PENDING NOTIFICATION OF NEXT OF KIN.

"Darrell?" Desjarlais said. "They did the same thing to you. It's the same place." He looked over at his nephew, but Night stayed silent. "We gotta tell this guy," he said, pointing backwards toward Eholt's car.

"No way, Randy," said Night. Fear shone in his good eye. "No way. You tell this guy and they'll finish me off. I know it. They'll come and finish me off. Don't do it. Okay? I'm asking you not to do it. Look, here he comes. Just take the ticket and let's get outta here." Night made a huge fist with his right hand. "I'm warning you. Don't say anything."

Eholt came back to the window, and handed the ticket over. After thanking the officer politely, Desjarlais asked Eholt what he knew about the body discovered near the power plant. "Have you found out who it was?"

Night windmilled his massive left arm hard into his uncle's chest in an effort to shut him up.

Something in Desjarlais's voice, and Night's barely restrained anger, set Eholt's heart racing. He had heard the call about the body over the radio earlier that day.

"I haven't heard much," Eholt said. "Other than someone being found frozen out there. If you don't mind my asking, why are you interested in it?"

"My nephew can't help thinking that it could have been him."

"Oh," Eholt said. His insides started to churn.

"Darrell, my nephew here. He was dropped off by the police last week at the power plant, and he can't help but think that maybe, you know, that it's the same thing that happened to him."

Eholt leaned forward, his elbows on the frame of the driver's window. He made eye contact with Night. "Did you talk to anybody about it?"

"No." Night seemed to be trying to make up his mind about what to do. After a few seconds he spoke again, his voice coloured with resentment. "Nobody would listen to me anyway."

"Well, Darrell, I'm listening now." Something in the way the officer was speaking inclined Night to trust him. So he told Eholt his story, staring off into the middle distance as he spoke. He seemed to be reliving the event; disgust and fear filled his voice.

"What is it you plan to do?" Eholt asked when he'd finished, thinking to himself, "God help us. The guy is saying two officers dropped him off. You have someone found in almost exactly the same spot a few hours ago, and Naistus found nearby less than a week earlier. Okay, what if? What if?"

"I'm not too sure," said Night. Planning was not his strong suit. The only thing he had discussed with his uncle and his friends was maybe talking to the media, so that's what he told Eholt.

Careful to say that he would not stop Night from doing so, Eholt asked for some time. He said he needed to notify his superiors so that a proper investigation could begin without tipping off whoever might have done this.

Night said he would not talk to anyone else, and told Eholt where he could get in touch with him the next day.

"Fair enough, I'll be there," said the cop.

The trust Night had felt while telling his story began to fade already. He doubted he would see Eholt again.

Before returning to his cruiser, Eholt asked Desjarlais for the ticket back. He ripped it in half and said, "Not tonight."

— — —

At about seven that evening, a group of city workers arrived with A-frame barricades, tarps and industrial heaters to try to loosen Lawrence Wegner from the ground. Foreman Brian Dalke's crew, with help from some of the police, started to build a tent over Wegner. Over the last few hours, Hargraves's four-by-four had flattened enough of a path through the snow that the police cruisers could drive into the field. The glare of their headlights illuminated the body. As Dalke shouted instructions, he noticed some large black birds nearby on the snow, probably attracted by the city dump. Ravens.

As Dalke lifted one of the tarps to drape it over the barricades, he glanced at the dead man lying face down in the snow. He paused near the man's right kidney where the T-shirt was raised. Dalke clearly saw a familiar imprint in the skin, several inches above the belt line.

"Hey, that looks like a boot print," he said out loud. There was no mistaking the hiking-boot tread, with its distinctive square pattern. No one seemed to hear, so he let it go and got on with the task at hand. Dalke never got another look at the curious imprint.

Using the industrial heaters, Bob Peters, the coroner and the city workers tried for the next half-hour to turn the corpse over. At first they worked to free him gently, almost delicately. Then, at 7:35, either out of frustration or because they realized the situation was hopeless, they wedged a flat little spade under his hip and flipped him over onto his left side.

"God, he looks really rough," Peters thought. Wegner's wrinkled face seemed to have taken the shape of the earth itself, and an ugly bruise marked his forehead over the left eye. Peters figured it had happened when the dead man had fallen.

Standing nearby, Dalke also saw the bruise, which to him looked like the result of a blow. But he said nothing and continued loading equipment back into his truck.

At about 9:50, an ambulance took Lawrence Wegner's body to St. Paul's Hospital, one of the last places anyone had seen him alive.

— — —

After an anxious and sleepless night, Bruce Eholt phoned the chief's office and persuaded Dave Scott to agree to an emergency meeting. He rushed over. Investigator Dennis Elias ushered him into the third-floor boardroom near Scott's office.

Eholt sat on one side of the large oblong table centred under a bank of lights recessed in frosted glass. Photographs of previous chiefs circled the wood-panelled walls. Scott, dressed impeccably as usual, came in a few moments later and took his seat at the head of the table.

Scott was intimidating. He had risen from media relations officer a decade ago to chief of the over three-hundred-and-fifty-strong Saskatoon Police Service. But Eholt checked his nerves and told his story in a plain-spoken, careful manner. As he talked, he secretly hoped for the chance to investigate further.

Neither Scott nor Elias interrupted Eholt's story for the fifteen minutes it took him to tell it, and when he finished they still sat silently. Eholt wondered if he had blown the meeting. He pressed on, insisting that if Darrell Night was telling the truth, they had to consider why Lawrence Wegner and Rodney Naistus had been found frozen to death in the same area.

Eholt cautioned against allowing Night's anger to fester. He didn't think the big man would stay quiet for long. "Let me go to his place," he offered. "I'll bring him in and we'll get a statement."

Scott agreed and told the constable to brief Deputy Chief Daniel Wiks, too. Eholt had succeeded; Darrell Night's case would not be ignored. "Find him today," ordered the chief. "I want him in here today."

THE SECRET GETS OUT

A FEW HOURS AFTER BRUCE EHOLT'S MEETING
with Chief Scott, Darrell Night and Randy Desjarlais pulled into
Desjarlais's driveway. As they got out of the car, Desjarlais pointed
across the street at a man in street clothes standing by his car.

"Darrell, that's the cop who stopped us the other night."

Desjarlais approached Eholt but Night stood firmly where
he was. Eholt and Desjarlais spoke for a moment. Night was
itching to get inside.

"He wants you to go the police station with him," Desjarlais
called back across the street.

"No way I'm doin' that, Randy. They almost killed me the
other night. I'm not about to let them finish the job."

Desjarlais and Eholt walked across the street to join Night.
Night towered over the five-foot-six-inch constable, but Eholt
wasn't easily intimidated. The three men talked things over.

"C'mon, Darrell," said Desjarlais, firmly onside with the
cop. "You should go with the guy. There's no way they should
have done that to you; you could be dead."

Faces began appearing in the neighbours' windows, watchful eyes letting the cop know that whatever he did would not go
unseen. It was all they could do. But these witnesses were enough
to waylay Night's fears, and he climbed into the back of Eholt's
car, finding it unreal that he had just volunteered to sit in the back
of a police cruiser again. At least this time he wasn't handcuffed.

The interview room on the third floor of the station contained nothing but a small round table, a few chairs and a telephone. With Eholt and Dennis Elias listening, Night told his story from the moment of his arrest to when the cabbie dropped him off outside his sister Sharon's place. He clenched and unclenched his fists like he wanted to hit someone as he spoke, carefully describing the drop-off, concentrating on the details as he stared into the middle distance, as if he were standing again on the snow-covered road in minus-twenty-five-degree weather wearing a jean jacket and running shoes.

Near the end, Night told Eholt and Elias he had seen the cruiser's number: 57. Draped over the trunk as Dan Hatchen had struggled to remove the handcuffs, Night had mistaken the 2 on Hatchen and Munson's car for a 5. After the interview, Eholt drove him home. Night's mistake was about to make the situation explode.

— — —

Over the weekend, the Saskatoon Police Service managers flew into a state of full-blown bureaucratic panic.

On Scott's orders, Deputy Chief Wiks knocked heads. No one on shift the night Darrell Night was dumped went unscathed. The officers of Car 57 denied categorically they had anything to do with Night, but Wiks sent them home anyway.

Word of Night's statement and the harsh treatment of the cops in Car 57 spread through the locker room and the dingy basement weight room. Over the rumbling bass of the stereo and the sharp clanging of free weights, cops bitched and took sides about Wiks's crusade. More than a few charged that Eholt was way out of line investigating fellow officers. He should have let Night make his own case.

Hatchen and Munson had their own problems. They had never asked Night's name when he was in the car, so they had no idea of his identity. When Lawrence Wegner's body was found on Thursday, Hatchen was worried it was the same man they had dumped. Now they had another kind of problem. Their guy had apparently made it home, but his mistake about the car number meant two colleagues were taking their heat.

Night's error forced Hatchen and Munson's hand. They admitted to Wiks that they were the ones who had taken Night out to the power plant, but maintained from the beginning that he'd asked to be let out of the car.

— — —

At about eight-thirty on the morning of February 7, 2000, Sergeant Bob Peters, Sergeant Al Carlson from Identification and a few trainee constables gathered in the St. Paul's morgue, watching pathologist Dr. Ranjit Waghray perform the autopsy on Lawrence Wegner. It had taken over three days for his body to thaw sufficiently for post-mortem examination.

According to Waghray's autopsy report, he found not only a bruise above Wegner's left eye, but also hemorrhaging under his scalp. At six centimetres by four centimetres, the bruise was large. He also observed some small abrasions on Wegner's hands and left forearm. No sign remained of the boot mark Brian Dalke thought he saw. "The back is unremarkable," says the report.

Finding no puncture marks or lesions anywhere on the body, Waghray concluded, "There is no external evidence of gross violence or trauma to the body."

His final diagnosis: "Hypothermia. Body found frozen on the ground."

The entire police force was in an upheaval because a native man—dumped in the same area where two other frozen bodies were discovered—was pointing fingers at Saskatoon police. And yet none of the officers attending the autopsy seized Wegner's scant garments as evidence. The clothing was stuffed into a garbage bag and returned to the family when the hearse carrying Wegner's body made the trip to North Battleford for burial.

— — —

Two days after the autopsy, Jocelan Shandler took her place in the long line of mourners filing past Lawrence Wegner's open casket in the band hall of the Saulteaux reserve. Several hundred people had crammed into the gymnasium-like room. Aside from Wegner's father, Shandler was the only white person there. One by one, people bent forward and kissed Wegner. It took over three hours for everyone to say goodbye.

When Shandler had arrived after the two-hour drive north from Saskatoon, Mary Wegner had hugged her tightly. Since Lawrence's death, Shandler had been punishing herself: he wouldn't have died this way if she had let him stay in the group home. But Mary and the family didn't agree. Lawrence had given her no choice. "You loved him like a mother," Mary said.

Shortly after the discovery of her son's frozen body, Mary Wegner had called Shandler and asked her to go out to where he'd been found. Standing in that desolate, windy field near the power plant, Shandler realized Wegner would have had no idea where he was. But how did he ever get out there?

The line at the casket edged forward; it was Shandler's turn to pay her respects. She was shocked by the large bruise over Wegner's left eye. Even the mortician's makeup couldn't obscure it. It covered almost the whole left side of his forehead.

Afterwards, finding herself beside Wegner's brother Wayne, she asked him if he had noticed the bruise. He had, and didn't know what to make of it either.

Shock subdued the family's capacity for suspicion in those first days after Wegner died. When his mother received the few pieces of clothing found on Wegner's body, she followed the

Cree custom of giving them away to relatives, including the two pairs of socks.

Wayne had picked up his brother's few possessions from Brent Ahenakew's apartment. Propped against the wall near Lawrence's mattress stood three pictures of the family, including one of Wayne's one-year-old son, Bailey.

"I feel so guilty, Jocelan," Wayne said. "I never phoned my brother the week before he died."

Shandler put her arms around him and they stood consoling each other for a long time.

The family buried Lawrence Wegner high on a hill overlooking the Cochin Valley, just a few miles from his mother's house.

— — —

Word of the frantic activity inside the police station had started to get around. On Friday, February 11, Gord Struthers, the city editor of the Saskatoon *Star Phoenix* approached Dan Zakreski's desk. For the past three years, Zakreski had worked as a provincial court reporter. He'd been at the paper for twenty years and was comfortable in the beat. Sources at the police station and in the legal community were his core contacts. Struthers's father was one of the paper's publishers, and Struthers had grown up around the *Star Phoenix*. He'd worked in the composing room and as a reporter before becoming city editor. Both men were close to forty and respected one another very much.

Zakreski recognized the nature of the grin forming on his boss's face as he handed him a sheet of paper.

"This could be big-game hunting," Struthers said.

Zakreski read the page quickly. Security guards at the University of Saskatchewan were spreading rumours that city cops had been dropping men off at the edge of town.

Zakreski had caught some newsroom chatter about Rodney Naistus, whose frozen body had been found on January 29 by Pat Lorje, the MLA. The paper had dedicated only a few skimpy lines to Naistus's death. Like many people in Saskatoon, Zakreski had assumed the guy had been drunk, fallen down and died. When a second native man had been found frozen to death on February 3, out by the power station, the paper still hadn't given it much attention.

But now Struthers asked Zakreski to do a feature about the frozen men and how they died. Zakreski started with Glenn Thomson, the media liaison at the SPS, but Thomson wasn't forthcoming.

Zakreski couldn't really start without a name, so he pushed harder.

"Okay, his name is Lawrence Wegner, that's all I'm gonna tell you," Thomson said.

Thomson was stalling, Zakreski figured, throwing him the bare minimum to get him off the phone. Standard procedure. But under the circumstances, Zakreski was encouraged by Thomson's cool reaction.

It didn't take many more calls for him to begin putting together a pretty good picture of Lawrence Wegner. He was from the Saulteaux reserve near North Battleford and was studying social work at the Saskatchewan Indian Federated College. Then Zakreski found Wegner's friend Alvin Baptiste. It was Baptiste's first contact with the media and he told Zakreski everything he knew. How they played darts together, how Wegner was quiet, loved his studies and sometimes got into trouble if he was into the drugs at night.

Baptiste said his first indication that Wegner was in serious trouble was when he hadn't shown up for school on Monday, January 31.

Zakreski took notes. He knew from the short notice in the paper that Wegner had not been found until Thursday, February 3.

"Students skip class all the time, is that unusual?" he asked.

"No, it's not, but it was weird for Lawrence. He never missed a class. He loved going to school. He wanted to get a social-work degree just like his mum, Mary."

Baptiste told Zakreski that Wegner had spent part of his last night with his roommate of the last few weeks, Brent Ahenakew. Zakreski also found Wegner's former group home operator, Jocelan Shandler, but she was reluctant to talk to him. Through sources, he found his way to Eliza Whitecap's house. He asked her if she knew a Lawrence Wegner. She told him that a man knocked on her door that Sunday night, but she didn't let him in because she did not know at the time that it was Wegner. She told Zakreski that they had called the cops.

"It's easy for you to track, you know. We reported it. We called 911. We saw him leave. He was just wearing a white T-shirt, out in that frigid weather. We tried to get help. We told the cops. They said they'd already sent a car. Last time I saw him he was headed down towards St. Paul's Hospital."

Now Zakreski knew he was onto something. If it checked out, Eliza Whitecap had called the cops asking for help the same weekend that Rodney Naistus had been found dead. He had uncovered an intersection between the police and at least one of the dead native men. And one thing was really bothering him. None of the people he'd interviewed had yet been contacted by the police. He couldn't believe it. Lawrence Wegner had been found over a week ago.

Zakreski spent the weekend stewing over the implications of his story. He started work on Monday, Valentine's Day, with another call to Glenn Thomson.

"Look, Glenn, I've found out a lot about Lawrence Wegner. I'm sniffing around here and, uh, I'm having people tell me that, you know, cops might have had something to do with this."

Zakreski was stunned when Thomson didn't respond with the categorical denial. In fact, he didn't say anything.

"Tell me you guys didn't!" Zakreski said. "I'm just trying to get a quote here. Give me the boiler—the categorical denial."

But Thomson wouldn't. Zakreski phoned back three times, but Thomson would only say that he couldn't talk and that there was a lot going on at the station. He asked Zakreski to give him more time.

Finally Zakreski headed over to the courthouse, where he bumped into Ernie Louttit, who was still one of the few native officers on the force. Zakreski asked him whether he'd ever heard of Lawrence Wegner. The look he got was one Zakreski called "the thousand-yard stare." But Louttit brushed him off with a curt "not now, got to go."

It was a brief walk from the courthouse to the office of one of Zakreski's best legal contacts. He had to talk to Silas Halyk, about an unrelated matter, but the visit was a chance to probe Halyk for any insight into this increasingly weird story. The lawyer cut an imposing figure. Well over six feet tall, with soft white hair and a customary smile, he had worked for the police union and also served as a defence lawyer. A successful legal career in a small city like Saskatoon meant walking a fine diplomatic line. Halyk, who had been called to the bar in the sixties and was now considered an *éminence grise* among the city's criminal lawyers, walked it well.

Halyk liked to meet people in his conference room, which he'd set up in the old drawing room of the century home that housed his firm. Big leather chairs studded with brass surrounded a heavy oak table, and the walls were panelled in elegant dark wood.

Zakreski mentioned the rumours about cops dumping native men outside the city, and suggested it all sounded a bit far-fetched. But Halyk immediately responded that in his long experience with the SPS and the police association he had never seen this kind of commotion and unease at the station. He'd sat in court long enough to remember the vagrancy laws in

Saskatoon and had heard judges sentence native men to a drive to the city limits to get them out of town. The rumoured behavior was not without precedent.

"Dan, they're going apeshit down at the police station right now, they're climbing the walls. I don't know what's going on, but something big is happening. If I were you, I'd stick with this one and keep an open mind."

Back at the office, Zakreski called Thomson again and didn't mince words.

"I'm going with the story for tomorrow morning. So if you're giving me the denial, can we just get it over with?" he said.

Thomson was firm in refusing to give a comment, but he promised the reporter he'd get a meeting with the police the next day if he would just sit on his article overnight.

Zakreski now had to face Gord Struthers. It wouldn't be easy to convince his editor that he wasn't being jerked around by the cops and that they should sit on such a hot story for one more day.

"I've got all the background I need for a really good feature on the freezing deaths of Lawrence Wegner and Rodney Naistus," Zakreski explained. "I've got the 911 call from Eliza Whitecap. I have everybody talking but the cops. They seem to want to sit down and talk."

Ultimately, Struthers decided to trust his reporter's instincts. They would hold off and hear what the cops had to say.

— — —

Jocelan Shandler had never returned Dan Zakreski's phone calls. But Shandler was receiving regular phone calls from another man. He'd begun phoning up to three times a day after Lawrence Wegner had been found on February 3, and had introduced himself as Sergeant McCaffrey. The first time he contacted Shandler, she thought her call display indicated that he was phoning from the Saskatoon Police Service, which confirmed for her his legitimacy, so she spoke freely to him. She'd even sent one of her group-home residents to Brent Ahenakew's apartment to ask questions about Wegner, hoping for something to tell McCaffrey when he next called.

During one phone call, McCaffrey became impatient, pressing Shandler in a new direction.

"Have you heard anything about Lawrence being put into a car?" he asked.

"No, I haven't heard anything like that."

He didn't seem satisfied.

"Have you heard anything about a twelve-year-old girl who might have seen Lawrence put into a car?"

She had never heard anything like that, she told him, and asked for a phone number where she could reach him.

He said he'd call her, and she never heard from him again.

For two weeks, Shandler had been telling the caller everything she knew about Lawrence Wegner and everything she could find out. Later she learned that no Sergeant McCaffrey worked for the Saskatoon police.

— — —

On the morning of Tuesday, February 15, Glenn Thomson called Dan Zakreski, just as he'd promised, and asked him to come immediately to the police station to meet with Chief Scott and the head of Major Crimes. Zakreski told Thomson he was also bringing his boss. Thomson said that would be a good idea and hung up.

Zakreski kept his Daytimer by his phone. His entry after that phone call was tellingly brief, even by his standards: "February 15th. Bad cops??"

At nine-thirty, Zakreski and Struthers entered a boardroom on the management floor of the police station, prepared not for a confession of wrongdoing but for some sort of counterattack.

Chief Scott strode confidently into the room. He was a strikingly handsome man who basked in the support of his entire force, support that he'd won back for the chief's office since taking over from Penkala in 1996. The beat cops called him a police officers' chief, someone willing to lobby for his people. The media savvy Scott had learned in his old job would be desperately needed today.

Scott began by thanking Zakreski for holding the story for a day and telling him that he respected him as a journalist for doing so. Zakreski kept his eyes down and his guard up, concentrating on his spiral-bound notebook. Flattery from the chief this early in the day could only mean he was being buttered up for something bad.

Scott started with a rather awkward turn of phrase, saying that a First Nations person had come forward and had said that they had been dropped off out by the city landfill, by city police officers.

Zakreski struggled not to look at Struthers. The reporter was already asking questions about the very similar circumstances under which Rodney Naistus and Lawrence Wegner had died. Now this. A third person, a live witness, had come forward to complain about how he had been treated by the police.

Scott went on to say that as chief he had exercised due diligence in identifying the two officers and suspending them. He stressed that this was in no way connected with the two other dead men. Scott said he wanted the *Star Phoenix* to know that he was taking this incident very seriously and that he was dealing with it in-house.

Zakreski was flabbergasted. He tried to stay focused, but couldn't get his head around the chief's words to think of a single question. Scott concluded his speech by saying that these were senior constables and that he knew it looked bad, but that he was handling it responsibly with a major internal investigation.

Zakreski finally opened his mouth to ask the names of the cops and the Indian who'd been dumped, but Scott wouldn't budge. Instead, he described how the native person had come forward to an officer, whom Scott did not name, and praised that officer's exemplary behaviour in bringing the matter straight to the chief.

— — —

Later that same day, February 15, Don Worme was sitting in his office, daydreaming about his family's recent vacation to Maui.

The Cree lawyer had spent the fifteen years since he'd graduated from law school becoming a successful and controversial criminal lawyer in Saskatchewan and cultivating his image as a "legal warrior," who would fight tenaciously for the rights of his native clients. He played on this theme publicly, on his licence plate—WARYER—and within the e-mail address for his aboriginal law firm—"legalwarrior."

Worme liked to dress in expensive black Hugo Boss suits, but there was no mistaking his aboriginal pride. His shiny black hair hung down his back in a ponytail. He would quip that his practice consisted mostly of defending drug dealers and murderers, but those around him witnessed a fierceness to his defence of natives, persecuted by a system he believed was heavily tilted against their interests. In his worst moments, the never-ending battles could lead to very dark moods. In the city cells, natives shared his name with those needing a lawyer and praised him as "a regular guy, just like you or me."

Don Worme was proud of his family name. Its history both amused him and fuelled his professional drive. In the early twentieth century, to help implement new treaties, the Canadian government assigned Indian agents to give native men and women English names. The agent who dealt with Worme's great-grandfather had laughed and slapped his knees when the man had given him his Cree name, which was also the word for a water-striding pond beetle. "A bug. Your name stands for a bug," the agent had said, but then couldn't think of an English equivalent. So he proposed the closest thing he could contrive, "A worm is like a bug. So we'll call you Worme."

Every time Don Worme signed his name he remembered the wound it represented and channelled his anger to fuel his spirit. He used "canofworms" in another e-mail address. His odd sense of humour helped him cope, and had come into play when he'd proposed naming his first-born daughter Terra.

"Ah c'mon," he'd pleaded with his wife, Helen, half in jest. "That way she would be Terra Worme, or Earthworm."

Helen put her foot down, and they compromised on Tara.

In the privacy of his office, Worme loosened his blue silk tie and undid his collar. He pulled the elastic hair band out of his ponytail, shook his head and let his hair fall freely across his shoulders. He sat back in his chair and propped his feet on a stack of legal files to let his lunch settle.

Dim sum at the Mandarin Restaurant on 20th Street had become an almost daily ritual. Helen, also a lawyer at the firm, would meet him there, along with any other family who had the time to drop by. Don's older brother, Dale, who wore his black hair in a pair of traditional braids, had joined them at lunch to look at Don's photos of their trip to Maui. Often his two other brothers, Darren and Kim, would eat with them too. Darren, who had been given up for adoption to a German family, had reconnected with his native brothers. He had also become a lawyer. Don now called Kim his brother, even though he was actually his nephew, the son of his dead sister, Pat. It was almost forty years since the terrible night Don's mother and sister were murdered in front of Don, Kim and Dale.

Worme was gazing at the photos on his wall of Helen and their kids and remembering Hawaii when he heard a light knock. Helen opened his door and peeked through. Her worried expression made him sit up.

"What's up?" he asked, brusquely. Worme, who jokingly described himself as having a sunny disposition, had long ago learned to habitually expect the worst.

"Someone to see you," she said. "This is one I think you better take, Don."

A few moments later Helen returned with a very large, slightly stooping native man, dressed in the uniform of the poor urban Indian: unlined jean jacket, blue jeans, white T-shirt and sneakers.

"Don, this is Darrell Night. He's from Saulteaux and lives in Saskatoon."

"Hey, Darrell," said Worme. Helen left, closing the door behind her. "So, what can I do for you?"

Night took his time answering. Everything about him was slow and deliberate. He sized up Worme through thick glasses, his one open eye squinting. Darrell had been drawn to the firm because of Helen's last name, Semaganis, which in Cree means "enforcer." The lawyer's strange sense of humour was about to meet its match.

"I think I need a lawyer," said Night, his voice heavy.

"What is it?" Worme asked. "What did you do?"

Night hesitated before he replied.

"Nuthin'." As serious as his situation was, Night wanted to enjoy the surprise he had in store for this aboriginal lawyer in expensive clothes.

"What is it then? Why do you need a lawyer?" Worme said, having assumed Night had gotten himself into trouble with the law.

"It's about the Saskatoon Police," said Night. "The bastards tried to kill me."

"What?!"

"They left me to freeze to death."

For the next half-hour Night described how the police had left him for dead. Worme immediately made the connection to the other men who had died under suspicious circumstances that winter. And now this man had survived, with an incredible story. What the hell was going on in Saskatoon?

"When was this, Darrell?" he asked "When did they do this to you?"

"Uhmm, it was a Friday. The night of January 28."

— — —

The *Star Phoenix* broke the story the next morning. The front-page headline on February 16 exclaimed, "Cops suspended: Police chief orders homicide investigation after Native men discovered frozen to death."

That morning, Chief Scott held a news conference with all the police reporters in the city. He reiterated the line he had given Dan Zakreski and Gord Struthers, and even credited the *Star Phoenix* with getting the story right. He had suspended two officers, he said, but stressed the investigation would be handled internally. He also announced that Major Crimes would look again at the exposure deaths of Rodney Naistus and Lawrence Wegner.

Around noon, Chris Axworthy, Saskatchewan's justice minister, made his own public statement, announcing an immediate and full investigation into the freezing deaths; the investigating task force would be composed of RCMP officers from around the province. With the story gone public, Scott's attempted in-house solution was overruled. The province was taking over.

One native man had brought the terror of the "starlight tour," long considered urban folklore outside the native community, to the public's attention for the first time. The photos of Lawrence Wegner's frozen body lying face down on the snow-covered prairie sped instantly across wire services to media all over the world. Saskatoon achieved instant notoriety as the little Canadian city where police dumped native people like human trash.

— — —

Although they had barely investigated Lawrence Wegner's death before Darrell Night's revelations, the SPS now worked until the deadline for transferring their files to the RCMP, seeking information that might prove Wegner had walked the five kilometres to the dump.

Just before midnight on February 16, SPS sergeants Bob Peters and Wilf Martin interviewed two employees of TCT Logistics at the trucking outfit's office on Dundonald, a kilometre north of the power station. William Robertson and Ron Skakum claimed they had seen an individual walking along the shoulder of Dundonald just as they had passed each other driving in opposite directions. Robertson thought the person was white but he couldn't remember him wearing glasses. Both men claimed the man was wearing just a T-shirt and jeans, although Skakum had only seen him from behind. Robertson had figured the man was wearing a T-shirt because he remembered seeing the man's bare arms. Neither had seen what he had been wearing on his feet. There was a subdivision less than a kilometre away, so they had both thought he must be headed there. Robertson and Skakum only called the police after hearing about a dead body being found near the power station.

— — —

Albert Chatsis stopped at the Mac's Milk store as he was driving home from his nightly walk. He usually treated himself to a drink, sometimes a hot dog. He rarely bought the paper. But the picture of a man identified as Lawrence Wegner on the front page of the *Star Phoenix* caught his eye. He thought he'd seen that face before. He left the store and was heading home when he realized that the face on the paper was the guy he'd seen beside the police car in front of St. Paul's.

The next morning he called Dan Zakreski at the *Star Phoenix.* Chatsis knew Zakreski's father.

"Hi, Dan, I wanna talk to you about something I seen."

But Zakreski told Chatsis he was too busy to talk and transferred the call to a colleague. When Chatsis started describing what he had seen at the end of January at St. Paul's Hospital, the colleague immediately had him back on Zakreski's line. Fifteen minutes later, Zakreski was sitting in Chatsis's apartment at Borden Place in the Confederation area. "So, tell me what you saw," Zakreski asked.

"It was on the Sunday, near the end of January. At around a quarter to midnight, I came up to St. Paul's Hospital. I was just going up the hill and I seen a police car on the left-hand side, and I went really slow."

"Why did you slow down?"

"I noticed that this guy was wobbling–and because he didn't have any clothes on—I thought maybe somebody ran out from the hospital to come and talk to the police about something.

"By the time I was a little closer, I catch a look at the guy. Even afterwards I keep looking from my rear-view mirror and the cop on the passenger side gets out and opens the back door and grabs the man by the head and, so he got into the car.

"He didn't have no jacket on. He had a wider face around his eyes and a very slim face on the bottom. I remember the reflection of his eyeglasses in the light. It caught my eye when I was driving by. It stuck in my head."

"Have you spoken to the police about this?" asked Zakreski.

"I never told anybody about it, until I called you."

— — —

The *Star Phoenix* continued to publish new details of how an unnamed native man had survived freezing temperatures after he was dumped by police, but Dan Zakreski still couldn't find the man to interview him. He desperately needed a name.

Finally he heard that Don Worme was representing the

man, and that Worme knew the identities of the cops responsible. Zakreski did not look forward to dealing with Worme, who was fiercely protective of his native clients and kept his distance from most reporters, especially Zakreski, whom Worme believed had burned him a few times. Their usual mode of communication was a cool animosity masquerading as professionalism. But Zakreski was desperate for an interview with the survivor, so he called Worme's office. Worme didn't call back. Zakreski decided to try his luck just dropping by.

— — —

Stacks of pink message slips covered Worme's desk. His secretary kept coming into his office while he was on one line, and slipping him notes about who was holding on the other. Everyone wanted to know the identity of the mystery man. Worme was still trying to digest what Darrell Night had told him during their first meeting. What happened to Night was an outrage, but Worme had developed a very cynical view of white attitudes toward the abuse of native people. "Here we go again," he thought.

He wanted to protect Night's identity for as long as possible. The first thing the lawyer had told Night to do was to see a therapist. Surviving his ordeal had been stressful enough, but it would be just as tough dealing with the impact of his disclosure. In Worme's estimation, Night's accusations against the SPS put him in considerable danger. Damned if the media were going to get to him and discredit him. No way. No name, and no pictures either.

The reporter was ushered into the boardroom with its original native paintings on the walls. After a short wait, Worme walked in, shook Dan's hand with a firm grip and asked the reporter to sit down.

"What can I do for Mr. Zareski, today?"

Zakreski didn't know if Worme was mispronouncing his

name on purpose. Perhaps it was Worme's way of maintaining the upper hand. Zakreski didn't bother correcting him.

"I'd like to meet with the native man who walked out of that field—"

"You'd like to meet him, would you?"

"Don, I just want to have a sit-down with the guy."

"Tell me, how would that be in the best interest of my client?" Worme was already irritated . "I know the game you guys play. If I give you his name, you'll be all over it and the next thing you'll do is dig up whatever dirt you can find on my client. Why don't you focus on the two cops who came forward?"

Worme figured Zakreski was actually just as desperate to publish the two officers' names as the native man's, so he goaded him with the information he'd gotten from his own sources.

"It was Hatchen and Munson, you know. They haven't denied taking him out there, so print that!"

Zakreski thanked him for the names, but circled back to his original request, promising he would not print the native man's name; he just wanted to hear him tell his own story.

"I've got the guy in my office. But you can't see him, and I can't tell you who he is." The lawyer was having some fun with Zakreski now.

When Zakreski rose to leave, he was bitterly annoyed. But he couldn't help but sympathize with Worme's position. He had a reason for his paranoia: the native man had taken on the cops.

— — —

Zakreski didn't have much chance to brood over Worme's attitude. His phone wouldn't stop ringing. His newspaper story had caused an uproar in Saskatoon's native community; everyone seemed to know someone who had been taken on a starlight tour, and now they were calling him.

"I know someone this happened to."

"They dropped my uncle off like that. It was in the summer. They've gone too far, now they're doing it in the winter. It's got to stop."

Another call was more specific.

"I'm just calling to set you straight on some facts in your article. Ya know, he was actually wearing something else."

Zakreski asked the man how he knew.

"I'm a family member and I've got the guy right here with me, is why. He doesn't want his name being used, but he wants to tell you what really happened."

Zakreski could not believe his luck. He heard the phone being passed from one man to the other. A deep, slow voice took the reporter through the story of what happened to him at the hands of the cops, and Zakreski wrote down every word. At the end of the account, Zakreski asked for the caller's name.

"No way, buddy, no way."

After he hung up the phone, with the unidentified man's story recorded, Zakreski thought about Don Worme. He didn't have the name, but it was still hard not to gloat.

— — —

Worme had good reason to keep protecting Night. He'd received two threatening phone calls, the second saying, "I got a bullet for him, and I've got one for you too."

Most of the time, Worme tried to see the humour in life. At least this second caller had been more polite. The first guy had been downright rude: "You fucking people, when we see you, you're dead."

— — —

On Friday, February 18, Don Worme drove into Prince Albert in his black Jeep Cherokee. He had organized a gathering with the Federation of Saskatchewan Indian Nations and the chiefs in charge of justice issues to discuss the incredible tension between the native community and the Saskatoon Police Service. He now represented the Wegner family, too, who had contacted him after Lawrence was found frozen to death. For Worme, the gathering promised an extraordinary moment. Darrell Night was going to meet Mary Wegner and her family for the first time.

While the FSIN—who were also assisting Naistus's family—and Worme had begun devising a strategy to demand a full independent government inquiry on the freezing deaths, the most memorable part of the meeting had not been the politics. It was the emotional greeting between Darrell Night and Mary Wegner.

"I want to say how sorry I am about how Lawrence had to die," Night said to her. The two came from the same Saulteaux reserve near North Battleford but they had never met. Mary Wegner still lived in her house on the edge of the reserve, but Night had grown up in Saskatoon. She had trouble controlling her emotions when she thanked Night for his courage in coming forward.

"I was just lucky," Night answered. "Lawrence never had a chance out there. I knew where I was."

— — —

When Don Worme returned to Saskatoon on Friday evening he parked in the gravel lot behind the firm and entered through the back door to pick up his messages. One of them was from Jason Roy, his nephew. The message was fairly detailed.

> Jason called about his friend Neil Stonechild. He and Neil had escaped from custody and were on the run. The police caught up with them. Jason gave a phony name and was released. The cops got Neil and severely beat him and put

him in the back of the police car. His face was gashed very deeply and he was covered in blood. Jason knew the cops had caused the injury on his face because seconds before Neil was fine. Jason couldn't help and had to walk away from it. He thought Neil would be taken back into custody, however six days later Neil's body was found. The cause of death was determined by autopsy to be hypothermia. Jason remembers that night was one of the coldest nights of the year. Later on Jason tried to get someone to listen to his story, but it fell on deaf ears and was brushed under the rug.

Worme scanned to the bottom of the note to read that Jason was trying to reach Neil's family in Manitoba. Jason thought that even ten years later, they would be still trying to get answers about Neil's death.

Worme already had three native families who wanted answers to terrible questions. He had Darrell Night asking him on a daily basis why Dan Hatchen and Ken Munson had tried to kill him. He was also representing the family of Lloyd Joseph Dustyhorn. Dustyhorn had been released by Saskatoon police in the early morning hours of January 19, 2000. A police officer drove him home and left him on his doorstep. Dressed only in a shirt, jeans, socks and boots, he had never made it inside the door, freezing to death on the stoop. And Mary Wegner wanted to know how her son could end up freezing to death at the Queen Elizabeth power station. Worme knew there were also questions from the family of Rodney Naistus, who wanted to know why their son was found frozen to death naked from the waist up on January 29.

Now this. The parallels were frightening, even to Worme, who thought he'd just about seen it all. He pressed his pen hard into the message paper, tracing the date in heavy black lines repeatedly, until it blared out from amongst the other words: Nov/90.

That date raised the ominous possibility that the Saskatoon cops had been taking natives on "starlight tours" for a very long time. Worme picked up the phone to call his nephew. The self-styled legal warrior had just stepped into the legal fight of his life.

"DECADE-OLD DEATH RESURFACES"

DAN ZAKRESKI SHARED THE CRIME BEAT WITH Leslie Perreaux at the *Star Phoenix*. The two were good friends and often went on fishing trips together. But these days Zakreski was consumed with his story about the recent freezing deaths and Darrell Night. He managed only an approving grunt when Perreaux suggested searching the newspaper archives for mention of any other natives who might have been dumped by the cops. Zakreski was swamped, so Perreaux dug in.

The research was time-consuming, and Perraux caught the occasional dismissive look from colleagues who seemed to think he was wasting his time wading through one large, bound scrapbook of back issues after another. Perreaux started with the section of the paper called "Police Briefs." It was the most basic of beginnings, but he wanted to make certain nothing obvious went unnoticed.

As he rummaged through the scrapbooks, he thought about the bewildering cruelty behind the practice he and Zakreski were investigating. He'd heard about South American cities where destitute street urchins were dumped and sometimes killed outside of town so the police could be rid of them. Could a similar thing actually be happening right here in Saskatoon? In Canada?

As he flipped through more old newspapers, Perreaux was somewhat appeased. He was finding no old reports of freezing deaths suffered by natives. He was exhausted and had just about decided to give up when a native boy was suddenly grinning up at him from an old school photo. The warmth of the boy's big smile compelled him to pause for a second. The accompanying headline startled him. "Family suspects foul play. Police say every avenue investigated." Perreaux read the article several times. The paper was dated March 4, 1991.

He looked over at Zakreski's desk and held up the scrapbook to get his friend's attention. He pointed at the picture. "Meet Neil Stonechild," he said. "He's been hiding in our archives for ten years."

Then Perreaux showed the article to Gord Struthers. The editor raised an eyebrow in his habitually understated manner, immediately realizing its significance. "Get on it. We'll put it up tomorrow, front page, headline, the works if you can source it all again."

— — —

"I've been waiting ten years for you to call," Stella said. Twenty minutes after finding the article about Neil, Les Perreaux had tracked down her number and reached her by phone in Cross Lake, Manitoba. Stella's immediate openness surprised him. He was a stranger phoning to ask intimate questions. He had anticipated a woman who just might want to leave such painful memories in the past, or who might be bitter and angry. Instead, Stella was serene and seemed relieved to be talking about Neil.

"I only want one thing, to find out what happened to my son. Why was he found way up in the north industrial area with only one shoe? Did you know they found him with just one shoe and clean socks?"

With the clarity of a mother who had spent every day since her son's death thinking about him, she patiently told Perreaux the same story she had told Terry Craig ten years earlier. He listened carefully, then told Stella it had happened again, and that one man had made it home alive to tell his story. Stella surprised Perreaux again by providing a witness of her own.

"There's Jason, of course, he saw the whole thing. Jason Roy saw Neil in the back of the police car. He told me Neil was looking out at him when they drove him away. I can get you his number, if you hold on a second."

The reporter could not believe his luck and thanked her profusely.

Before she let Perreaux hang up, Stella reminded him of the very thing that had struck him about the picture in the old newspaper. "Neil was just a boy. He never had a chance to grow up. Maybe now that you're writing this, they'll take another look at what happened to Neil."

— — —

After talking to his nephew, Worme called Neil Stonechild's mother. Within seconds he and Stella were talking as if they'd known each other for a lifetime. When she asked him about his own family, the lawyer launched happily into stories about his children.

In turn, Stella told him more about Neil; she had always fiercely maintained that she would one day learn how he'd died. Worme wanted to help her. He had a soft spot for mothers, having lost his own so long ago, and Stella's warmth and commitment made that old wound ache. Here was a woman who had patiently waited ten years and still had the fortitude to ask calmly whether there was anything *she* could do to help *him*.

Worme offered to represent her. He scribbled the details of her call all over his secretary's note about Jason, writing in one corner that Constable Ernie Louttit had worked on the file on his own time.

He then dictated into his tape recorder the letter his secretary would send to Stella, which would legally commit him as her lawyer. "We commit ourselves toward ensuring that Neil's life was not lost in vain and that justice is achieved," he said.

Considering the pace of the justice system, Worme realized he would be working with Stella for a very long time.

Stella had confided to Worme that she had given Les Perreaux Jason's phone number. Concerned for his nephew's safety, he called and tried to persuade him not to speak out publicly. Not to worry, Jason said, he would speak only on the condition of anonymity. Worme insisted, but in the wake of the recent deaths, Jason was desperate to tell his story.

When Perreaux called on February 21, Jason refused to talk on the phone. Instead, against his uncle's advice, he asked the reporter to meet him in a restaurant at the Confederation Mall.

Perreaux arrived by cab to find a young man in his mid-twenties shuffling around outside, looking down at the concrete sidewalk, stepping on and off the curb while he nervously smoked a cigarette. Roy jumped into the cab before Perreaux had a chance to get out.

"Let's drive around a bit so we can talk. Then we can go into the mall," Roy said. As the cab drove around for a few minutes, Perreaux got the distinct impression that Roy feared someone was watching them.

When they finally got to the restaurant, it was packed. At first, Perreaux doubted they'd find a table. Roy relaxed slightly after a coffee, but his hands still shook and his eyes watered. He was visibly terrified. The fear, he told Perreaux, had never gone away.

"You can't identify me, okay, I'm still afraid of the police, especially now." But still he described to the reporter what he remembered happening the night of November 24, 1990.

"Neil was screaming my name, telling me to help him. Seeing him sitting in that car like that, I was in no position to want to get in that car with him. So I lied." He was forthcoming about his lengthy criminal record and didn't hesitate to tell Perreaux that he'd lied about his identity and about knowing Neil because he was wanted by police. Perreaux took notes furiously as Roy gave him everything except the false name he'd used with the police.

"I'd rather not say. The only people who know that name are the two cops from that night and me."

— — —

Around six o'clock on the day Perreaux met with Jason Roy, Don Worme received a fax from the *Star Phoenix*—the draft of Perreaux's article. He read the opening line: "It's a −24 degree November night in 1990, when a young native man disappears."

The next morning, Tuesday, February 22, 2000, Worme picked up the paper. "Decade-old death resurfaces" read the big headline. Underneath it another headline announced, "Neil Stonechild's family questions why he froze to death in this field." A picture of the snowy field was stretched across the top third of the page. Neil's school photo was superimposed on the top left-hand corner of the field. Looking at that boyish face grinning out from the top of page one, Worme reflected for a moment about Stella's loss. It would be up to him to make sure the Saskatoon Police Service couldn't shake this new headache on their hands, one they likely thought had been laid to rest ten years ago.

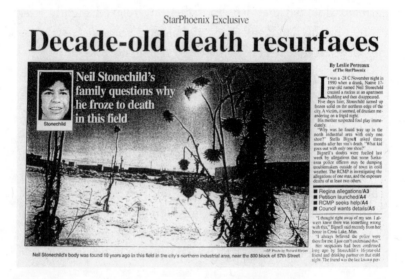

StarPhoenix Exclusive

Decade-old death resurfaces

By Leslie Perreaux
of The StarPhoenix

Neil Stonechild's family questions why he froze to death in this field

Stonechild

It was a -28 C November night in 1990 when a drunk, Native 17-year-old named Neil Stonechild created a ruckus at an apartment building and then disappeared.

Five days later, Stonechild turned up frozen solid on the northern edge of the city. A victim, it seemed, of drunken meandering on a frigid night.

His mother suspected foul play immediately.

"Why was he found way up in the north industrial area with only one shoe?" Stella Bignell asked three months after her son's death. "What kid goes out with only one shoe?"

Bignell's doubts were fuelled last week by allegations that some Saskatoon police officers may be dumping troublemakers outside of town in cold weather. The RCMP is investigating the allegations of one man, and the exposure deaths of at least two others.

■ Regina allegations/A3
■ Petition launched/A4
■ RCMP seeks help/A4
■ Council wants details/A5

"I thought right away of my son. I always knew there was something wrong with this," Bignell said recently from her home in Cross Lake, Man.

"I always believed the police were there for me. I just can't understand this."

Her suspicions had been confirmed long ago by Stonechild's 16-year-old friend and drinking partner on that cold night. The friend was the last known per-

Neil Stonechild's body was found 10 years ago in this field in the city's northern industrial area, near the 800 block of 57th Street

PART III

LEGAL CHEATING

Prologue

Beligerent drunk gets ride to highest power in land

By Brian Trainor

Hawk and Gumby were assigned to the Riversdale area of the city for the year. Two young constables, eager for the excitement that they felt came with policing and working in Car 6 provided them with more than enough action. The days were considerably quiet, as they were throughout the city. However, the nights brought problems.

The July night was clear and warm as the sun had just set, leaving the sky aglow with a faint

orange hue. Driving west on 19th Street, a call was heard from Car 5 requesting help at the Salvation Army. The men in five were trying to get a drunk into the back of their car, but the man was not co-operating. Being two blocks away, Car 6 volunteered to assist.

The two constables were standing on the sidewalk amidst a growing crowd of men who were enjoying their dilemma. The drunk was seemingly wrapped around the rear door of the patrol car and dislodging him would take considerable force. Gumby walked up to the two officers and took control. He felt that using tact rather than braun may work in this instance and offered to take the fellow home instead of the drunk tank and promising on his mother's grave, managed to convince the man to climb into Car 6.

Getting directions that were very vague and to the west, Hawk drove off along 20th Street, hoping the passenger recognized something that looked like home. All the way, the two officers were regaled with tales of violence — how horrible things were and how their passenger could break their necks using only his big toes if he had the mind to.

As the streets zoomed by, the stories got more threatening. The volume of his voice rose and the acts of violence grew more pronounced. Threats that heads were going to roll began and soon Gumby had to close the sliding window to prevent any attempt at assault.

By the time the men got to Montgomery Place, their passenger turned into their worst nightmare, according to him, though neither cop had spoken a word the entire trip.

As they continued south along Dundonald, the tirade continued until they passed the last street light and entered the darkened countryside. An uneasy silence had overcome the man in the back. Sensing that this wasn't the way home, the drunk began to demand he be taken to the "highest power of the land."

A few quick turns and the car came to an abrupt stop in front of the Queen Elizabeth Power Station. Climbing out and opening the rear door, Hawk yelled for the man to get out, advising him that this was the place he had asked to go to.

Quickly gathering his wits, the drunk scrambled out of the car and into the thickets along the riverbank, disappearing from view. One less guest for breakfast.

Trainor is a Saskatoon city police officer.

SPS officer Brian Trainor's Saskatoon *Star Phoenix* column from summer 1997.

BIZARRO WORLD

MEMBERS OF THE NEWLY FORMED RCMP TASK force into Darrell Night's drop-off and the freezing deaths of the local native men had barely found hotel rooms in Saskatoon when they, like everyone else, read the headline about the decade-old Neil Stonechild case in the February 22 *Star Phoenix*. They were already looking into the deaths of Lawrence Wegner, Rodney Naistus and one other man who had died within hours of being released from police custody. Fifty-three-year-old Lloyd Joseph Dustyhorn was brought in for intoxication on the evening of January 18. After being kept under observation in a cell until the early hours of January 19, when he was released and transported home by city police, he froze to death on his doorstep.

RCMP Superintendent Darrell McFadyen had been handed overall leadership of the largest task force in Saskatchewan's history. His lead investigator was Sergeant Ken Lyons, a veteran detective with a shaved head and the build of a fullback. Lyons's first challenge had been to find dozens of hotel rooms for his team. Local hotels were filled with competitors and fans of the Brier, Canada's premier curling event. The only hotel in town with any vacancies was the Sandman, a nondescript airport hotel still under construction, located off Circle Drive in northwest Saskatoon. Only the second floor was fit for human habitation. Despite the constant racket of drywallers and other construction workers, and notwithstanding fire alarms at all hours and sporadic access to hot water, the Sandman was to become Project Ferric's home base. (The task force's odd name had come from the RCMP's custom of designating investigations alphabetically in much the same way as meteorologists name hurricanes; "Ferric" had no significance beyond beginning with F.)

The *Star Phoenix* article quoted allegations from an anonymous "friend" who had seen Neil driven away by two cops in the back of an SPS cruiser as he screamed, "They're gonna kill me." The article's appearance blindsided the RCMP. To buy time, they told the media that the task force was already looking into four freezing deaths—a fourth man, thirty-three-year-old Darcy Dean Ironchild, had been found frozen on his doorstep on February 19—and into the Darrell Night case; they were not currently investigating the Stonechild matter.

Behind the scenes, however, McFadyen was wasting no time. He phoned Saskatoon Deputy Police Chief Dan Wiks the morning the story appeared and informed him that the RCMP would look into the Stonechild case as soon as they had freed up an investigator from the other files.

Investigating another police force is never easy. The Saskatchewan Justice Department had further complicated things by publicly yanking the matter out of the SPS's hands. The brief conversation between Wiks and McFadyen was cool but professional. McFadyen asked for the original investigation file. Wiks told him that he and other management-level officers had been turning the 4th Avenue station upside down looking for the file. Unfortunately, Wiks told him, the Stonechild file had been destroyed.

— — —

On Wednesday, February 23, Don Worme was relieved to be back on the road in his black Jeep Cherokee. He needed to clear his head from the chaos. So he did what he always did to ground himself, he headed southeast of Saskatoon back to the Kawacatoose reserve, where he had grown up with his grandfather and his brothers.

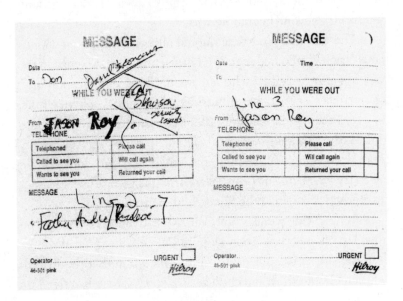

Although he was trying to get away, he could never manage to turn his cellphone off. Around eleven in the morning, he took a phone call from Ken Lyons. Given Worme's newly acquired clients, the two men had already become acquainted. Through the static on the line, Lyons reassured Worme that, contrary to the *Star Phoenix*'s report that morning, Project Ferric was going to investigate the Stonechild case and that unsuccessful attempts had already been made to secure the original investigation file. All that remained of the file, it seemed, were some notes saying it had been shredded.

Lyons said the SPS had told him they kept the file as long as they were required to, but he also said he thought the file was not supposed to be destroyed for ten years.

Worme did the math. If what Lyons was saying was true, Worme told him, the file had been destroyed at least nine months prematurely, since Neil had died in November 1990.

Lyons concluded by assuring him that they would continue looking into the destruction of the file and whether the SPS should have held onto it. Either way, there was not much left to work with.

Worme's mind wandered as he watched the road. His nephew, Jason Roy, had really pissed him off by talking to the *Star Phoenix* against his objections. But he was worried about the kid, too. The paper had not yet identified him, or Darrell Night, but he knew it was only a matter of time. Journalists were calling from as far away as Washington, D.C. Since Jason's initial call less than a week earlier, they had spoken several times a day. Neither mentioned that ten years ago Worme had dismissed Jason's garbled attempt to tell his uncle what he had seen.

"Great, a witness and no file," Worme thought. "Welcome to Bizarro World." Bizarro World was Superman's freakishly upside-down parallel universe. After Dale, Kim and Don had moved in with their grandfather, the boys had gone mad for comics, and Dale had taught his brother Don to read from *Superman* and *Conan the Barbarian*.

The Jeep rolled to a stop at the foot of the small snow-covered hill at the cemetery, and Worme stepped out. He climbed a bit and then stood listening to the poplars whisper as the wind rubbed their bare limbs against one another. His mother, Margaret, was buried a few yards to the north under the snow. His grandfather, who died in 1979 at the age of eighty-three, lay pretty much where Worme was standing. Nothing marked the graves; here and there prairie grass poked through the snow.

Worme remembered his grandfather, Edward Worme, as a big man with a wide smile and heavily callused hands. The day the little boy arrived to stay, Edward had given him a piece of fur. Don had carried it everywhere, burying his nose in it for comfort, just as he had with his mother's winter coat. Life with the irrepressible, rebellious "great man," as Worme always described him, observing his struggles against the white government for the right to make a living with his farm, had served as an unforgettable lesson in courage when facing injustice.

Without his grandfather's influence, Worme felt he never would have become a lawyer. Cheeky almost from birth, he had been a spirited kid, tantrums, the works. He remembered hoofing his Uncle Vince in the balls once for no reason. When he was fourteen he quit school, but his grandfather said that if Don was old enough to quit school, he was old enough to fend for himself. He drove the teenager to Highway 6 at Raymore and left him at the side of the road clutching a small yellow plastic bag containing a few of his things.

Worme had hitchhiked to Regina, and then for the next couple of years he wandered through Saskatchewan, Alberta and British Columbia. He once lied about his age to get a job cutting metal for boxcars. One of his bosses had such a violent temper, the crew nicknamed him the Tasmanian Devil. When Worme had had enough and came back to Saskatchewan, he discovered that his older brother, Dale, was at university studying geology. Not to be outdone, he decided to finish high school himself, and then went on to university, doing well enough to get into the law program at the University of Saskatchewan.

At his graduation he gave one of his professors—the lawyer who had prosecuted his mother's murderer back in 1964—some small black licorice cigars with red sprinkles on the end. They were the same kind the lawyer had given four-year-old Don to bolster his confidence before testifying against Francis Littlechief.

After a few minutes, as he always did at the cemetery, Worme took out a couple of cigarettes and placed them on the snow near the graves. He added a promise to his mother and grandfather: he would fight with every ounce of his strength for Neil's mother, Stella, and for Darrell Night and the families connected to the recent deaths.

— — —

Ken Lyons pulled Corporal Jack Warner off the Wegner file and assigned him to lead the new Stonechild investigation. Warner had heard of Neil Stonechild for the first time, like his Project Ferric colleagues, when he read that week's story in the *Star Phoenix*.

Warner was a friend of Lyons, and a respected detective with the Major Crimes unit in Regina. In his mid-forties now, he and Lyons had grown up together in Kennedy, a small town in southern Saskatchewan. After joining the RCMP, Lyons had stayed in the province, whereas Warner had gained a lot of his early field experience in the Yukon, before returning.

The two men could not have looked less alike. Shaven-headed and burly, Lyons usually wore a suit and tie, and could never be mistaken for anything but a cop. Warner was tall and thin and favoured tweed sport coats, resembling an English professor more than a police officer. Giving up cigarettes had led to the perpetual smoking of Amphora pipe tobacco. Warner was on his second marriage and had six kids. One of his sons had followed his father's career path into the RCMP. On downtime at his beloved country cabin, out of cellphone reach, Warner read voraciously, everything from Leon Uris, James Michener and John Steinbeck, for instance, to Saskatchewan's own Guy Vanderhaeghe.

Lyons had told Warner that Don Worme was representing Jason Roy, the anonymous witness in the February 22 newspaper article. Their paths had crossed on a few murder cases, Warner investigating suspects Worme was hired to defend. Worme's impressive skill in cross examination had won him Warner's respect. The cop had a sense it was mutual, which could only help, since Jason Roy was the first person Warner wanted to meet.

The file on Neil Stonechild's death was nowhere to be found. After 1992 the SPS's computer system was improved so that any investigation report was stored digitally as it was being dictated. But Neil had died in 1990, so his file was only on paper. When the station was renovated in 1998 and 1999, Chief Scott approved a culling and destruction of files. The SPS normally kept all operational files, but to clear up much-needed space, the SPS deferred to the looser restrictions of the 1990 Police Act. According to the act, sudden-death files, like Neil's, could be destroyed after only three years. The Stonechild file had been destroyed.

— — —

In the relative quiet of room 218 at the Sandman, down the hall from the noise and clatter of the Project Ferric "war room," which ran twenty-hour days, Warner laid the few Stonechild records he'd assembled on the bed. Sitting forward on his desk chair, smoking his pipe, he hunched over them like a poor man surveying his meagre worldly possessions.

The coroner's office had forwarded the coroner's declaration and the autopsy report. A so-called "hard copy" or computer record showed the date of Neil's death with a brief comment, "DEATH OTH CAUSES," and the name of one suspect, "Pratt, Gary Leslie." Because it was dictated after the SPS upgraded its computer system, Warner also had a copy of SPS Sergeant Bob Morton's 1993 report, in which he claimed to have destroyed Neil's clothes as per Sergeant Keith Jarvis's instructions.

Warner took note of the names Morton and Jarvis. He still didn't have the slightest idea who was on shift the night Neil had died. Shift schedules for 1990 had been thrown out long ago.

Morton's photos from the scene and the autopsy were stored as exhibits, separately from the file, and had not been shredded. Warner went through the pictures one at a time. He didn't like what he saw.

— — —

Don Worme's Saturday did not get off to a good start. Up early, in bare feet and a white robe, he was looking forward to a cup of strong coffee and a bit of peace and quiet before driving his daughters Tannis and Rhiannon to hockey and ringette practice. He lived on Temperance Street in Saskatoon's east side, not far from the university. The modest two-storey house stood only a couple of miles from his mother's old neighbourhood across the river, near St. Paul's Hospital and the Stroll. Now his neighbours were fellow lawyers, doctors and other professionals.

After brewing his coffee, he flipped through the February 26 Saturday edition of the *Star Phoenix*. He swore under his breath and felt his blood pressure begin to rise as he read one of the headlines, "Beligerent Drunk Gets Ride to Highest Power in Land." The paper had dug up an article from the archives, a column published in its Sunday supplement in the summer of 1997 by SPS officer Brian Trainor. For almost three years, Trainor had written a series of columns about police life from the inside, called "Tales from the Blue Lagoon." In the late nineties Chief Scott had asked him to stop, and he did.

After reading this particular column through, Worme sat back in disbelief. In detail and in a mocking tone, Trainor described two police officers, nicknamed Hawk and Gumby, picking up an intoxicated native man. They mock the man's request to be taken to "the highest power in the land" by dumping him near the Queen Elizabeth power station. The resemblance to Darrell Night's ordeal was eerie.

> A few quick turns and the car came to an abrupt stop in front of the Queen Elizabeth Power Station. Climbing out and opening the rear door, Hawk yelled for the man to get out, advising him that this was the place he had asked to go to.

> Quickly gathering his wits, the drunk scrambled out of the car and into the thickets along the riverbank, disappearing from view. One less guest for breakfast.

Breakfast at the drunk tank, Trainor had meant.

The paper also published a response from the SPS on the old column, which distanced the force from responsibility and claimed that Trainor had written the piece on his own time. The force didn't know whether his story was fact or fiction. Worme had no doubt that the nicknames hid real officers who might still be on the force. For all he knew they might have driven Naistus and Wegner to their deaths.

So slow learners did not miss the point, the paper ran a stark rundown of the facts of the first two months of 2000 along-side Trainor's column. For Worme, the SPS's repeated position that they had never heard the stories about officers dumping people on the outskirts of town—and that the Darrell Night drop-off was an isoloated incident—was wearing thin.

— — —

Later that morning, Jason Roy was taking a shower when the phone rang. He grabbed a towel, and went out to the living room to answer it. He was living at Snowberry Downs with Vanessa Kayseas, a gorgeous Saulteaux woman with long black hair, and their two-year-old daughter, Taylor. Roy was unem-ployed and Kayseas studied social work at university. She had just run out to the convenience store across the street.

Roy's circle of friends had always been small. Kayseas, for example, had once lived with Neil's old best friend, Jeff Crowe. She and Crowe had a seven-year-old boy named Ryland, who was living with her grandparents in Wadena, Saskatchewan. Roy and Cheryl Antoine had split up long ago; their daughter, Justine Antoine Roy, was eight and lived with her mother. Kayseas had known Cheryl Antoine since they were kids. For better or worse, everyone seemed to have known everyone else, at some point. Similarly, with limited incomes, they'd all lived in the same few apartment buildings. Snowberry Downs was one. Twin Gables, where Roy had seen the cruiser carrying Neil emerge from the alley, was another.

If Jason Roy hadn't quite hit bottom, it was not for lack of trying. He was twenty-six and balding, with a face puffy from booze, drugs and chronic insomnia. He looked at least ten years older. Nightmares still haunted what sleep he managed to get. He faced the anger and fear in Neil's face almost every night. By 1996 Roy's B and E's and petty thefts had landed him in the correctional centre in the north end of Saskatoon.

Being with Kayseas and their baby girl had helped Roy calm down. He had also built a relationship with a French-speaking Catholic priest from Prud'homme, Saskatchewan. Father André Poilievre, a bald, athletic fifty-five-year-old, had also lived in Paris and Canada's north. He had battled alcoholism himself years earlier, emerging from his struggle with his own demons to dedicate his life to working with street kids. In Saskatoon, that meant mostly native kids like Roy. They'd first met in 1989 when Roy was enrolled at Joe Duquette High School, which specialized in helping high-risk students caught up in street life. Father André had since helped him through at least a half-dozen stints in rehab, never giving up on him. Gradually, Roy began to trust him. In 1996, when he was doing time in the correctional centre, Father André was serving as the chaplain there, and he had even confided in the priest about that last time he had seen Neil alive.

Roy reached for the phone while still trying to tie the towel around his waist. It was Vanessa. Water dripped onto the floor. His heart began to pound when he heard the panic in her voice.

"What's going on, Vanessa? Slow down," he said.

"They're arresting me, Jason. They're taking me down to the police station. I can't talk now. Make sure the baby's safe. And call Don. Do it now!" The line went dead.

Roy dialled his uncle's cellphone immediately.

— — —

Don Worme had jumped into his Jeep as soon as Jason told him that the SPS were arresting Vanessa. He tried the chief's office on his cellphone as he raced downtown. He didn't reach Dave Scott, but someone else told him that Constable Brad Senger was the one driving Kayseas to the station in Car 54.

He managed to get Kayseas released within the hour, but by then she had been strip searched. She looked dazed. No charges were ever laid. The story she told Worme astonished him.

She had been about to use the pay phone near the convenience store when a man called her name. She turned around and saw it was a police officer asking her to come over to his unmarked car. He identified himself as Robin Wintermute. Kayseas didn't know this, but Wintermute was the dog handler who had searched the scene where Lawrence Wegner had been found. The officer did not explain how he knew her name, but said they'd received a tip that she'd been selling drugs earlier that morning at the convenience store. That was preposterous, she told him. He typed her name into his mobile data terminal; it showed she had an outstanding parking ticket for forty dollars. He read her her rights and said she would have to come down to the station.

She said that one of the strangest parts of the ordeal was that the cop driving her to the station kept radioing in to the dispatcher every few minutes to describe what intersection they were passing.

After promising her he would find out what had happened, Worme called the RCMP and demanded help protecting his clients. For the moment, that meant hiding Jason and Vanessa at the Sheraton Cavalier Hotel, downtown.

— — —

On Saturday night a crowd of mostly natives and a few whites began to gather in the Saskatchewan Indian Federated College gymnasium. As they headed to their seats, each person took a candle. Driven by outrage over the freezing deaths, including that of Lawrence Wegner, who had studied there, a group of older local women activists had organized the protest. They called themselves Grandmothers for Justice.

The unofficial leaders of the Grandmothers were two seasoned native activists, Bernelda Wheeler, former host of the CBC Radio program *Our Native Land,* and Marjorie Pratt Truro, one of the only Canadians involved in the American Indian Movement's standoff the with the FBI at Wounded Knee in 1973. Although the pair had marched on Parliament together, lately age and health problems had toned down their activities. But the revelations of the past weeks spurred them to to get back on their political feet.

Also in the crowd was a vice-chief of the Federation of Saskatchewan Indian Nations, Lawrence Joseph. Joseph served as the FSIN's spokesman on justice issues. Over the past two weeks he'd repeatedly castigated the police with fiery invective and inflammatory rhetoric. Angry as he was himself, Worme was concerned because he thought Joseph was polarizing the situation.

When over four hundred candles had been handed out, Marjorie Truro went to the podium to rally the crowd with songs and speeches.

Then the crowd began a slow walk to the police station. Other protestors followed in their cars. Grandmothers for Justice were determined that similar marches and vigils would happen weekly in the coming months to show the authorities that police could not brutally mistreat natives without consequences. If the Saskatchewan Minister of Justice Chris Axworthy thought he could stem the rising political pressure by taking the investigation out of the hands of the SPS and handing it over to the RCMP, they wanted to prove him wrong. Like Don Worme, they wanted an independent inquiry into abuse of natives at the hands of police and nothing less.

— — —

A few days after Kayseas's arrest, Father André got a call from Jason Roy, asking for a meeting. When the priest pulled up in his white Ford pickup truck, Roy jumped in the cab and wasted no time saying he was afraid the SPS were following him.

He had never been publicly identified as the witness in Neil's death, but so what, he said. Why else would the cops be intimidating him and his family? Vanessa was worried sick about their baby. And he didn't feel safe even in the hotel.

Father André offered Roy and his family the empty apartment in the basement of the rectory on Windsor Street, across the tracks from Woodlawn Cemetery. They stayed there for the next two nights. Father André came by in his truck each morning to check in. On the third morning, as he was backing out of the rectory driveway, he noticed a police cruiser go by on an adjoining street and make a U-turn. He pulled out and waited just across from the rectory, to see what the cop was up to.

The cruiser passed the rectory very slowly. From his truck, Father André could look down at the driver. The cop locked eyes with the priest and refused to look away until the car had passed.

Father André went back into the rectory. "Buddy," he said to Roy when he got inside, "I don't know what's going on, but I don't know if this place is safe for you either."

Father André had accompanied Roy several times to Worme's office since the boy had contacted his uncle. When they went this time, the priest explained that even the church was no longer a sanctuary for Roy.

Worme phoned Jack Warner and demanded a meeting to get Roy and his family some further form of RCMP protection. The media pressure to identify Roy was escalating each day and Worme wanted to hide his client somewhere out of town. At a preliminary meeting, the RCMP had seemed open to the idea. With Vanessa's bizarre arrest and the priest's tale of cops watching the rectory, Warner agreed to meet Worme at the Bessborough Hotel the next day. It was all getting too crazy, Worme thought as he hung up the phone. Bizarro.

— — —

On Monday, February 28, the *Washington Post* put Saskatoon's shame on international display. The respected newspaper published a lengthy feature detailing all the freezing deaths, describing the troubled relations between natives and the SPS, and quoting Jason Roy, without naming him. Also quoted was former premier Allan Blakeney, who confessed, "As much as it pains me to say it, this remains a racist province."

— — —

Jack Warner made his first contact with the man who had led the original investigation into Neil Stonechild's death, former SPS sergeant Keith Jarvis, on March 3. When he retired in 1993, Jarvis had moved to the west coast, where he worked as an apartment-building manager in Burnaby. Warner reached him there by telephone.

Taking notes as he talked, Warner briefly explained who he was and the reason for his call. Jarvis sounded congenial but claimed to have heard very little about the RCMP's investigation. Neither had he read anything in the media about Neil Stonechild. The name, he said, meant absolutely nothing to him.

Warner tried to jog Jarvis's memory. After considerable prompting, he recalled doing an investigation of a sudden death in Saskatoon's north end and that the person was a native youth found frozen to death and wearing only one shoe. Although his memory was sketchy, he remembered Pratt as the name of an original suspect.

When Warner described Jason Roy's account of the evening, Jarvis told him categorically that he remembered no allegations that Stonechild had been in the custody of Saskatoon police on the night he was last seen. Nor could he check his notebooks from the fall of 1990; Jarvis claimed to have destroyed them after retiring.

Although the conversation was not very satisfying, Jarvis had been friendly and he agreed to talk to Warner again any time. Warner had been careful not to push too hard and scare him off. "I'd guess there's more water in the well," he told Ken Lyons later.

— — —

Around midnight on March 4, Darrell Night got up from the table at the Albany on 20th Street where he was drinking with some buddies. As he walked toward the washroom, he felt someone jostle him from behind and then hit him in the kidney hard enough to make him double over. When he put his hand on his back it came away covered with blood. Someone beside him said, "Jesus Christ, man, you've been stabbed."

"I don't know what you're jumpin' up and down about," Night said, "I'm the one covered in blood. Someone call an ambulance."

Barely conscious, Night managed to call Don Worme from St. Paul's. Worme raced down to the hospital. When he got there he was stunned that the police had not set up any kind of protection for his client. He didn't know who had stabbed Night, but he was not about to take any chances. Not knowing what else to do, he phoned Warner, who came over and assigned someone to guard Night until morning.

Over the next couple of days, Worme found out the police

were treating Night's stabbing as a fight between a couple of drunks. No more than that. His assailant was never apprehended and no charges were ever laid. Night stayed in hospital for over a week and underwent surgery, before being released.

After helping out with Night, Warner had no trouble getting Don Worme to agree to a private meeting with Jason Roy. Warner had agreed to protect Roy and his family by sending them out of town for a while. But first he wanted to hear Roy's story for himself. He'd seen the reports in the media, but as a cop he was naturally skeptical.

Warner drove his unmarked car into the Confederation Mall parking lot in the early afternoon of March 7, and spotted Roy right away. Shoulders hunched, one hand in the pocket of his windbreaker, the other bringing a cigarette to his mouth, he was standing just outside the door of the Robin's Donut Shop, where they had agreed to meet. Warner offered him a seat in the car while he went inside to get them coffee.

"Two creams, two sugars, right?" Warner asked when he returned, handing Roy the paper cup and settling back behind the wheel.

"Mmm—uh, thanks," said Roy awkwardly, not used to being offered coffee by a cop. For the next few minutes, Warner listened to Roy without interrupting. Roy reached the part of his account at which the cruiser with Neil in the back stopped him at the alley.

"They asked me my name and CPICed me," explained Roy, surprising Warner with his fluency in police jargon. Warner noticed him begin to tap his fingers as though he were typing on a keyboard. Canadian Police Information Centre queries entered through mobile data terminals in police cruisers were routed through RCMP headquarters in Ottawa. If Roy was telling the truth, a computer record had to exist.

Hiding his excitement, Warner asked the young man if he had complied and given the cops his name.

"No."

"Well, what name did you give them, then?"

"My cousin's name, Tracy Horse—he doesn't have a record." Roy told him how the officers had CPICed his cousin's full name and birth date, and then simply let him go. He had never revealed to anyone the false name he'd given police on November 24, 1990. His eyes moistened as he described Neil's bloodied face in the back seat of the cruiser.

By end of the interview Warner was a lot less skeptical about Jason Roy. He had sounded genuinely guilty about not getting into the car with his friend, as if getting arrested himself might have changed the outcome.

His coffee cup empty, the young man slumped against the passenger door.

"There's one thing I don't get," Warner said, after a moment's consideration.

"Eh?"

"Why has it taken you ten years to come forward?"

Roy frowned. He looked across his coffee at Warner as though he thought the cop had lost his mind.

"It hasn't taken me ten years," said Jason. "I've been telling people all along, including the cops."

Warner drove directly back to the Sandman and faxed a request to Ottawa headquarters for a CPIC search of all computer queries made from SPS mobile data terminals for November 24 and 25, 1990.

Headquarters worked fast, and sent the list back the next day. The computer record showed that at 11:56 on the night of November 24, 1990, Badge 80, Constable Brad Senger, pressed the send button on the mobile terminal in the cruiser he was patrolling in with Larry Hartwig. The first entry shows that Senger initially put the name Tracy Horse and the date of birth into the system. His second entry, made immediately afterwards, queried the middle name Lee.

— — —

On March 9, armed with facts from Ottawa that corroborated Jason Roy's story, Jack Warner and RCMP Superintendent Darrell McFadyen went to see SPS Deputy Chief Dan Wiks. Wiks said he was unaware of the assertions made in the newspaper about a witness seeing Neil in the back of a police cruiser. Warner was astonished; there had been weeks of intense media coverage of the freezing deaths and a front-page article about Neil Stonechild. Warner and McFadyen also told Wiks that the same witness had told a detective at the time that he had seen Neil in the back of a police vehicle. Wiks did not address this directly; however, he did say that if it were true, he could only believe that word would have spread throughout the police service and caused a furor.

In mid-March Warner made the six-hour drive to Winnipeg to meet Stella Stonechild Bignell. She had moved there temporarily from Cross Lake so that Norman Bignell, whom she'd married in 1993, could upgrade his trade skills at a local college. As he pulled up to the house on Maryland Street, Warner had second thoughts about coming alone. The neighbourhood was rundown, and in the fading light of late afternoon, the protective grilles that had been installed on the windows of many of the houses cast shadows like prison bars. But the last thing he'd wanted was for Stella and her sons to feel intimidated by the presence of two cops. When Warner knocked, a young man in his twenties answered the door. Tattoos covered his lean, muscular arms. He introduced himself as Jake Stonechild, Neil's younger brother.

At the kitchen table, over cup after cup of tea, Warner talked for the next six or seven hours with Jake, Stella and Neil's older brother, Marcel. They'd felt immediately at ease with him, more so than Warner could have hoped, and the hours flew by. Stella's complete absence of bitterness and her sincere determination to know what had happened to her son worked their usual charm. She offered full access to her family, or to anyone she knew who had seen Neil before he'd disappeared. And she confirmed that Jason Roy had told her years ago the same story he'd told Warner about seeing Neil in the back of a cruiser.

By the time Warner left, it was too late to visit Neil's sister, Erica, who lived two hours away at the Valley River reserve, so he booked himself into a motel.

The next morning, on March 15, the real value of Stella's grant of access to her family made itself apparent. Ever since she had been born with a thick mane of black hair, everybody had called Erica Gypsy, and from the way her brothers talked about her, she was no pushover. Without a prior call from Stella, Warner would never have gotten through her door. Even so, she welcomed him by asking, "Why the hell should I trust you?"

When they went inside, Erica looked him in the eye and asked him if he was serious about finding out how her brother had died. When Warner replied, "Absolutely," she considered him for a long moment. Then her tone changed and, with an openness reminiscent of her mother's, she spent the next two hours telling him what she remembered.

The viewing at the funeral home was still vivid for her— the marks on Neil's face, her anger at seeing his long black hair cut short and ragged. She remembered the shock of feeling the bumps on his skull and her overwhelming sense that his death wasn't an accident. She also told him the family had gone to the police station repeatedly to collect his clothes, and had been repeatedly sent home empty-handed. Erica was still fuming.

Warner headed back to Saskatoon. These interviews had brought to mind a case he'd investigated in the early eighties. A teacher from the Onion Lake reserve had been brutally assaulted and murdered. Her body had been burned and found buried to the waist in garbage. He'd never solved the case. Warner and Ken Lyons still told each other that they would not retire until they had found the killer. Inspired by Stella and her family, and by the trust they'd given him, he was beginning to feel the same burden of responsibility for Neil Stonechild.

— — —

Despite his experience and age, Jack Warner was still a relative youngster amongst the other officers in Project Ferric, which had grown to include thirty-two people. With one veteran after another, he simply spread the autopsy photos of Neil Stonechild on their desks without saying anything more than "Have a look." Silently, the officers would lean forward, concentrating, sometimes rotating the pictures for a different angle. Typically, they'd linger the longest over two photos in particular.

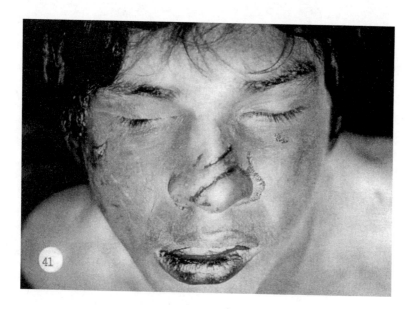

One showed parallel two-centimetre-long cuts across Neil's nose. The other focused on a curious indentation in the skin, circling Neil's right wrist. Just above the indentation, and between the base of the thumb and index finger, an abrasion partially obliterated the blue ink of Neil's tattooed initials. Each cop who saw the photos concluded the same thing: the marks were made by handcuffs and the boy had been beaten.

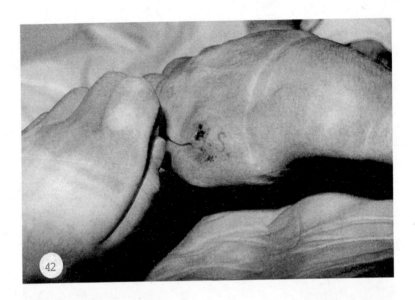

But Warner needed a scientific perspective on Neil's injuries. Given that the marks on Neil's face had not been noted by the coroner, Brian Fern, and that his own documents showed that Fern had regarded Neil as a native young offender who'd likely frozen to death after drinking too much, Warner felt it wise to look outside Saskatchewan for such expertise.

He settled on Alberta's chief medical examiner, Dr. Graeme Dowling. Dowling had over twenty years' experience in forensic pathology and Warner had worked with him before.

By the end of March, he and Ken Lyons had drafted a letter

to Dowling, in Edmonton, asking for his help, based on the photos, the autopsy report and the coroner's declaration. Their overarching concern was to get Dowling's opinion on Neil's injuries: was it more probable that they were caused by an assault or by falling into the snow? Specifically, were the blackened lips in the photos due to injury or to freezing, were the marks on Neil's face more consistent with a blow with a blunt object or something sharp, and what was the cause of the mark on the right wrist?

Warner knew that in forensic pathology, as in homicide investigations, things were always messier than in the popular dramas on TV: criminals did not often confess and dead bodies did not easily yield their secrets. Still, he must have hoped for more analysis than the three short and far from definitive paragraphs he got back from Dowling.

Dowling always cautioned his university students against believing that autopsies are "the be all and end all of death investigation."

Nowhere was this more important than with hypothermia, or what Dowling preferred to call "cold exposure," in which nothing of significance usually presents itself at the autopsy. Examinations typically reveal only minor scrapes to the skin caused when the victim, close to death, becomes disoriented and falls to the ground.

In his reply to the RCMP, Dowling showed that he would sooner be accused of being vague than of venturing into potentially ill-considered speculation. After briefly explaining that the discoloration of the lips was a change connected with freezing and thawing and was not an injury, he focused his remaining two paragraphs on the injuries themselves:

> All of the injuries depicted and described are minor "blunt" injuries called abrasions (otherwise known as scrapes). They are caused by the skin coming in contact with a blunt,

as opposed to a sharp, object such that some of the skin is scraped away. Although the injuries on the nose aren't completely clear in the photographs, I do believe that these are also abrasions . . . . I do not believe they have been produced by a sharp object such as a knife. The same applies to the minor injuries on the right hand . . . .

With respect to whether these injuries were caused by an assault or by a fall, this is not a question that can be answered by looking at the injuries in isolation. There is no visible difference between the injuries caused during the course of an assault as opposed to those which result from a fall.

Then, perhaps self-conscious about not being more definitive, or perhaps observing the quality of the snow in the autopsy from the vantage point of someone who had experienced Prairie winters, Dowling ventured a bit further:

In this case however, if you look at the injuries in the context of the position in which Mr. Stonechild's body was found (i.e., face down in frozen crusted snow), it appears to me that his injuries would be entirely consistent with his falling onto the snow at this site prior to his death.

No sooner had he begun to move in the direction of that conclusion, however, than he pulled up short, following his own investigative tenets. He had not examined the scene, after all, nor was there any way for him to know the quality of the snow at the time of death itself. Dowling wrote:

Just to be clear, I cannot definitely say whether any of these injuries are a result of an assault as opposed to a fall. I can only say that the injuries are consistent with his collapse into the hard snow just prior to his death.

Dowling had not ruled out the possibility that some injuries had been caused by force from a blunt instrument, but Warner was no closer to finding out whether the wrist marks had been caused by handcuffs. He needed a scientific way of measuring Neil's abrasions from the photos themselves.

A casual phone call with RCMP Identification Specialist Ken Bullock in Regina gave Warner a new idea. Bullock mentioned having worked once with a civilian named Gary Robertson whose office was in Nepean, Ontario, near Ottawa. "This is what he does. He specializes in taking precise measurements of objects using computers. It's called photogrammetry."

Warner stumbled as he tried to pronounce the word. "Never heard of it," he said. Still, he looked into Gary Robertson and the science of photogrammetry. The practice had been used in investigations of several air crashes. Starting with high-resolution computer scans of an image, practitioners like Robertson convert the two-dimensional image into a three-dimensional model by calculating unknown measurements from comparisons with the measurements of the known objects in the picture.

Robertson, a member of the American Society for Photogrammetry and Remote Sensing, had written a number of articles on the subject and taught courses to police. He had been working with RCMP units since 1987, and had also employed photogrammetry on airplane crash investigations, including the Dryden, Ontario, and Swissair disasters. Most importantly for Warner, Robertson had used his expertise examining imprints on human tissue.

Warner called Robertson at his office. He explained the troubles he'd had trying to determine the cause of Neil's wounds using only the autopsy photos, but deliberately held back his own suspicions. Robertson was being asked only whether he could determine with accuracy the dimensions of the wounds and what might have caused them. The scientist responded confidently. Aside from the photos themselves, all he wanted were the precise dimensions of the autopsy table in the St. Paul's Hospital morgue so that he had some known reference points. Warner provided Robertson with what he needed and waited for the results.

— — —

Throughout March 2000, Don Worme and the RCMP were finalizing arrangements for Jason Roy, Vanessa Kayseas and their child, Taylor, to live outside Saskatoon for added security. Fear had so gripped Roy that Kayseas had taken charge. His collapse had begun when he'd watched the first news reports of Darrell Night's early-morning walk out of the frozen prairie.

Kayseas adamantly opposed moving out of the province, or to any place where she knew no one. She felt safer living closer to family. They settled on Wadena, a two-and-a-half-hour drive southwest of Saskatoon, where her son, Ryland, lived with her grandparents.

By April, they were living in a house rented in the name of an RCMP officer. When they left Saskatoon, they had agreed not to tell anybody where they were going or how long they would be gone. But Kayseas was in denial. She kept telling herself that they were going to Wadena to live near her grandparents and spend more time with family. The truth came back to her, however, every two weeks when an RCMP officer visited to check up and give them four hundred dollars for expenses. Like it or not, she and her family were living in protection. Their new home was a two-storey 1940s house, with two bedrooms, a spacious kitchen, dining room and basement, which they left only to buy groceries.

Kayseas cooked and cleaned and the kids (Ryland had moved in with them) went to school. They did everything they could to feel like a normal family, but Roy's fear had turned to outright paranoia. He frequently ran upstairs to peek out the bedroom windows. He never felt safe at night. He had moved their mattress into the living room and frequently lay there with his eyes wide open, listening for the slightest sound. He'd get up and look out the window before dropping off into a restless sleep. Sometimes he slept with a knife, convinced someone would break into the house in the middle of the night and kill his family, convinced the police wanted to hurt them to make him pay for talking.

Night after night, Kayseas cried herself to sleep. Roy was sinking into a paranoid depression, and he was taking them all down with him.

"We're not expendable Indians, we're not. We have value and worth as much as the next person," she'd tell herself.

— — —

Jack Warner phoned Keith Jarvis a second time early on the afternoon of April 3. Although hamstrung without Jarvis's note-book, Warner now knew from Stella and Jason Roy that Neil had gone missing on the night of November 24 and that Roy had met with Jarvis while he was investigating the case.

Jarvis explained that in 1990 he was working in Morality, the section that handled all sudden deaths that were deemed not to be homicides. While he never attended the scene, he said this time that he remembered "the Stonechild matter, a youth found with one shoe, dead in an area there was no explanation for." He also remembered that the canine unit had been called in to look for the shoe but hadn't found it. He said he probably would have received the file a day or so after the discovery of the body, but recalled that he did not attend the post-mortem.

Without disclosing the CPIC information he had about Hartwig and Senger questioning Jason Roy, Warner asked the former investigator about his contact with the young native. Jarvis said he had not called Roy in for an interview, and he denied hearing any suggestion at the time that a member of the

SPS had been involved with Neil Stonechild's disappearance. He was certain about this; if there had been any such suggestion, everyone would have been talking about it.

Jarvis now remembered visits by Neil's mother and sister to the station. They had suggested, he recalled, a possible suspect whose name he thought had been Kenny Trottier. Warner had heard only of Gary Pratt's name coming up at the time, but Jarvis insisted he remembered the name Trottier. In any case, the mother and daughter had refused to say where the information had come from, so he hadn't pursued their tip.

He also said that the file had been open for a month or so, but he couldn't recall any suggestion of foul play. Since nothing more surfaced, he had closed the file. And nobody had subsequently suggested the matter had not been properly investigated.

They talked for over forty-five minutes. Warner had asked again about his notebooks. This time Jarvis didn't claim to have destroyed them, but said he had turned them in to the SPS, which should have kept them for ten years. That meant his notes prior to 1990 would have been destroyed, but the SPS might still have his notes from November and December of 1990, the time of Jarvis's investigation.

— — —

In the second week of April 2000, SPS constables Dan Hatchen and Ken Munson were charged with forcible confinement in the dumping of Darrell Night. However, the RCMP eliminated the two officers from suspicion in the deaths of Lawrence Wegner and Rodney Naistus. Despite the twenty-hour days logged by the men and women of Project Ferric for nearly two months, the investigation into the freezing deaths was sputtering and in danger of stalling completely. What made the difference in the Night case was the fact that the victim had survived.

In the Stonechild case Jason Roy had provided Warner with his only real breakthrough. Warner and his team had spent hundreds of hours isolating each CPIC query made on each SPS computer terminal in late November and early December of 1990. This exercise gave Warner a fairly clear idea of who was on shift when Neil died. Next came weeks conducting two hundred interviews with witnesses, including many Saskatoon police officers, some of whom were retired and no longer lived in the city.

The RCMP investigators queried each SPS officer they interviewed regarding Jason Roy's scenario from the night of November 24, 1990. The SPS officers who had been on the job in late 1990 seemed to be suffering from almost total amnesia. One exception was Eli Tarasoff, who said he'd read the file at Stella's request and had felt that it did not reflect a thorough investigation. He'd confronted Jarvis and found the lead investigator to be "kind of flippant about it." Tarasoff's adopted son, Dion, was native and had been a friend of Neil's. "When natives were involved," Tarasoff said, "he [Jarvis] did not take it serious."

Ernie Louttit talked about his dealings with the Stonechild family. He said he found the investigation to be less than adequate but was blown off by Jarvis when he confronted him. Louttit made no mention, however, of copying the investigation file.

Roy's scenario did not ring a bell with Sergeant Dennis Read, but Read's irritation with Jarvis as a lazy investigator was obvious. He vividly remembered Jarvis once dumping a murder investigation and leaving the file to an inexperienced officer to carry on alone.

Tom Vanin, who was staff sergeant of Major Crimes at the time, said he remembered Neil's body being found in the field and that he had expected the case would be handed over to Major Crimes, but that it had never happened. At one time, homicide investigators visited the scenes of all sudden deaths but, Vanin explained, the policy had changed. Regardless, homicide investigators should have been called out to the scene of Neil's death. "I guess they went out and found no bullet holes or stab wounds and determined it wasn't a homicide and sent it to Morality," surmised Vanin.

At least two other officers, however, felt otherwise. One described Jarvis as meticulous, and the other commended him for working his way up through the ranks by doing his job well.

In the end, the hundreds of interviews yielded nothing but rumours and old grudges. No one seemed to remember much of anything. How strange, thought Warner, that police officers trained in keeping notes and remembering details could recall so little.

TRUTH AND LIES

WHEN KEN LYONS FIRST APPROACHED LARRY
Hartwig in early May 2000, he asked the SPS officer what he
knew about the deaths of Lawrence Wegner and Rodney Naistus.
Aside from hearing rumours around the station, Hartwig said he
knew nothing about them. Then he volunteered that he'd known
Neil Stonechild.

On May 7 the two men met briefly in the boardroom at the
RCMP detachment in Saskatoon.

"You mentioned earlier that you knew about Neil Stonechild," Lyons began. Hartwig said he had known Neil and his
mother well, having arrested Neil often. Lyons tried to capture
and summarize everything he said. Hartwig described Neil in
somewhat contradictory terms—as a nice kid, but real bad, with a
lot of enemies. Hartwig had heard the call for officers to the discovery of Neil's body. Hartwig said Neil's death in the north end
did not seem right. He was basing his comments on rumour and
innuendo, he added, but it did not surprise him that Neil was
found dead and beat up. Lyons had stopped taking point form
notes and did his best to record Hartwig's account verbatim.
Hartwig's memories of 1990 were cryptic and jumbled.

All I knew is the guys arrested him in the 3300 block 33rd
Street. They were going to a call of a suspicious person or a
B & E in progress. They found Neil. He was drunk at the

time. They arrested him for intoxication.([Hartwig]paused)
Then in a questioning voice [Hartwig said]: "Why would
they have driven him around trying to find out who
he was?" Then they found some guy and asked him
who he was. Then some guys are saying things like
they're going to kill me, or they're going to beat me up all
the time.

Hartwig thought he could remember who his partner was
in 1990: Ken Munson. But he couldn't recall the Stonechild
family complaining about the lack of a proper investigation or
Scott defending what the police had done. Hartwig did, however,
offer to try to locate his old notes and turn them over.

Lyons and Hartwig next met on May 15, downtown at
Grandma Lee's coffee shop. Hartwig said he had recently moved
and was having trouble finding his notebooks. Hartwig did however produce three pages of SIM printouts from the Saskatoon
police records. SIM was the name commonly used for the
Saskatoon Police Service's electronic information management
system. Back in 1990 SIM was merely an index of complaints
with basic information that referred back to a paper file. The
records Hartwig produced documented his dealings with Neil,
twice in April of 1989 and once in October 1990, when he had
stopped him for driving without a licence.

The RCMP now hoped that some electronic records of
telephone numbers dialled into and out of Hartwig's and
Senger's private lines might provide them with more information on who was talking to whom. Warner had obtained a
warrant in mid-April. Under Part VI of the Criminal Code,
"Invasion of Privacy," Warner had to show that other investigative procedures had been tried, and that wiretaps were an
investigative necessity. Warner knew that monitoring communications during the hours immediately following the first
formal interview with a suspect were critical. Hartwig had

been the more senior officer back in November 1990, so the RCMP decided to formally interview him first and see what he would do.

Lyons formally interviewed Hartwig at their next meeting, just before eleven on the morning of May 18. During the first thirty seconds Lyons offered Hartwig his right to legal counsel, without delay, which made it clear to Hartwig that he was suspected of being involved in the death of Neil Stonechild. Hartwig asked only for a member of the police association to attend. "I don't need a lawyer, eh," he said. "I've done nothing wrong."

Hartwig agreed to answer a few questions while they waited for a union representative to arrive. Whereas the first two conversations had been cordial, this interview became immediately intense. Hartwig started shuffling through his papers, including his notes from the time, which he had managed to find. When he came to the pages from November 24, 1990, he insisted he'd worked the night shift alone, from eight that night until eight the next morning.

In preparation for the interview, Lyons and Warner had learned a lot from talking to Bruce Genaille and Jason Roy. Genaille had told them that two police officers had pulled him over thinking he was Neil. The CPIC information received from Ottawa clearly showed that Hartwig had CPICed the name Bruce Genaille.

Lyons finally spelled out his suspicions for Hartwig. He did, in fact, have Neil in custody that night. Lyons also told him that during their previous conversations he had been hoping that Hartwig would provide some reasonable explanation for taking Neil into custody. Hartwig had said he had entirely forgotten the incident, but Lyons was only too glad to refresh his memory.

"Well . . . great," said Hartwig, pausing. "Uhm, how do we know that I was the person that had Neil in custody?"

"Well, do you want to get into it?"

"Yeah, you betcha. I wanna find out, buddy."

Lyons hesitated because the union representative still hadn't arrived. Hartwig was beginning to lose patience.

"Fuck!" Hartwig dragged the curse out into a sort of exaggerated, disbelieving sigh. He had insisted that he had a damn good memory and now he was apparently involved with an incident that he didn't recall. "You know how many times I've abused a prisoner?" Hartwig said, defiantly making a big zero with his fingers.

"Larry," Lyons said after they'd spoken a little longer, "after reviewing everything that is known, there's no doubt in my mind, and the other investigators', that Neil Stonechild was in your custody."

"Fuck!" said Hartwig.

"I've got a real fear," Lyons continued. "My fear is this. I know you're in a bad spot."

"Uhm-hmm," affirmed Hartwig. "If I screwed up, or if I made a mistake, I'm the first guy to admit it." Pushing Lyons for information, he asked, "Was the warrant on the system that night?"

"Yeah."

"It was? Fuck!"

Lyons continued to fill him in. Hartwig hadn't worked on his own the night of November 24, 1990. And he had pulled over Bruce Genaille, mistaking him for Neil.

"He's actually Neil's cousin," said Lyons.

"Bruce Genaille? Fuck." Hartwig seemed stunned.

"Tracy Horse wasn't Tracy Horse," Lyons added.

"Oh, fuck. Okay. Nobody, nobody, nobody has ever said in my hearing, or my range of hearing, 'They're gonna kill me.' I would remember that," said Hartwig.

Lyons suggested Hartwig had made a mistake and that's all it was.

"Well, yeah, but hey, I don't like making mistakes, buddy."

"Who was I working with?" Hartwig asked, moments later.
"Brad."
"Brad?"
"Senger."
"Senger?" Hartwig repeated.

Warner was sitting in a room nearby, monitoring the conversation. He was paying particular attention to any talk of Senger.

"Have you talked to him today?" Lyons asked.

"No, I haven't talked to Brad about this at all."

Hartwig continued to answer Lyons's questions, but claimed he had to pick up his kids at 3:45. Lyons assured him that no matter what happened in the interview he would be going home.

"Well, damn rights!" Hartwig shot back. "I've done nothing wrong," he said. "I've made a mistake, on my notes, right?"

"More than your notes," answered Lyons.

"Fuck," sighed Hartwig for the umpteenth time.

Lyons pushed harder now, saying that the only answer to what had happened could come from Hartwig.

"The sinister side of things, we've talked about—" said Lyons

"Right."

"Beat him and left him for dead—"

"Right."

"That didn't happen?"

"No."

"What did happen?" Lyons asked.

Hartwig cursed and wondered again where his representative from the association was.

"You wanna know what I think happened?" said Lyons. He ran through a version of the night's events. Hartwig and Senger got a call. They were obviously looking for Stonechild. Hartwig had dealt with Neil a month earlier. These kids were all raising hell. They found Neil and he somehow became injured.

"Didn't happen," Hartwig insisted. "If he was injured, I would have taken him to hospital."

Lyons pointed at his own nose and told Hartwig that the kid who saw Neil in the cruiser mentioned marks across Neil's face.

Still monitoring the interview, Warner listened carefully as Hartwig became increasingly anxious to know whether the RCMP had spoken to Brad Senger. Lyons kept putting off an answer, saying they'd get into that later. He pushed ahead with his scenario. The CPIC records showed that Hartwig had punched in Neil's name between those of Bruce Genaille and Tracy Lee Horse.

"Holy fuck!" said Hartwig, taking his curse to a whole new level.

Then Lyons tempted him with an out. Perhaps Hartwig had wanted to give the kid a break, not taking him into custody but taking him off somewhere and leaving him with an "All right, buddy, you're on your own."

Hartwig repeatedly said he couldn't remember anything and that the whole episode didn't sound as if it would have been important enough for him to put in his notes. "If I took Neil any-where," he said, "it would've been home."

"Has somebody talked to Brad Senger?"

"Somebody, yes," said Lyons.

"Okay. Now? Or has?" Hartwig pressed.

"Will be, they should have him right now."

"Well, I'd like to talk to Brad, 'cause if there's something there that can jog my memory, that would be great." A few min-utes later he said again that he'd like to talk to Senger to see if he remembered anything about that night. Lyons took a run at Hartwig's own memory loss.

"Larry, I have to be honest. I don't completely believe you when you say you don't remember what happened, okay?"

"Ken, I don't wanna say I don't care, but—"

"But you don't, yeah, okay," said Lyons, and laughed at

Hartwig's attitude. "Okay, how can we determine what happened there?"

"Don't know, unless you talk to Brad and find out if he's got anything recorded in his notes, eh?" Hartwig repeated he couldn't remember anything about the call and only had Neil down as GOA (i.e., Gone on Arrival).

A little later, he wanted to know what this guy who'd called himself Tracy Horse looked like, asking several times to see a picture.

"I'll just slip out and see if I can find a picture," said Lyons, grabbing the excuse to step out of the room. He also told Hartwig that he'd allow an acquaintance to see him. At 11:16 he left the room. The tape machine, which had been recording the conversation, kept rolling for about a minute. As Hartwig sat there, alone in the room, shuffling his papers he had only one comment on his situation: "Fuck!"

Moments later Nick Hartle, a Saskatoon RCMP officer, knocked on the door and walked in.

"Hi, guy."

"Man, this is serious stuff," said Hartwig.

Ken Lyons and Jack Warner listened from another room.

"Frick, I've gotta have something to jog my memory. Obviously now there's something there, because I was there, I dealt with Neil that night, I dealt with this other guy who called—said his name was Tracy Horse. And now I gotta remember him. 'Cause obviously there's something there."

Hartle began to ask Hartwig what he remembered, but the officer cut him off.

"And I handcuffed him! And they said he had a—like he was pointing to his eye, had bruises." Hartwig sighed, and cursing again, insisted he remembered none of it. "I gotta talk to Senger. I gotta see if he's got notes on this. This is not good. I dealt with this guy, he's found dead four days later, eh! And I have no notes and I can't remember anything about it."

Hartwig was finding it increasingly difficult to contain his agitation.

"I says, I want an association rep before we're gonna go on the record. I wanna get this taken care of and I wanna do it now. So holy fuck! Talk about getting hit with a baseball bat, eh. I couldn't believe it when he told me that I'd CPICed, that I'd actually dealt with Neil, I had him in handcuffs. He was in my frickin' car. Why didn't this come up ten years ago? Right? I would have been able to remember ten years ago. Right?"

Hartle blamed the media.

Warner shook his head. If Hartwig knew Neil, as he'd volunteered to Lyons when they first spoke, then why had he not come forward ten years ago when Neil's body was found?

Hartwig's repeated insistence on seeing Senger was the cue Warner and Lyons had been waiting for. Warner had to leave soon and interview Senger. Lyons had gotten all he would out of Hartwig today. What bothered Warner most was that he'd never heard Hartwig lead with outright denials. In Warner's experience suspects would almost always start denying whatever they were accused of from the beginning. But not Hartwig. He had relied on his notes, or comforting lack thereof, and had maintained he just simply could not remember anything. "The guy's waffling," he said as he left.

Warner bolted out of the 8th Street detachment. Hartwig would surely call Senger as soon as Lyons let him go. But Lyons knew how to stall him. He'd planned a little drive by Snowberry Downs to jog his suspect's memory after the interview was over.

— — —

Shortly after eleven-thirty, Lyons entered the interview room again. He told Hartwig he'd spoken to Warner, but he didn't have a picture of the witness. He agreed to let Hartle stay.

Hartwig wanted to see Senger's notes and said he'd be willing to talk with Senger even with Lyons and others around.

"The thing is, Larry, it's not a question of—if it did happen. It's what happened." Lyons pointed out that sometimes witnesses were credible, sometimes not, but in this case the RCMP had a record, a CPIC record from the mobile data terminal in the cruiser.

"If you're saying I was there and if you're saying there's a witness that put me and Brad there, I was there," Hartwig conceded. He said he'd never had a knock 'em out, drag 'em out fight with anybody, he'd never smacked anybody around. And, he added immediately, "I've never given anybody a screen test."

The expression caught the other two men in the room by surprise.

"What's a screen test?" asked Lyons

"Well, you—I learned that from the feds. Guys? Eh?"

"I missed that one, too, then," said Hartle, who had been silent since Lyons had returned.

"The screen test," explained Hartwig. "You're, uh, driving down the street, you hit the brakes and the guy [in the back] hits the—the silent patrolman."

Hartwig had just been told he was a suspect in a criminal investigation, had insisted he had never abused a prisoner in any way and then proceeded to give an explicit description of how to smash a detainee into the metal barrier separating the back and front seats of a police cruiser. Lyons and Hartle both laughed awkwardly.

At around 11:50, Hartwig agreed to drive over to Snowberry Downs apartments on 33rd Street. As they were leaving the interview room, Hartwig asked again to see Senger. The RCMP were talking with him right now, Lyons told him.

"When they're done, can I talk to Brad?"

"Yeah."

"Good. Ken, I wanna find out, eh, I wanna remember," Hartwig said as Lyons led him out.

— — —

Around noon Warner knocked on Brad Senger's door.

Warner introduced himself and said he had new information about the Stonechild case; it was important they talked. Senger asked Warner to come in, but claimed he couldn't remember him. That struck Warner as odd; he had spoken to Senger during the early stages of Project Ferric.

Warner's investigation had shown that Senger was barely out of the police academy when he partnered with Hartwig on Neil's last night. Warner took Senger for the weaker of the two men, definitely the follower in the pair.

Senger was making lunch for his two small children and was not pleased about Warner coming to his house, but Warner pressed ahead. Lyons could keep Hartwig occupied for only so long.

Warner informed Senger that his former partner, Larry Hartwig, was being interviewed at the 8th Street detachment. He succinctly laid out the facts. There was a witness and there was no doubt in Warner's mind that Neil Stonechild had been in Senger and Hartwig's patrol car that night. Warner tried to encourage Senger to talk, telling him that another member of the Saskatoon police had told Warner that Senger would tell the truth. He also questioned Senger about whether he was covering up for his partner.

Warner then floated the possibility of a public inquiry resulting from Project Ferric's investigation, which would be very messy for the people involved. The truth, he suggested, should come out now. Warner had not told anyone about Senger or Hartwig, and it was up to them whether they wanted to tell anyone they had been interviewed. He asked if Senger could find any of his notebooks.

Senger went downstairs and returned a few minutes later with his notebook from November 1990 and handed it to Warner, who flipped briefly through the pages. The handwriting was very legible, typical of someone freshly graduated from police college.

Senger offered the same sorts of denials Warner had just heard from Hartwig. He insisted he knew nothing about Neil Stonechild and that he really couldn't help with the investigation. Senger failed to mention that he had taken the call the day Neil's body was found. Warner left about twenty minutes after arriving, but told Senger that he'd be back later in the day with more questions.

True to his word, he arrived back at Senger's house at five o'clock with Lyons. They brought him photocopies of his notebook. Whereas Hartwig clearly did not want to do a polygraph exam, Senger seemed more open to the idea. However, Senger's willingness was just the first step; it could take months to get him to take the test.

— — —

Murray Zoorkan's kingdom had no windows. In January 2000 he'd started the SPS's one-man cold-case squad, looking into old unsolved murders. His first job had been to hunt all over the building to find remaining records. The renovation that had resulted in the shredding of the Stonechild file had also caused a temporary reduction in available office space. Consequently, every day when he opened the door to his office, Zoorkan had to corkscrew his six-foot-three-inch frame into a closet at the back of a room used as a classroom for police training courses.

As he manoeuvred his large frame into the tiny room on the morning of July 19, 2000, he found himself thinking about Project Ferric. The RCMP had been eager to examine the notebooks of some of the SPS officers originally involved in the Stonechild case: René Lagimodiere, Bob Morton and the lead investigator, Sergeant Keith Jarvis. Zoorkan had helped search back in February, but had found nothing and agreed that they'd likely all been shredded during the renovation.

By summer Zoorkan had added another windowless room to the domain of the SPS cold-case squad, an airless two-metre-by-three-metre vault in the basement past the parking garage, the weight room and the central storage area where the spare uniforms were kept. He set up a few large metal filing racks and dubbed it the "murder room." There he stored old cardboard boxes full of original files and notebooks that he'd found scattered throughout the station. Officers handed him old murder files in the hallways. Given permission to look everywhere in the station, he'd even uncovered an old case filed in Scott's office by a former chief. Over a few months of organizing the material, he had four or five "murder boxes" of documents relating to unsolved cases. He hadn't had the time yet to go through each in detail, but he'd at least sorted the boxes chronologically.

"It's not brain surgery," he said to himself as he headed to the basement. "If the notebooks are anywhere they're down there."

He squatted down and pulled out the box on the bottom rack. It held the files for Joan Foulds, a Saskatoon teacher beaten to death in the summer of 1990. Zoorkan's hunch was based on more than timing. Joan Foulds's murderer had never been found, and Zoorkan knew that Sergeant Milton Atwell, the chief investigator on the case, was so determined to ensure that the case would one day be solved that he'd ordered that all the notebooks of anyone connected to the case be gathered up and stored in one place.

Zoorkan sifted through the material Atwell had collected. In less than ten minutes he'd found what he was looking for. Keith Jarvis had been involved in the Foulds investigation, and his notebook for 1990 was nestled in the box. Zoorkan checked to make sure it was Jarvis's, and then, to avoid disturbing anything, left it as he'd found it. Zoorkan immediately called Warner.

At the end of May, Project Ferric had been scaled down, and several members had been sent back to their home bases and other duties. Warner was back in Regina, but he continued looking into Neil's case, commuting regularly to Saskatoon. When he got Zoorkan's call, he said he'd come up immediately.

A little more than two hours later, Warner and Lyons followed Zoorkan down to the murder room. They gave him time to photocopy the notebook before taking the original, thanked him and climbed back into their van.

Low clouds threatened rain on the cool July day, as Warner and Lyons barrelled down the Trans-Canada Highway in their grey van, headed for the Major Crimes office in Regina. Only a few weeks earlier, Warner had spoken for a third time to Jarvis. Jarvis now remembered Stella and Neil's sister Erica coming into his office more than twice and expressing concern about the investigation. He also recalled for the first time being aware of a complaint about Neil, originating from Snowberry Downs.

Warner smoked his pipe at the wheel while Lyons read the notebook. For most of the two-hour trip back to Regina, they discussed the meaning of the entries written in Jarvis's sloping hand. Critical facts leapt off the pages.

Jarvis's entries for the Stonechild investigation were on November 29 and 30 and December 5. The gap was odd; Jarvis must have taken some time off. In total, it looked like Jarvis spent part of only three working days—about twenty hours—trying to determine what had happened to the seventeen-year-old.

His notes showed that he worked a twelve-hour shift, from three in the afternoon to three in the morning, on the first two days of the investigation. The first entry in the notebook about Neil, on November 29, made no reference to time of day. Framed above and below by a solid line of ink and wedged between an unrelated matter and an entry at 7:20 p.m. that said that the deceased was possibly Neil Stonechild, Jarvis had written three phone numbers and the phrase, "Lucille Neetz, found on person of deceased Confed Dr." As an afterthought in a cramped hand, he had inserted the words "sister" and "mother" above the name of Neil's former girlfriend. Warner wondered where the information had come from and why Jarvis had not indicated a time.

Another entry, again without a time reference, was even more baffling to the investigators as they batted ideas back and forth in the van. At some undetermined time after 4:45 p.m. on November 30 Jarvis had written:

> *On Nov 24/90 2351 hrs*
> *Deceased @ party 306–3308 33 St W*
> *Comp: Trent Ewart*
> *382-4588*
> *Wanted deceased removed due to intoxicated.*
> *Cst. Hartwig and Senger attended @ 2356 and*
> *Cleared 0017 hrs on Nov 25/90*

The notebook contained no indication that Jarvis had spoken to the two officers.

Warner was stunned. He knew a few things about the storage of police records. Hartwig and Senger had entered "GOA" into their cruiser's mobile terminal at Snowberry Downs on the night of Neil's death; if Jarvis had queried the name "Neil Stonechild," no record of the dispatch would have come back to him.

"There are only two ways he got that information," said Warner. "Either he did a physical or manual search, or somebody told him. So if he did a search, what led him to do one, and if somebody told him about the complaint, who was it?"

The brief entries in Jarvis's notebook for November 30 also shed a different light on his involvement with Jason Roy. The second time they had spoken with him on the telephone, Jarvis had told Warner that he did not call the boy in for an interview. Jarvis's notes showed, however, that Jason actually called Jarvis at 6:52 p.m. to say he had been with Neil most of November 24, and that Jarvis had arranged to meet Jason where he was staying at Avenue P South. Jarvis arrived there at 8:45 p.m. and spent fifty-five minutes taking a statement. Jarvis hadn't written a single note about their discussion.

Jarvis's notebook showed that he had indeed taken four days off. When he arrived back at work, he was working the day shift, eight in the morning to eight at night. Around 3:45 p.m., he had checked in with Dr. Jack Adolph, the pathologist who had performed the autopsy on Neil. Adolph had advised him that Neil may have been dead since November 25. Jarvis also wrote, "There was no evidence of any trauma to the body whatsoever." The same entry went on to say that, pending the arrival of a toxicology report from the Regina Crime Lab, the Stonechild file was "concluded at this point."

None of it made sense to Warner. Adolph had detailed several injuries in the original autopsy report. He had called them "superficial," but that didn't necessarily mean insignificant. Most interesting was the possibility that Neil had been dead since November 25.

Jason Roy had given the name Tracy Horse to Hartwig and Senger and been CPICed at 11:56 p.m. on November 24. He'd told Jarvis about seeing Neil in the back of the cruiser driven by the cops who'd checked him out. And Jarvis's notes showed that he knew police had investigated a complaint involving Neil about the same time that night. But right after Jarvis heard from the pathologist that Neil could have died on November 25, he'd closed the file.

Zoorkan's discovery of Jarvis's notebook was one of those moments an investigator waits for. This, thought Warner, was their big break.

— — —

Keith Jarvis ushered the two RCMP officers into the common room of the apartment building in Burnaby, B.C., that he managed with his wife, Dianna. It was about three on the afternoon of October 12, 2000.

Warner and Lyons had flown out the night before from Regina. They'd stopped by briefly to give Jarvis a copy of the notes he'd thought were either lost or destroyed, so that he could review them overnight. Lyons had also shown Jarvis the graphic autopsy photos on his laptop of the injuries to Neil's face and wrist.

The three men arranged themselves on the couches in the common room. During the drive from their hotel, Warner and Lyons had settled on an approach. Warner was far from convinced that Jarvis's memory was so lousy, but the partners agreed not to grill the former SPS sergeant.

They began by taking some basic biographical information from Jarvis, and made it clear that their interest in speaking with him was connected to his role as the original investigator in Neil Stonechild's death. Warner tried to keep his questions open-ended. Could Jarvis tell them what he remembered from the point when he had first heard about the body being found?

Jarvis stammered his way through an outline of the investigation that more or less reflected what he'd written in his notebook. Either he was nervous or was having difficulty remembering.

In passing, he mentioned the original autopsy reports, "which came back, ah, natural causes, hypothermia, and no signs of, ah, apparent violence."

Jarvis concluded his summary by saying that he had retired in 1993. He laughed suddenly, which surprised the two investigators, and then added, strangely, that since 2000 he had had two or three discussions with Warner and Lyons. Unprompted, he carried on: "And the recent one was, ah, October 11 where I did observe some photographs, ah, photographs of the face of the deceased and his hands, the face has two lacerations of the nose, ah, and the hands, there's laceration, or appears to be laceration by the heel of the—the hand and marks of a circular type, ah, design going across the, ah, the backs of the hands closer to the wrist, other than that I would only—I could only speculate as to what those, ah, markings could be."

Neither Warner nor Lyons pursued Jarvis's last remark. Instead, Warner told him they wanted to go through a number of relevant points. He should feel free to speak up if anything came to mind as they talked.

For fifty or so resolutely cordial minutes, Warner and Lyons worked to get Jarvis to decipher the most puzzling aspects of his investigation. They asked where he'd gotten the information behind his first entry about Neil's death, the untimed notation about former girlfriend Lucille Neetz accompanied by several phone numbers. Jarvis tried to explain that the information had come to him after 7:20 p.m., when he had written that the deceased might be Neil Stonechild. Warner gently explained the obvious: the notes are in chronological order and Lucille's name and the phone numbers come before the entry at 7:20. Jarvis stumbled and stammered, finally admitting that he really could not say where the name and numbers had come from.

During their previous conversations with him, Jarvis couldn't remember talking to Jason Roy. Now, seeing in his notebook that he had visited Jason and had talked to the boy for almost an hour, Jarvis remembered he had taken a statement.

He also now remembered specific details of that conversation with Roy. Jarvis credited his renewed recall to speaking with Warner and Lyons, "and, ya know, refreshing memories and so forth." Jason had told him that he and Neil had split up at some point and that he'd given a phony name when the police had questioned him because he was unlawfully at large. However,

Jarvis was evasive when they came to Jason's telling him about Neil's being in the cruiser. "I'm not sure," Jarvis said, "if he told me that Stonechild was in the back of the police car or if I learned that from the result of our conversations." Jarvis hesitated and stuttered. If Jason had said such a thing—which, Jarvis allowed, he might very well have—then it would certainly be in his written statement, which had presumably been shredded along with the original investigation file.

Next they asked what had compelled Jarvis to conduct a manual search of the dispatch records, which had led to his discovery that Hartwig and Senger had been sent to Snowberry Downs where Neil was drunk and causing a disturbance. Hartwig and Senger had not left a written report about going to Snowberry Downs because they had typed into their mobile terminal that Neil was "GOA" or Gone on Arrival, and they had been unable to locate him. Someone had to have told Jarvis about the dispatch for him to go to Communications to get the details. The next entry in Jarvis's notebook, at 6:52 p.m., was Jason's call to say he had been with Neil on November 24.

Jarvis fumbled through his answer. "I think it might have been a combination of things, ah, a combination of the complaint to Snowberry Downs that I became aware of, ah, I can't remember how we—how I became aware of that, ah, whether it was through you or—or Jason Roy, talking with him, ah, the close proximity of the Snowberry Downs, two individuals who were, ah, checked at the same time, you've got Snowberry Downs a problem there at the same, ah, the 7-Eleven store that they went to was all, it's all in close proximity to each other and, ah, it makes sense that, two-and-two-make-four type of thing."

Jarvis's memory came around somewhat. He said that he believed Jason had told him there had been some kind of contact between the SPS and Neil, and the SPS and himself.

Warner asked Jarvis who he thought would have been the last person to have seen Neil Stonechild alive.

"Based on what I know, ah, going on the reports it would have to be approximately Jason Roy and/or, ah, the officers who checked them that night," Jarvis replied. He now insisted that he must have spoken to Hartwig and Senger. "I'm sure I would have approached them either personally or by virtue of a memo. I think I approached them personally." His notebooks recorded no such contact.

Jarvis added his own musings to the investigators' pursuit. "Now the only concern I have, not concern but, ya know, a question that comes to my mind, is if he was checked that night why was he not arrested? He was unlawfully at large from a group home."

"Keith," said Warner, getting up and moving to the door, "do you mind if I just consult with Ken outside here just for a sec?"

"Sure, sure," said Jarvis. Warner and Lyons stepped into the corridor, closing the door behind them. They didn't leave Jarvis alone in the common room with his thoughts for long, and when they got back Warner told Jarvis they had covered what they needed to unless he had something to add. Jarvis seemed to relax, thinking the interview was over. Lyons jumped in. Careful not to sound threatening, he hesitated as he spoke, giving the impression that the ideas were just forming as he articulated them.

"You mentioned the circular marks that you saw on the wrist the other day, yesterday, Keith," Lyons said, referring to the autopsy photos. "In your view, are you able to offer up an opinion—as you certainly aren't going to be qualified as any expert that's for sure." Lyons was intentionally selling Jarvis's twenty-seven years of experience short.

Jarvis floundered. The pictures showed that his notes for December 5, 1990, were fundamentally incorrect about there "being no trauma whatsoever" on the body. Jarvis had missed the autopsy, and the only time he went to the morgue, with Morton to get a fingerprint, he had failed to look closely at the body, saying it was not his job.

"Well, I—I could only speculate. I mean these—these were photographs that were seen on your laptop, Ken, that were from the original, ah, Ident photographs I surmised—I could only offer up an opinion, ah, the marks—I have seen marks very similar to that myself over the years as a police officer. It can be the result from someone being placed in handcuffs who has been detained, it could be from many things."

"Yeah," said Lyons, encouraging the stumbling Jarvis to continue.

"Often times you don't even have to put handcuffs on tight and people move their hands around and you can get marks."

"That's right."

"It could be from anything, really, looking at it, looking at the marks in the photographs, ah, I'm not an expert, but I would say it would probably be consistent with handcuffs."

— — —

The old-fashioned water fountain stuck out from the wall so close to the floor that Murray Zoorkan seemed to fold almost in half as he bent down to fill his water bottle.

It was about 6:20 p.m. on November 13, 2000. Zoorkan had stayed late to catch up on paperwork. A couple of weeks earlier, Deputy Chief Dan Wiks had appointed him special liaison to Project Ferric. He was to be the RCMP's connection on the inside, someone to help them understand how the station worked, to get them in touch with its culture.

"Murray!"

Still bent over, Zoorkan saw Constable Larry Hartwig approaching from the Traffic Section. Hartwig wore his emotions on his sleeve. Even the way he walked showed a level of aggression. After his interviews with the RCMP in the spring, he'd vented angrily to anyone who'd listen.

Without preamble, Hartwig launched into another tirade

against the RCMP. Brian Trainor, the cop who had written the controversial "Blue Lagoon" column for the local newspaper, wandered over. Two other officers soon came out of their offices to listen to Hartwig rant.

Hartwig was furious with the RCMP for treating him as a suspect. Ernie Louttit, he bellowed, was saying that Gary Pratt might be responsible for Stonechild's death. Hartwig knew Louttit. They'd gone through police college together. He told Zoorkan, incorrectly, that Stonechild's missing shoe had been found in Pratt's car.

Zoorkan tried hard to remember everything Hartwig was saying so he could write it down later. When Zoorkan took up his new assignment, Wiks had warned him against doing any investigating for Project Ferric on his own. But in this case, Zoorkan could argue that Hartwig had initiated the contact. As he listened to Hartwig rage on, he began to wonder if he might be able to convince the constable to submit to a polygraph exam. When Hartwig slowed down a bit, Zoorkan seized the moment.

"Did you do anything wrong?" he asked.

"Absolutely not," said Hartwig.

Zoorkan proposed the polygraph, but said that first he had to check with his RCMP contacts at Major Crime headquarters in Regina. Late the next afternoon, Zoorkan approached Hartwig at his desk in the hit-and-run detail in Traffic. He told Hartwig that the RCMP had agreed, that things could be cleared up if he'd consent to a polygraph.

Hartwig became confrontational. "Who asked you to talk to me?" he said.

"What do you mean? No one asked me. You started this at the water cooler."

"Are you recording me?" Hartwig asked.

"No, check me," said Zoorkan.

Zoorkan's height added to his aura of calm, which seemed

to have a placating effect on the quick-tempered Hartwig, who cooled off slightly. Hartwig explained he was just worried because everyone, including the RCMP, had lied to him.

"It doesn't really matter, if you're telling the truth," said Zoorkan. Polygraphs were regularly used as an investigative tool, he said, trying to persuade him.

But Hartwig brushed Zoorkan off. He said he couldn't talk about it at the moment; he was going deer hunting and would not be around for the next six days.

Zoorkan told him to call when he had the time.

"I want to clean it up, you know," said Hartwig.

"It's not goin' away," said Zoorkan.

"I know."

— — —

Since Project Ferric began, the RCMP had made a point of keeping Deputy Chief Wiks up to date on their progress. On November 16, three days after Zoorkan had run into Hartwig at the water cooler, Warner's boss, Darrell McFadyen, telephoned Wiks to let him know that they were attempting to persuade Senger and Hartwig to agree to polygraph tests.

Zoorkan approached Hartwig one more time at the station about taking a polygraph, shortly after he'd returned from his hunting trip. Hartwig refused even to have coffee with him.

— — —

Through the fall of 2000, Gary Robertson, the photogrammetrist contacted by Jack Warner, compared specific parts of the stainless steel table in the St. Paul's Hospital morgue, such as drains and water jets along table's side, to his high-resolution scans of the Stonechild autopsy negatives. The known measurements of the table became objective cross-references as he proceeded.

Robertson wrote the RCMP back in November to say that he had determined the exact measurements of the injuries to Neil's nose and wrist. They were of the same dimensions and appeared to have been made by the same object.

Robertson made his measurements not knowing that Warner had a specific object in mind: Peerless handcuffs, the type used by the Saskatoon police. Only after receiving Robertson's letter did Warner ship him a set of the cuffs for comparison.

In Robertson's experience, the elastic nature of skin made it difficult to compare marks or blemishes with physical objects, but in his report delivered in January 2001, he concluded, "The Peerless handcuffs matched the imprint as to dimension and orientation." He allowed for a margin of error of half to one millimetre.

Warner read through the report with Lyons at the RCMP's Major Crime headquarters in Regina. He held up a photograph that had come with the report. In it Robertson had used computer technology to overlay the image of a section of the handcuff on the autopsy image of Neil's face. The cuff sat precisely within the parallel gashes across the bridge of the boy's nose.

A perfect fit, thought Warner.

— — —

In the grungy common room of the Saskatoon Correctional Centre on a mid-February afternoon in 2001, multicoloured race cars made one boring pass after another across the TV screen. Gary Pratt (or Charlie Brown, or just Chuck, as he was known on the street) sat among the other prisoners half-heartedly watching the race. Pratt looked forty—ten years too soon. A muscular five feet ten inches and 185 pounds, with lean cheeks and sunken eyes that gave him a wild, hungry look, he resembled actor Christopher Walken, with curly blond hair.

A guard came in and told him the RCMP had arrived to see him. Pratt knew it was Jack Warner and he knew what it was about, but he still stood up with so much nervous energy that he looked like he was going to bolt. Not that there was anywhere to go.

Pratt had actually contacted Warner first. The Saskatoon police had shown up a few times at the correctional centre, saying they wanted to take him downtown for questioning about Neil Stonechild. He'd refused, insisting he had nothing to tell them. They didn't have the authority to take him from the centre, but he was scared. So he'd phoned around and found Warner who, Pratt had heard, was investigating the SPS. Warner had already visited a couple of times. Pratt learned from Warner that he was the Saskatoon Police Service's prime suspect in Neil's death; the only way to clear his name was a polygraph exam.

Pratt had always maintained that he'd had nothing to do with Neil's death and had consented to go downtown to RCMP headquarters for the test. Now he feared he would face twenty years in prison if he failed.

Warner pulled out his handcuffs. Protocol, he explained. As they left the building, Pratt felt as if he were in the movies. There were a couple of SPS cruisers parked nearby, so Warner told him to walk between him and another officer who'd come to help. They pushed him into the back seat of their car, got in and headed off at high speed. Pratt turned around once, sure the Saskatoon police were following them, but no one else in the car seemed to think so. As the unmarked RCMP car flew down Circle Drive, Pratt's heart pounded and sweat began to soak his shirt.

When they arrived at the RCMP detachment on 8th Street, Pratt was left alone in a small room with a single pane of glass along one wall that he couldn't see through. He assumed Warner was on the other side.

The polygraph operator soon arrived and explained that the machine measured nervousness and changes in skin temperature. As they put the electrodes on, Pratt felt as if he were in some kind of electrical experiment. "Great," he thought to himself, "it measures how nervous I am and I have sweat running down my arms."

For what felt like three hours, he answered the operator's questions about whether he'd been the one who had dropped Neil off. When it was over, Pratt watched the man leave the room, his impassive expression giving nothing away.

Fifteen minutes later he came back and gave Pratt a serious look.

"Gary, you lied," he said.

Gary put his head in his hands and started to cry. The operator kept talking.

"That break and enter in 1986. You did that right?"

"Yeah, I guess so," he replied, sniffing.

"Well, you lied about that on the test. About everything else you told the truth. You did not kill Neil Stonechild."

Gary Pratt was no longer a suspect for the RCMP.

On the way back to the correctional centre, Warner gave Pratt a few cigarettes, looking away as he slipped them into the torn hem of his jacket.

LUCKY SHOES

AROUND MARCH 19, 2001, ERNIE LOUTTIT WAS
rumaging through his basement. His regular partner, Constable
Dean Hoover, had just made the Emergency Response Team,
and had been designated as a sniper. Louttit had been a marks-
man in the military. He'd told Hoover that he'd dig through his
barrack box in the basement for his old sniper's tables and any
other useful army training materials. As he started going
throught the old papers, he'd come across his photocopy of the
investigation report into Neil Stonechild's death.

"Don't tell me that's what I think it is," his wife had said
when he'd come upstairs and shown it to her. She told him to get
the file out of the house as quickly as possible. The file was a hot
potato, and she knew it. Louttit didn't want it around, so he'd dug
out Warner's card and phoned him immediately.

Warner had spoken to Louttit about Neil's case a year ago, in
March 2000, and then again in June. He'd faxed Warner the page
from his old notebook that described his conversation in the
arcade with Jake Stonechild. The two men knew each other,
having worked together in Meadow Lake, Saskatchewan, on a
missing-person case in the mid-nineties.

Louttit's story about finding the file struck Warner as very
peculiar. Louttit had never once mentioned copying the original
investigation file. Warner suspected Louttit had never actually
forgotten about it, but Warner wanted to see the file far more

than he cared about challenging Louttit about such suspicions. He told Louttit to meet him at the police station with the file the next day.

"How many pages are in the file?" he asked casually.

Louttit counted them out. Twenty-one, he said.

The next morning Louttit and Deputy Chief Wiks met Warner at the station to hand over the report. Warner looked Louttit in the eye and asked if he had known he had the file all along. Louttit stuck to his story.

Warner looked carefully at the report. He counted only twenty pages. Warner remembered clearly that Louttit had said twenty-one. Scanning the chronology and narrative of the pages, though, Warner thought the file seemed fine. Louttit had also given a copy of the file to Wiks. Warner politely asked Wiks whether he had been given the entire package, but the deputy chief shrugged his question off.

Warner had been dealing with the SPS for more than a year. Privately, he could only characterize the relationship as adversarial. But as much as he'd have liked to challenge Wiks, he would draw more water from the well, as he often reminded himself, if he remained low key. He had the Stonechild file in his hand to prove it.

Warner read the file as soon as he could. Jason Roy had always maintained that he had told Jarvis about seeing Neil in the back of the police car. Now, looking at Roy's handwritten statement, there was no mention of seeing Neil. Thinking back to their interview in March 2000, he considered the possibility that Roy had lied, but decided against it. He believed Roy, but phoned Don Worme the next day to tell him they'd have to talk to Roy about his statement in the case file because it could affect his credibility.

He also gave Worme an update on the case. Among other things, Gary Robertson's report had suggested that the force of the blow that caused the marks on Neil's face may have also broken his nose. Also, if there had been a struggle, DNA might still be present under the boy's fingernails. He wanted to exhume Neil's body for a second autopsy.

— — —

Over the last year, Don Worme and Jack Warner had steadily grown to like each other. Warner offered him details about the investigation during regular phone calls and also phoned Neil's mother once a week, so Worme was also hearing Warner's news from her.

The exhumation made sense to Worme, and with his blessing Warner called Stella. He explained as gently as he could why it was necessary to re-examine Neil's body. With no X-rays on file, no one could know for certain if Neil had suffered fractures to his nose or cheekbones, as the photos suggested. Family members had also mentioned the bumps on his head. Warner wanted to find out whether these bumps were actually injuries to the skull. They might also find some DNA evidence that could be profiled. Stella's pain carried over the crackling phone line from Cross Lake, but she did not hesitate to give her consent.

On March 26, there was a terse message from Warner waiting for Worme when he got back to the office. Warner was annoyed because a reporter had caught word of the exhumation. And now reporters from Saskatoon were calling Stella about it, upsetting her terribly. Worme had some work to do to fix things up.

He called Warner to assure the RCMP officer that the leak to the press had not come from his firm. Warner believed him. By Monday, April 16, all the arrangements had been made. Worme phoned Stella to tell her that the exhumation would take place on April 24 and that the body would be sent to Edmonton, where the examination would be performed by medical examiner Graeme Dowling, who had already helped Warner with Neil's case.

— — —

Warner was still sleepy at six o'clock on the morning of April 24 as he stood by Neil's grave at Woodlawn Cemetery. This was only the second exhumation he'd ever attended. Erica and Jake Stonechild and John Nyssen, Saskatchewan's chief coroner, stood with him as the funeral-home attendants lifted the cheap casket out of the ground.

When the casket was opened in a nearby shed away from the family, Warner saw a bouquet of red plastic roses glowing a garish red against the remains of a dark pullover sweater and a brown long-sleeved button-up shirt. Neil's socks were still white. A rosary lay near his crossed hands, which were across his abdomen. A partially disintegrated religious card with a picture of Jesus was on top of his chest, near the rosary. A small metal chain with a small heart pendant was also loosely placed on the sweater. The ring Erica had given him was clearly visible on his left little finger.

Warner's thoughts turned to Neil's mother, who had not attended the exhumation; she did not want to see her son this way. It had always bothered her that she could not afford to have Neil's body transferred to Waywaysecapo, Manitoba. She wanted so badly for him to lie near his grandfather, on the reserve named after her great-great-grandfather.

The RCMP flew Neil's body to Edmonton. Unfortunately, Dowling's examination yielded little. The bumps reported by family members had been caused by the first autopsy. Following the usual procedure, an incision had been made over the vertex, the highest point of the scalp. Then the scalp was peeled back and the skull cut open to allow for the examination. Some of his hair had been shorn off in the process. The scalp was then packed with a drying agent before it was sewn back in place over the skull. This material had caused the bumps Erica and others had noticed. X-rays showed no evidence of fractures. Warner's hopes for recovering DNA material were also thwarted; the embalming process and the decade the body had spent buried in Saskatoon had made this impossible.

Warner and Lyons had hit a low point in their investigation; however, one good thing would come of Neil's disinterment. Neil was to be flown to Manitoba in a brand new casket, courtesy of Warner and the RCMP.

— — —

Around two o'clock in the morning that same day, Marcel Stonechild's wife, Brenda, gave birth to their third child. They named him Gabriel, after the angel. As soon as he could tear himself away from his wife and newborn son, Marcel drove the five hours to bury his little brother.

The native ceremony was held at two o'clock on April 26 in the community hall on the Waywaysecapo First Nations reserve. Stella's wish to see Neil come home had finally been granted. There was no eulogy, but some relatives stood to say a few simple words. Erica read a dedication, saying how much she missed her Harry. It was incredibly serene, thought Warner, who had driven there with Lyons, almost as though Neil had died in his sleep from a protracted illness. The speakers showed no hint of anger or resentment. Nobody mentioned how he had been abandoned to die a lonely death. A single mourner stood expressionless and played his bass guitar.

The pallbearers, including Marcel and Jake, lifted the casket onto a horse-drawn wagon. They sat with the coffin on the wagon while others walked behind. Drummers followed the procession of mourners to the small cemetery in a lush green field.

Warner stood off to the side, watching while Stella threw a handful of dirt onto Neil's gleaming new casket as it was lowered again into the ground, this time to stay.

— — —

The pressure on the Saskatoon Police Service was building. Senger and Hartwig remained suspects in the Stonechild case. The newspapers were filled with stories of Saskatoon's new mayor, Jim Maddin, a former cop, dealing with a litany of complaints about Chief Dave Scott from all quarters: Scott would not take direction or follow the will of the police commission. He was accused of killing community policing initiatives; the commission had watched three community police stations fail. Now Scott was shutting down a bicycle patrol and had made it clear there would be no new foot patrols either. The mayor wanted more officers on the streets, but the chief gave nothing but excuses for why it couldn't be done. Scott also resisted increased police involvement in the city's race relations committee.

On June 21, Maddin made his biggest decision since taking office eight months earlier and decided not to extend Dave Scott's tenure. Publicly, he offered vague explanations, saying only that the commission wanted a new direction for policing.

The move created a wave of opposition. Scott's supporters sent several letters and petitions to city hall, many calling for Maddin's resignation or vowing that Maddin would only be mayor for one term. Prominent native voices stayed quiet.

While the drama over Scott unfolded, Warner retreated to the toughest part of his investigation. He was writing his final report and documenting his investigative findings. There was a lot to sort through. He studied all the mobile data terminal and CPIC data repeatedly. He checked and rechecked records to make certain his conclusions held up. He had completed his final interviews and had compiled about eight ledger-size notebooks of material on the Stonechild case. He wrote multiple drafts of his fifty-page report. At the end of June he handed it over to his boss. On July 3, 2001, Darrell

McFadyen delivered the cover letter and the investigative brief by hand to Richard Quinney, the executive director of public prosecutions at the provincial ministry of justice in Regina. The cover letter was damning.

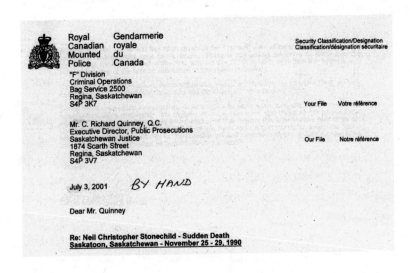

. . . . . There is compelling independent evidence through CPIC records to show that Constables Hartwig and Senger did have Neil Stonechild in their custody. There is compelling evidence to suggest that Neil Stonechild had been struck on the face with a set of handcuffs and that he had handcuffs on his wrists prior to his death. There is compelling evidence to show that the outstanding warrant for Neil Stonechild was on the CPIC system and that the system was working properly at the time he is believed to have been in custody. What we have not been able to determine is what transpired between the time that Csts Hartwig and Senger encountered Neil Stonechild and the date his body was discovered.

The inspector concluded his letter by offering to have the investigative team meet with Quinney to discuss what criminal charges if any might be appropriate in this matter.

— — —

Throughout July, Mayor Maddin's opponents grew more vocal. He shot back with a blunt assessment of Saskatoon's sinking reputation in the summer of 2001.

"I am not very proud of the fact that the city of Saskatoon and the Saskatoon Police Service is indeed in the microscope by agencies such as the Saskatchewan Human Rights Commission and Amnesty International. We are on watch, we have been placed on watch with respect to policing in our city, and that doesn't please me much, nor the members of the board," he declared.

Amnesty International's conference was held in Regina that summer and even featured an address from Don Worme. Amnesty's list of human rights abuses was a chronicle of torture, killings and persecution from some of the most troubled parts of the world. Detailed stories of the native men dumped outside Saskatoon to freeze to death were included in the three-hundred-page report. Canada had joined the list.

And as if to drive the point home, Dan Hatchen and Ken Munson were finally going on trial in September.

— — —

During that summer Vanessa Kayseas began to utterly resent being stuck in Wadena and to blame Don Worme. Whenever his number appeared on the call display, she'd think, "Oh, God, here we go again." His calls prompted Jason Roy to become either manic or paralyzed with fear.

Roy became so convinced that his presence was endangering his family that he left. He went to Saskatoon on a binge and then the police moved him to Regina. Now Kayseas was all alone in a house she'd never wanted to live in.

"This fucking investigation is taking over my life," she muttered to herself, blaming the police now, too. The move to Wadena, having to leave school and her social life, and now Jason gone: first the cops had taken her downtown and humiliated her, now they were taking away her security and her family.

Roy came back and left several times. The previous summer he'd been admitted to the Poundmaker Lodge addiction-treatment facility in Edmonton to stop drinking, clear his mind and stabilize. But he was falling back into his old habits and Kayseas was now spent. She had been putting up with his deterioration for more than a year.

"Okay, this is enough," she finally told him. "I can't be doing this anymore. I love you, but we can't spend the rest of our life here in Wadena. This isn't who I am." She felt vulnerable; it was a small town and the RCMP detachment shut at six o'clock. At least in the city they had lots of friends and a community to help protect them. She yearned to be back in Saskatoon. In early fall Kayseas took her little girl back to Saskatoon and resumed her studies at the university. Roy couldn't yet face Saskatoon again, so he decided to spend some time in Edmonton.

— — —

Even though he was running late, as usual, Don Worme took a long sip of strong coffee at the counter of his spacious kitchen. It was just before nine o'clock on the first day of Dan Hatchen and Ken Munson's trial, September 11, 2001.

"Hatchet" and "Munster," as Worme had taken to calling them, faced charges of unlawful confinement and assault for dumping Darrell Night in sub-zero temperatures. An all-white jury had been chosen the day before.

Worme had left the silk tie he was planning to wear somewhere in the kitchen. As he searched he caught a glimpse of the TV on the counter tuned to CNN and then watched breathlessly as a jetliner crashed into one of the twin towers of the World Trade Center in New York City. He stood mesmerized along with the rest of the world as footage of that morning's devastating impact was repeated over and again.

He suddenly realized that if he didn't leave immediately, he would miss the beginning of the trial. He dashed to the truck and turned on the radio. He'd catch whatever news he could during the ten-minute drive to court.

Publicity surrounding the trial had turned the event into a media circus. The Court of Queen's Bench was a stone's throw from the river and the Bessborough Hotel, a downtown landmark. The RCMP had set up a surveillance unit in a suite overlooking the courthouse. Worme met Darrell Night outside and they entered wearing bulletproof vests. They were flanked by Night's older brother, Merv, and his uncle Leo, each of whom weighed about 270 pounds and stood six and a half feet tall, even bigger and more intimidating than Darrell.

Night was the first on the stand. He described his arrest and subsequent drop-off by Hatchen and Munson in the bitter cold before dawn. He told the court about walking to the Queen Elizabeth power station, where a foreman let him in. His story was now familiar to anyone who read the local newspaper. He told about the handcuffs being fastened so tightly that they left imprints on his wrists for days afterwards, and about how meeting Constable Bruce Eholt during a routine stop for a traffic violation had convinced him to come forward to make his complaint. He made no attempt to hide that he was an alcoholic and on social assistance.

When asked what shoes he was wearing when he was arrested, he used his hand to lift his foot and showed the court a worn sneaker that looked as though it had once been white. He said he was wearing the very same sneakers that night, and had since taken to calling them his "lucky shoes."

Mid-morning, Judge Eugene Scheibel paused to speak of the terrorist attacks in New York and Washington. He expressed concern that the jurors would be too emotionally distracted to do their job. The jurors stepped out to discuss the issue, only to return quickly, resolute in their commitment to see this trial through.

To Worme, Hatchen and Munson sounded arrogant and self-serving on the stand, more worried about the trial's effect on their careers and families than about the impact of their actions on Darrell Night. From the beginning, they did not dispute leaving the native man near the power plant on the night in question, but to them they hadn't committed a crime, merely an error of judgment. Both officers said they were ashamed of what they had done, but claimed they were only doing as Night had asked.

According to Munson's statement, taken in February 2000, Night had pleaded with the officers, saying, "Come on, guys, you don't have to do this, let me go and I'll walk back from anywhere, just drop me off." Worme listened incredulously. It was "Belligerent Drunk Gets Ride to Highest Power in the Land" all over again.

Munson and Hatchen had both said in their statements that they'd felt Night could take care of himself, despite the cold, his light clothes and the fact that he'd been drinking. Hatchen claimed only to have worried a few days later when he'd heard about the discovery of Lawrence Wegner's frozen body. They had never asked Night his name, so they had no way of knowing whether he was the one who had turned up dead.

As Worme watched the two officers brazenly play down the seriousness of their actions during the nine-day trial, he couldn't help but wonder what would have happened if Night had died out there. Hatchen and Munson's computer records and notes for around five that morning showed absolutely nothing about any contact with him. They showed only that the two cops had attended a weapons disturbance at Avenue Q and 21st Street, then gone directly to a parking complaint at Clancy Village. Nobody had witnessed Hatchen and Munson arrest Night. His body probably would have been discovered by accident, like those of Lawrence Wegner, Rodney Naistus and Neil Stonechild. The toxicology report would have shown that Night had been drinking. His corpse would have provided negligible evidence of any contact with the police. The bruise on his forehead where he said he'd banged his head getting out of the cruiser could just as easily have happened when he collapsed into the snow. Handcuff marks could have been attributed to the cuffs of his jacket. Any lawyer could reasonably argue that he had found his own way out there.

Aside from Night's survival and willingness to speak out, the crown attorney argued in his closing statement that the only reason this trial was happening at all was that the victim had mistaken the car's number, 27, for 57. Given the discovery of the other bodies and the immediate suspension of the cops who drove Car 57, the pressure on Hatchen and Munson to come forward had been enormous.

On September 20, 2001, the jury filed back into the courtroom and delivered its verdict on the counts of forcible confinement and assault. They found the officers guilty of the first charge—they'd crossed a line when they'd decided not to take Night to the drunk tank and driven him out toward the Queen Elizabeth power station—but not guilty of assault. The SPS fired both officers immediately.

In Saskatchewan, talk of Hatchen and Munson's verdict was just dying down when, on September 28, CBC Radio broadcast news from coast to coast of a major development in the Stonechild case. Based on sources at the highest level of the Saskatchewan Justice Department, the report claimed that government prosecutors were preparing to lay a charge in connection with Neil's death. The only remaining decision was whether it should be for manslaughter or criminal negligence causing death.

Government officials responding to the story would say only that the RCMP report was still being reviewed and that it was far too early to consider laying charges.

Weeks passed. Months. No charges were laid.

On October 30 Hatchen and Munson further inflamed the animosity of Saskatoon's aboriginal community toward police when at their sentencing hearing they unexpectedly asked to be dealt with by a traditional native sentencing circle. In the same breath with which they spoke of the need to heal the rift between natives and the police, Hatchen and Munson's lawyers made it clear they had no intention of giving up their right to appeal the conviction, even if the sentencing circle went ahead. They still maintained that their clients had committed an error in judgment, not a crime.

When Worme called Night at the elders' lodge in the Saulteaux reserve—he'd gone into hiding there after the stabbing and returned after the trial—he said there was "no fuckin' way" he was doing a sentencing circle with Hatchen and Munson.

Scheibel sentenced the pair on December 7, 2001. He made it clear that he thought their request for a sentencing circle defied "both reason and logic":

> The complainant has indicated he is not prepared to participate in a sentencing circle, given the attitude of the accused. Who could fault him for refusing to participate in what he sees as a sham? One lacking in sincerity, one lacking in true remorse and one where those who have inflicted the wrong accept no responsibility for their actions. In that situation, what possible benefit could there be in holding a sentencing circle? There can be no healing, only the reopening of old wounds.

In deciding on a sentence, Scheibel said he had taken into account the fact that it had not been established beyond a reasonable doubt that Hatchen and Munson were motivated by racism, that the two police officers had been fired after the verdict and had lost their pensions, and that they and their families had been publicly humiliated and were in financial ruin. He sentenced Dan Hatchen and Ken Munson to eight months in a provincial correctional centre.

— — —

RCMP investigations into the deaths of Lawrence Wegner, Rodney Naistus, Lloyd Joseph Dustyhorn and Darcy Dean Ironchild had failed to produce any criminal charges. Facing mounting political pressure from native leaders and from Don Worme, the government called inquest after inquest through 2001 and early 2002. By definition, an inquest allows juries to determine the cause of death but not to assign guilt. The inquests allowed the government the benefit of taking public action, while avoiding the commitment of a full public inquiry.

As the court had been debating Hatchen and Munson's sentencing circle proposal, an inquest was underway into the freezing death of Rodney Naistus, who had been found in a light industrial area just north of the power plant the same morning Darrell Night had been dropped off. Polygraphs had cleared Hatchen and Munson. No police involvement was proven in Naistus's death. The jury concluded that, most likely, after drinking at downtown bars, Naistus had gone out to a house party about a kilometre from where he was found. He may have wandered away from the party and frozen to death.

This result was almost identical to those of earlier inquests into the deaths of Dustyhorn and Ironchild. Dustyhorn had been released from an SPS holding cell on January 19, 2000, despite obvious signs he was hallucinating. He was found three hours later frozen to death outside his west end apartment. The jury found his death to be accidental, the result of a drug overdose. Ironchild had been taken into custody on February 18, 2000, for public drunkenness. Around midnight, after a few hours in custody, he was released and sent home in a taxi. He was later found dead in his house. His brother told the inquest that Ironchild might still be alive had police taken him to hospital and not sent him home. The inquest ruled that his death was accidental, the result of a drug overdose. Neither jury found any responsibility on the part of the police.

— — —

Jack Warner and Ken Lyons had almost given up on Brad Senger. Back in May of 2000 they'd met with him and Larry Hartwig, offering them both polygraph exams to clear their names. From the beginning, Hartwig had refused; however, Warner thought Senger might still agree. But by the time Warner handed in his investigation report a year later, neither suspect had come around. In writing his investigative summary, Warner put their decision into context, saying, "Both are experienced peace officers and appreciate that a polygraph is nothing more than an investigative aid which has no standing in the courts. They would, through the same experience, know the polygraph has the capacity to a large extent, of clearing them."

Many of their fellow SPS officers, however, weren't taking the pair's no for an answer. After Murray Zoorkan's efforts to persuade Hartwig had ended in a shouting match, co-workers, tired of being smeared by the negative publicity, had put extra pressure on Senger, telling him if he had nothing to hide he should go ahead and "do the damn test."

Warner still wanted polygraph results for these two. Months of wiretaps on Senger's and Hartwig's home phones, and on

Hartwig's phone at the hit-and-run desk in the Traffic Section, had turned up nothing of consequence.

Senger finally relented in December 2001. Warner and Lyons called in Sergeant Charles Lerat, the RCMP polygraph expert in Saskatchewan, and a friend of Warner's. The aboriginal officer, just shy of his thirty-fifth birthday, had spent his entire career in the province. The polygraph test was scheduled for December 12, 2001, at the RCMP subdivision in Prince Albert, where he was based.

Warner settled in to monitor the proceedings and Lerat began his routine around ten-thirty that morning. He would take Senger through the three stages of the standard polygraph exam. First, the pre-test involved a series of general questions designed to make the subject openly declare times when he'd lied or acted dishonestly. The second stage of the test involved the three precise questions, called "issue questions." This was the electronically monitored portion of the test. Lerat would apply electrodes to the subject's body and ask the three questions about the events at issue. Once the wires came off again, Lerat would then conduct the third stage, the post-test. This would allow him a chance to elicit any further admissions in the emotional aftermath of the second stage, or even an outright confession.

As the pre-test began, Lerat introduced himself as Chuck. He wanted Senger to feel comfortable. Senger, dressed in jeans and a sweatshirt, was polite and said he'd prefer to be called Brad. Lerat reminded him that he was allowed to have a lawyer at any point, that the test was voluntary and that he could choose to end it whenever he wanted.

Senger was well aware that he was a suspect. Upon arriving, he had signed a police warning telling him that he could be charged with criminal negligence causing death. Senger kept his preliminary answers to a brief "uh-hmm" as Lerat led him through the basic facts surrounding Neil's death, such as when and where he was found, and his missing shoe.

Q. What name are you usually using? Is it...it is Brad or Bradley, or...?
A. Brad.

Q. Brad. Am I allowed to call you Brad?
A. Yup.

Q. Okay. Uh...Stan introduced us. As I said before, my name's, uh...Chuck LERAT.
Uh...Brad. I'm. a. uh...Sergeant with the RCMP. You know that.

P197

This is Exhibit *P197* in the
Hearing of the Commission
⸻ ⸺ Inquiry.   ⸗CH .

Next, Lerat detailed the events of November 24, 1990: Neil in the back of the police car, Hartwig and Senger querying Neil's and Bruce Genaille's names, and Tracy Lee Horse, the name provided by Jason Roy. Senger again limited himself to answers like "right" or "uh-hmm." When asked, he claimed he barely remembered working with Hartwig and that only his notes had reminded him that they'd been partnered that night.

"There's absolutely no way that I can recall doing that possible street check on that particular night at that particular time with any of these individuals," Senger said and paused. "I don't know what else to say—discuss. There's not much there."

He did, however, remember that Hartwig had been driving that night. They'd answered a call involving the murder of two small children in a custody dispute, and had had to tell their mother that she had just lost both her kids.

Lerat asked him to talk more about Hartwig as a partner.

"Uh, well, what do I remember? He's very argumentative."

"Oh?"

"I don't want to say 'redneck' but—that covers it."

As if he regretted being so blunt, a few seconds later he added,

"Like, I'm concentrating on the negatives. On the positives, uh, he's honest to a fault."

"Okay."

"He will absolutely never, ever not back you up. If there's anything going on."

Lerat worked his way toward questions concerning Senger's character, memories of things that made him feel guilty.

"What have you done?"

"Oh, on a breathalyzer test, I ignored a fellow's reading. Uh, his reading was point two-four. His second reading was point two-seven. And I lowered his second reading to be point two-six."

"What was the reason for that?"

"For the sole purpose that I didn't have to put up with this drunk to do a third test."

Lerat pushed for more.

"I went shopping one day and I bought—we went shopping at Canadian Tire and bought a whole bunch of items and—including a rake, and the clerk rang in all the items and we're driving home and, uh, they didn't charge me for the rake."

"You didn't take it?"

"No, I didn't go back and say, listen you didn't charge me for the rake." He paused. "That was nine years ago. It was a long time ago."

Warner was monitoring the test from a nearby room. Senger repeatedly claimed that he couldn't remember much about the night of November 24, but he had no difficulty recalling exactly how long ago he'd walked off with a rake. Now that Lerat had worked through his questions about dishonesty, he would begin a line of questions directly probing the circumstances connecting Senger to Neil Stonechild on the night of his death.

"I've got a list of questions down here—"

Senger seemed to know the routine, and tried quickly to deflect Lerat's line of questioning by interjecting about his partner, "Before you go on to the questions—When this initially came to light, my initial reaction was that I didn't remember. Then I told you that I went back to the apartment and drove around. And of course Hartwig talked to me numerous, numerous times about this."

Warner listened as Senger described Hartwig's conversations with him.

"He was hounding and you know, 'You have to remember. You must remember.' Like, I was, I don't remember."

Warner thought it sounded a lot as if Hartwig had tried to influence Senger's memories.

"Uh, he told me that him and I were—went to this call. He remembers dealing with two individuals. He gets out of the car, he says, this is his words. He says, 'It's cold outside. Why don't one of you guys—you guys want to sit in the car?' One guy sits in the car. We run both of their names and he lets them out of the back and this guy that was sitting in the car, he leaves. And we go and we carry on doing whatever. He's adamant, adamant that I remember this."

"You may have remembered querying him and if he was taken any distance and then kicked out of the car," Lerat challenged him, "whether it be to avoid booking him that night or anything like that, you—you would know. And I can guarantee it, Brad. You could remember that regardless of what Hartwig says." He insisted that Senger wouldn't just forget what had happened.

"I can't agree with that," Senger sighed. "Because you're making an inference that this person was driven, this person was arrested, this person was in a police car. I'm telling you that Hartwig is telling me this because this is his memory of the events."

Lerat wasn't buying Senger's story. He spelled things out in blunt terms for him. "I mean before you started to rationalize and all kinds of things, it's pretty black and white. Either you had him in your custody or you did not have him in your custody."

"Yeah," agreed Senger.

Lerat quickly moved toward asking the three issue questions. As a police officer, Senger was well aware these would be electronically monitored and would later serve as the basis of measuring his honesty.

"Between November 24 and November 25 of 1990, did you have that Neil Stonechild in your custody?"

"No."

"Between November 24 and November 25 of 1990, was that Neil Stonechild ever in your custody that night?"

"No."

"Between November 24 and 25, 1990, were you one of the officers who had Neil Stonechild in custody?"

"No."

Lerat had already gone through one entire tape. His next question took a different angle, rattling Senger.

"Did anyone tell you they had Neil Stonechild in their custody that night?"

"Yes, Hartwig. He said that he put this fellow in the car—but he didn't know it was, or is—we don't know who it was."

Warner listened patiently. Senger had gone from saying he could not remember Neil being in their car to saying Hartwig had told him he had put Neil in the car. And now Senger was saying "we."

"When was the first time he would have told you that?"

"He told me that, uh, shortly after he was interviewed at the 8th Street station."

Warner had monitored most of Larry Hartwig's formal interview with Ken Lyons back in May 2000. Hartwig had said repeatedly that he needed help remembering the night of November 24, 1990. Most of it was a complete blank to him. But most of all, he'd wanted to speak to Brad Senger about it. A very different picture was emerging from Senger's exam. According to Senger, shortly after the interview Hartwig had remembered putting Neil in the cruiser. Lerat kept pursuing the details of Hartwig's call.

"What happened then?"

"He told me where he was, what he was doing. He told me what he had said. He asked if I remembered anything about the incident that happened and then he said, 'They're accusing us of killing Stonechild.'"

It took a few more brief questions from Lerat to prompt him, but Senger eventually continued.

"He went on further to say that, after we checked the apartment and the second call came in on O'Regan Crescent, he had said that must be Neil Stonechild and we ran out of the building and went and ran to O'Regan Crescent to check around for Stonechild. Because he said he knew Stonechild."

At 13:04. Lerat left the room to score the test. He came back ten minutes later. As he turned over the third tape, he informed Senger that, according to the test, he had told some of the truth but not all of it.

"I've told you the truth. I've told you the truth how many times? I didn't put anybody in the back seat, I didn't handcuff anybody." Senger paused. "Who knows, I don't know who was in my custody. If I had someone in my custody that night, I don't know who it was."

Lerat continued with Senger through the post-test portion of the examination until just after two p.m., but Senger admitted to nothing. As part of his evaluation, Lerat had a choice of three boxes he could tick off to indicate whether Senger was telling the truth: Yes, No or Inconclusive. Lerat checked the No box, which meant Senger had been, as the test termed it, "deceptive." Lerat concluded that Senger was not responding truthfully to the three issue questions and did have Neil Stonechild in his custody on the night of November 24, 1990.

NO CHARGES

ON THURSDAY, FEBRUARY 14, 2002, WAYNE WEGNER hugged his mother, Mary, in the packed courtroom of the Court of Queen's Bench in downtown Saskatoon. The Wegner family sat waiting for the inquest jury, composed half of whites and half of aboriginals, to declare how Lawrence had come to freeze to death two years earlier.

As with Rodney Naistus and the other freezing deaths, no charges had been laid. Many Saskatchewan natives suspected the inquests were just political gambits to avoid a full public inquiry into the abuse of natives at the hands of the Saskatoon police. Flawed as they were, the inquests were the only hope for the families of the dead men, including the Wegners.

The testimony in the Wegner inquest under coroner Hugh Harradence had dragged on for over a month. Wayne, his mother and the rest of the family had watched and listened in frustration and dismay. They felt that the lawyer for the SPS, Barry Rossman, and the lawyer for the coroner, Lane W. Wiegers, were portraying Lawrence unfairly as a schizophrenic drug addict. Why weren't they talking about how he'd gotten miles from downtown in sub-zero weather wearing only jeans, a white T-shirt and two pairs of clean socks? His shoes were never found. The condition of the socks made it clear that he couldn't have walked out there.

Wegner's drug problems were no secret, but the autopsy had shown only elevated THC levels from the hash he'd smoked with friends shortly before his death, and therapeutic levels of his prescription drugs for depression. There was no toxicological evidence that he'd used morphine the night he died. The lawyers' character assassination of Wegner had left the family feeling that they were powerless and that the inquest was a smokescreen designed to avoid discussion of the glaringly obvious. Suspicion of police involvement and anger at their shameless mistreatment of Saskatoon's native community hung over the proceedings.

Benita Moccasin, Darlene Katcheech and Albert Chatsis testified to seeing a native man being shoved into a police cruiser near midnight outside of St. Paul's Hospital on the night Wegner disappeared. For their protection, the two women's names remained subject to a publication ban. Their testimony was explosive. They both were certain that they had seen their friend Lawrence Wegner loaded into a police car on a Sunday night in January. Eliza Whitecap and her daughter, Jennifer, testified that Wegner had been at their door just before midnight that night. They'd realized it had been him when they saw his photo in the newspaper a few days later. He was not wearing shoes and was yelling, "Pizza, pizza."

Wayne and his family did not like the way the native eyewitnesses were treated on the stand. The gracious manner in which the lawyers had questioned the medical experts disappeared when they cross-examined the three witnesses. Rossman, Wiegers and Harradence attacked their credibility.

Despite what they had seen outside the hospital, the testimonies of Chatsis, Moccasin and Katcheech was not without flaws. For one thing, Moccasin and Katcheech came forward as witnesses only after the inquest was underway. They had not been interviewed by the RCMP as part of their initial investigation. After hearing the stories about Darrell Night's abuse at the hands of the police, they had been too scared to speak up. Once they heard on the news that the inquest would proceed, they came forward to testify as a matter of conscience. And the inquest paused so the RCMP could investigate.

The delay in coming forward came back to haunt the two women on the stand, jeopardizing their credibility. Rossman argued that Moccasin and Katcheech were inventing their story as they went along. They testified that they had witnessed the scene outside the hospital on the Sunday night Wegner died, estimating the date on the basis of the light traffic on the evening in question and the memory of a looming term paper deadline. Under intense cross-examination, in the end they could not be absolutely certain of the date.

Like the women, Chatsis had seen two police officers questioning a man in a T-shirt and glasses outside the hospital. And also like the women, he was fairly certain it was the Sunday night Wegner died, but could not prove it.

Then Chatsis went further than he had in his original statement to the RCMP. He claimed that when he parked his car for his walk in Diefenbaker Park, he saw a police cruiser across the river, driving along Spadina toward the power station. He said he recognized the car as a cruiser when it was illuminated by the passing headlights of another vehicle. According to Chatsis, the cruiser stopped a couple of times near the power station. At one point he saw three individuals standing outside the car before it drove off. The timing was possible. If a police cruiser had left the hospital shortly after Chatsis passed and headed to the dump and power station along the river, he might well have arrived at Diefenbaker Park in time to see it driving along the opposite river bank. However, a recreation of the situation during the inquest showed that while these claims were possible, they were implausible. The distance from Chatsis to the scene he described was almost a kilometre. It was also very dark.

Chatsis, too, had damaged his credibility by waiting almost a year to come forward with these additional details. His only explanation for the delay was that he had not made the connection between the scene at the hospital and the scene at the riverbank until a friend had jogged his memory.

Other witnesses contradicted the women's story. Two truck drivers said they had seen someone who might have been Lawrence Wegner walking south towards the dump along the railroad tracks that led out of town. Their descriptions were vague, though, and they had done nothing to help the man at the time, coming forward to police only after the body had been found. With them too, there seemed to be some uncertainty about the date.

Some other bizarre twists marred the inquest. During her testimony, Jocelan Shandler did not mention the strange calls she had received for almost two weeks after Wegner's death from the mysterious "Sergeant McCaffrey," quizzing her about what she knew about Wegner and his family. She had told the RCMP about the caller at the outset of their investigation. The RCMP later confirmed that McCaffrey was not a member of the SPS. But no one asked Shandler about the phony police officer on the stand, so she never mentioned him, mistakenly under the impression she was allowed only to answer questions put to her. She went home deeply troubled and unable to sleep. Hoping to force an opportunity to tell the jury about the mysterious calls, Shandler confronted Hugh Harradence, who was presiding over the inquest, and said she would take her story to the media. She was not recalled as a witness.

To test the theory that Wegner had walked along the tracks to the dump, an RCMP officer, dressed in a parka rather than a T-shirt, walked the route with only socks on his feet. His socks became filthy and tattered. No one ever explained how Lawrence Wegner had supposedly managed to walk to the field where he died without shoes and without soiling his socks.

On the second-last day of the inquest, the jurors asked for a definition of "homicide." The Wegner family hoped that this request meant that the jury might come forward with more than just another list of recommendations.

The jury deliberated for thirteen hours. As they were ready to announce their conclusions, Wayne Wegner held his mother close. They were terribly disappointed with what they heard. The jury found that Lawrence's death was too suspicious to be ruled accidental, but they were unwilling to declare it a homicide.

Despite the family's disappointment, they remained polite and dignified. After the jury finished, Wayne stood and thanked them. "It's been a difficult process. We appreciate what you have done."

Wayne left the courtroom certain that his brother did not walk out to the field where he died, that something else had happened to him. One particular moment from the inquest would remain vividly with him. The jury and the family had visited the sites involved in the case. When they were near the railroad tracks the two truckers had claimed they'd seen Lawrence following, Wayne knelt down and put his bare hand on the track bed. When he lifted it, his palm was black with dirt and sticky creosote.

— — —

Jack Warner had finished his report on the Stonechild investigation at the end of June 2001, a year and half after taking the assignment. The Saskatchewan Justice Department had been sitting on the file ever since.

Since first meeting her, Warner had phoned Neil's mother weekly with progress updates on the case. Her courage and openness to whatever needed to be done, including Neil's exhumation, had initially inspired Warner. But as months passed and he had less and less to report, the calls, so weighted with disappointment, had become a burden.

Finally, on August 8, 2002, more than a year after he'd handed in Warner's report, Darrell McFadyen got the call from the justice department. As soon as Warner heard the news, he boarded an RCMP plane and flew northeast from Regina to see

Stella in Cross Lake. The broad green and silver carpet of conifers and lakes flowed past beneath the plane. In his sadness, Warner barely noticed.

As always, Stella greeted him with a smile and a big hug, thanking him for everything. They sat down for tea. Sensing something was wrong, she cut through the small talk about the flight and the weather.

"Jack, just tell me what you came to tell me," she said.

"The report we sent to the justice department," Warner hesitated. "I'm sorry, Stella, but they've decided not to lay charges."

For a moment Stella was too shocked to speak. "Why?" she asked.

Warner explained that the RCMP had submitted all the evidence he and his team could find, but that too much of it, like the polygraph exams, could not be taken into court.

"It's hard to prove," he said, his words sounding hollow and inexcusable to his own ears.

As a homicide investigator, Warner knew that convictions often came from circumstantial, not direct, evidence. Warner had done his job. His investigation produced compelling evidence that Neil had been in Hartwig and Senger's custody the night he died, that suggested Neil had been struck in the face with handcuffs and that he had handcuffs on his wrists prior to his death, and that the CPIC system had shown that there was a warrant out for Neil's arrest at the time. The RCMP, though, had been unable to determine what had transpired between the time Hartwig and Senger encountered Neil and the date his body was discovered.

The Saskatchewan Justice Department's decision in the Stonechild case was questionable at best. Warner, however, was a detective and a pragmatist, not a lawyer. He thought at this point it was better to continue investigating and strengthening the case. Warner could keep the file open.

"Now I'll never know," Stella said.

"Don't think like that, it's open with us, open all the time. One of these days, something will happen, it's just a matter of time. I've seen it before."

Chances were good, he assured her, that the justice department would call a public inquiry into Neil's death. And he would keep investigating, too.

Although she had every reason to be disappointed and disillusioned, Stella believed him. "They better watch out," she said, a spark rekindling in her voice. "I know you're a determined man."

— — —

From the beginning of Project Ferric, Justice Minister Chris Axworthy had argued against an inquiry because it would compromise the RCMP's investigation. Now, in the fall of 2002, Worme was being told that a provincial commission investigating how the justice system treats aboriginals was going to preclude an inquiry for the same reason. Worme was furious at Lawrence Joseph, vice-chief of the Federation of Saskatchewan Indian Nations, for agreeing to it. The commission was just another toothless attempt by the justice department to buy its way out of a tough spot. Over Guinness with friends at the Freehouse bar near the court, Worme did not hesitate to condemn the commission as a compromise that Joseph and other native leaders in the FSIN had been foolish to accept.

Privately, he continued to argue for a full, independent public inquiry into Neil's death. He emphasized that the RCMP had concluded that Neil had had contact with members of the SPS on the night in question, and that no one had yet been able to explain the circumstances of the boy's death.

The provincial government finally relented. On February 20, 2003, in a release to the media, the new justice minister, Eric Cline, announced the Commission of Inquiry into Matters Relating to the Death of Neil Stonechild. Under the terms of reference, the commission, which was scheduled to begin in September, was supposed to "inquire into any and all aspects of the circumstances that resulted in the death of Neil Stonechild, and the conduct of the investigation into the death of Neil Stonechild." One of the province's most distinguished judges, Mr. Justice David Wright, who had been practising law for half a century, was chosen to conduct the public hearing. Worme had gotten what he wanted.

In March, the Court of Appeal upheld the convictions against Hatchen and Munson. A year and a half after being convicted, the former police officers turned themselves in to the Saskatoon Correctional Centre to begin their eight-month sentences.

Throughout the spring and summer of 2003, the lawyers, including Worme, sparred in preparation for the Stonechild inquiry. They sent technically worded legal briefs back and forth to each other about what evidence should be included or excluded. They argued to have their clients receive formal standing at the inquiry, which meant the government would cover their legal fees. They would also get advance release, called disclosure in legal circles, of thousands of pages of confidential documents from Warner's investigation.

Worme had made good on his word to Stella that he wouldn't give up until the province called a public inquiry.

— — —

In July 2003 the preparations for the inquiry gained momentum. New Chief Russell Sabo had made Deputy Chief Daniel Wiks the SPS's point person for the Stonechild file and Wiks suddenly took issue with key elements of the RCMP evidence. Meeting with Darrell McFadyen and his investigators, Wiks told them he wanted to get another opinion on Robertson's photogrammetric analysis. He also questioned for the first time whether there was any evidence of blood on Neil's jacket. Too bad, thought Warner to himself—doing forensic work on the jacket would have been possible had the SPS not thrown away the clothing. In his analysis, Robertson had come to the explosive conclusion that Neil had died within forty-five minutes of receiving his facial injuries. But, insisted Wiks, this conclusion strayed too far from Robertson's area of expertise for the police lawyers and they wanted to argue before Justice Wright that he should therefore rule this section of Robertson's report inadmissible.

— — —

The July sun shone brightly off the white cement and the rough water of the G Ward pool on 5th Street East. Parents jostled for a better view of their kids, some of whom struggled with the front crawl, while others splashed wildly just to keep their heads above the surface. Water slopped across the deck, soaking parents' feet as they shouted encouragement from the edge of the pool.

Well back from the good-natured chaos, in the shadow of the overhanging change-room roof, Don Worme sat on a plastic chair leafing through the Saskatoon *Star Phoenix*.

Concerned that her husband was not spending enough time with their kids, Helen had announced earlier that morning that she was going shopping with Rhiannon, which left Worme no choice but to ferry his sons Donovan and Eli to the pool with their nanny for swimming lessons.

If Worme was aware that he was the only Cree man on the pool deck, he showed no sign of it. His feet propped casually on an empty plastic chair, he wore a crisp white T-shirt, grey shorts and expensive-looking sandals. The shirt was one of his favourites. The black and white photograph on its front depicted four Indians from the late 1800s holding rifles with the words "Fighting Terrorism Since 1492."

The cellphone rang. The phone was Helen's and he fumbled with it as he tried to answer. Worme lost his own phone a couple of times a week. The caller was one of the contractors who was installing stonework around the pool on the large acreage Worme had just bought, twenty minutes northeast of Saskatoon. The ranch-style house sat on a high bluff near Highway 41, with a stunning view of the city's skyline to the west. He had planned for the stones to be laid around the pool in the shape of a guitar, a Fender Stratocaster to be exact. The design was causing a bit of confusion.

The move from downtown to the two-hectare ranch was almost done. Artworks they had acquired from well-known Saskatchewan aboriginal artists still leaned against the walls as he and his wife put the final touches on the house, with its cathedral ceilings, burnished hardwood floors, a Jacuzzi in the master bedroom on the main floor, and a wide-screen TV and pool table in the basement, with a walkout to a hot tub and swimming pool. A little over fifteen years out of law school and the man who had watched his grandfather forced into bankruptcy by white bureaucrats now barbecued Angus steaks on a two-thousand-dollar Weber grill.

Before Helen had pressed him into parenting duty, he'd planned to go to the office and review a CD from the office of the Stonechild commission containing the disclosure material related to the upcoming inquiry. His two boys were still thrashing away in the foaming water in front of him, so he decided to have another look at that CD. He walked to the Jeep for his laptop, bought a coffee from the snack counter on his way back and set up the computer on a plastic table. Worme pressed back against the wall of the change room to avoid anyone, accidentally or otherwise, seeing the images of Neil's exhumation on his screen.

He turned to a photo showing the panels of the coffin removed for the examination. Grimly, he forced himself to look.

Ten years in the ground had left Neil unrecognizable. But something in the way the boy lay in his coffin still conveyed the spirit that had once driven him to endure two cracked ribs in a wrestling match. Whatever his faults, Neil had been a warrior.

Most remarkable, however, were the brilliant red roses clustered on Neil's chest, as red as they'd been on the day of the funeral. The first time he'd seen the photo, it had taken him a few seconds to realize they were plastic, all the family could afford. But that burst of colour had remained on the dead boy's chest for the past thirteen years, a token of Stella's determination, placed above his heart for comfort in the darkness.

Worme gazed across the pool, ignoring the laughter and shouting, and thinking of the small piece of fur his grandfather had given him after his mother's murder.

"Daaaaad," a child's voice shouted.

Worme's younger son, Eli, was running toward him in bare feet, clutching a sheet of paper. His nanny trotted after him. She reached out to slow him down on the slippery cement.

"Daaad," repeated Eli, reaching his father's side out of breath and laughing.

"Careful, careful," said Worme, smiling in reassurance to the nanny. "What is it? What do you have here? I thought you were swimming and here you are drawing pictures."

Eli had tried to draw the scene at the pool. Random squiggles of blue filled the page with water, while misshapen stick figures represented his father and brother.

"Can I keep this?" Worme asked. He gave his son a light pat on the head. "Off you go. We'll go home soon, okay? Donovan is almost finished."

Nodding proudly, Eli headed back into the happy fray with his nanny.

Worme turned back to the gruesome contents of his laptop.

PART IV

WHERE DO WE GO NOW?

Prologue

Saskatoon, Sask
Apr. 21/64

Regina v. Francis Littlechief

Donald Worme (age 4)

Dale is my brother. Sister Pat is my big sister. I live at my Grandpa's out of Saskatoon.

I lived with Pat and my mother's name was Margaret. Kimmy lived there too. He was smaller. Pat was his mother.

I know Francis Pat's husband. He is here. There was a fight there. I was home.

We ate in the kitchen. Mummy came up with the axe and Francis took the axe and hit mummy on the head and her eye with the axe and Francis hit Dale on the head with a knife.

I ran under the kitchen table, not the one we eat off of. I said to Francis not to hit me and Marleen ran out the back door and Francis ran out after her.

Kimmy was in the kitchen. He was crying.

I ran out the front door. I opened it and went to the woman next door.

No-one hit me.

FAMILY AND FRIENDS

ON THE NIGHT OF SUNDAY, SEPTEMBER 7, 2003, Jason Roy lay alone in a tent in his mother's backyard. The Stonechild commission of inquiry was scheduled to begin the next morning.

Vanessa Kayseas had kicked him out of the house. They had been arguing constantly. He had no job, and Kayseas was fed up. Between her job as a school guidance counsellor and raising her son and their daughter, she was run off her feet. Roy was seldom around, and when he was he did little but talk about the inquiry.

He listened to distant thunder. Saskatoon, which had seen its share of droughts, was enduring one of its driest spells in 135 years. Searing heat and strong winds sucked the moisture out of the air and brought hordes of grasshoppers. Tonight, though, a late-summer storm was building.

Roy's nerves were frayed. For years now he had tried to turn things around. He had stayed out of trouble with the law since his last stint in the correctional centre, although he still struggled with alcohol. He had even managed to get his high school diploma. Still, he felt things never seemed to play out well for him. The inquiry had not yet started and already the deck seemed stacked against him.

For one thing, Mr. Justice David Wright had ruled that Don Worme would be in conflict representing both Neil Stonechild's mother and Roy. So Worme's brother Darren Winegarden was now his lawyer. Roy liked Winegarden, but worried that he might be out of his league, since most of his work up to now had been litigation for the FSIN.

Roy was the inquiry's principal witness, so Wright gave him partial standing. But partial standing meant he would not receive the thousands of pages of confidential disclosure documents and his lawyer's fees would be paid only for work related to his testimony. But the inquiry would not be happening without him, he reasoned. It looked like even SPS Sergeant Keith Jarvis was going to have standing. It seemed so unfair. Sure Jarvis could be affected by the inquiry's findings with respect to his investigation, but so could Roy's credibility as a human being.

Roy was also annoyed with Joel Hesje, the inquiry's chief counsel. He had gone to the inquiry offices across from the Bessborough Hotel to meet the heavy, soft-spoken man, who'd been born and raised in Saskatchewan. Things got off to a bad start when Hesje proposed recording their conversation. Roy did not like tape recorders and rarely allowed himself to be taped. Hesje, a city lawyer with the air of a country boy, argued gently that he was just using the recording to make sure his notes would be accurate. Understanding that the tape would not be used for any other purpose, Roy had acquiesced. Next thing he knew a transcript of their conversation had been distributed under the rules of disclosure to all the other counsel preparing for the inquiry. Darren Winegarden complained, to no effect. Hesje called it a misunderstanding.

Roy had told his story to many people over the years. He'd told Jarvis within a day of Neil's body being found. He'd told several of his close friends. He'd told Stella. He told social worker Diana Fraser, Kilburn Hall therapist Brenda Valiaho and Father André Poilievre. He'd told his uncle, Don Worme, who'd brushed him off initially. He was tired of being listened to but not heard.

In the tent the heat weighed him down. He wanted to fall asleep but couldn't. His swirling thoughts dug up the old nightmare he had lived with for years after Neil died, the dream about being pushed down the elevator shaft at the police station. It always left him panicked and paralyzed about the future and now that future was only a few hours away.

A few days earlier, Roy had attended a vigil for the Stonechild family, who had just arrived for the inquiry. More than one hundred people showed up. Roy's own brother, Laurence, had performed a spectacular hoop dance. Talking to people he had not seen in years had stirred up old emotions and bolstered his courage. Both Stella and Marcel had wished him well, telling him to be strong.

"Just be yourself and tell the truth. That's all you have to do," Stella had said as she'd hugged him tightly.

The thought of Stella's comforting words finally lulled him to sleep.

What seemed like only moments later, a ferocious white light startled him awake. Sitting upright, he unzipped the flap and looked out at the night sky. Dozens of lightning bolts struck the ground around the neighbourhood; so many at once he could not count them all. The thunder was deafening. But there was no rain, just lightning turning night into day.

How the hell was he supposed to get any sleep now, he wondered. Then it came to him. It was Neil, making his presence known. Loud and clear.

— — —

The next day, September 8, the first of the inquiry, was grey and humid. The forecast called for thirty degrees Celsius, the kind of weather that made Stella's temples ache. She and Norman waited for Don Worme in the apartment the commission had arranged, back in the old North Park neighbourhood from her first days in Saskatoon. They also had been given a room in the Radisson Hotel, where the first inquiry sessions were taking place, so that Stella could rest her back during the long days of testimony.

As they were flying in the other day from Cross Lake and the fields below had rushed up toward the descending plane, Stella had had to push back a sudden flood of memories of Neil. He had been lying down there, right beneath her, not far from the airport, in the freezing cold, alone. This was her first trip to Saskatoon since she and Norman left in 1993. It was also the first time, strangely enough, that she would meet Don Worme in person. At the airport, when he hugged her, she surprised him by saying, "You don't look anything like Benjamin Bratt."

Worme was at a rare loss for words. He stood substantially shorter than the athletic TV star.

"Every time you called me, Don, I'd think, oh, it's *Law and Order* calling me again."

"Sorry 'bout that. Maybe you can think of me more as a Johnny Depp. How's that?" he replied with a grin.

While driving to the airport to pick them up, Worme had listened to the news on local radio. The host talked about the inquiry "looking into allegations that cops were dropping off aboriginal people outside of town to sober them up instead of taking them to the drunk tank." The bias of the station was all too familiar: Indians equal drunks.

Irritated, Worme had switched stations. The CBC was discussing new SPS Chief Russell Sabo's June 2003 admission that Darrell Night's abandonment was not an isolated incident, and that Saskatoon police had dropped off other native people as far back as 1976. The admission was remarkable, because for almost thirty years the SPS had maintained that starlight tours were nothing more than the stuff of urban legend.

As Worme hugged her, Stella's anxiety was instantly apparent. She said that she was terrified of breaking down on the stand. She had never testified in court, but Worme assured her that she didn't have to say anything if she couldn't remember. She had imagined she would testify second or third; he had to tell her that she'd be the first witness.

The drive to the Radisson Hotel took only a couple of minutes. The Radisson and the nearby Sheraton, where many of the other inquiry sessions would take place, depending on which had space available, were only a few hundred metres from both the courthouse and the river.

— — —

Stonechild family members Jake, Erica, Dean and Marcel were waiting for them in the lobby. A sweeping curved staircase led up to the mezzanine level where the inquiry would begin shortly. Because of Stella's bad back, they took the elevator to her day room so she could rest. Everyone talked about the amazing storm the previous night. The place where Jake was staying had been hit by lightning, and he looked at them with a big grin. He had had the same thought as Jason Roy: "Neil is telling us he's there, it's his way of showing us he's here."

When the time came, Stella held onto Norman's arm, knees and legs shaking, as they walked out of the elevator and across the upper mezzanine, past lawyers and witnesses drinking coffee. She tried to ignore a dozen camera lenses focused on her as she walked into the Michelangelo Ballroom. There was nothing Italian about it. No windows, even. Just a huge chandelier, desperately trying to compensate for an otherwise very ordinary hotel banquet hall filled with rows of cloth-covered collapsible tables and hard, stackable chairs.

Stella looked at the large raised podium, set up for the judge. Beside it, to the right, was the table where she and the other witnesses would testify. Three columns of tables for the lawyers led out from the podium. In their dark suits, the lawyers were busily arranging black legal briefcases and document boxes on their allotted tables. Journalists were plugging in their recording equipment and settling into the back row.

At the front, near the witness table, Joel Hesje sat with his assistant and dozens of binders of evidence stacked on a table against the far right wall. Behind him sat Barry Rossmann, representing the SPS, and one table back, Jay Watson, Constable Brad Senger's lawyer.

Darren Winegarden, representing Roy, had the table behind Watson, toward the back of the room. Winegarden and his client both looked nervous.

In the centre column directly in front of Justice Wright sat lawyers Silas Halyk and Catherine Knox, representing the FSIN. Larry Hartwig's lawyer, Aaron Fox, had the table directly behind them.

At the front, to Stella's left, was the table at which she and Norman would sit with Don Worme. A microphone and lectern set up for lawyers examining the witnesses stood just a few steps in front of them.

Worme was very unhappy with the seating arrangements. Drew Plaxton, representing the Saskatoon Police Association, was sitting directly behind him, and would likely be able to hear everything he said to Stella. He feared Plaxton's proximity would intimidate his client. But Stella had learned to ignore the negatives in life, and she would ignore Plaxton, too.

Behind Plaxton, at the back of the left column, just in front of the public seating, was Bruce Gibson, representing the RCMP.

Along the entire left wall, camera operators from local and national broadcasters lined up to record every moment of the inquiry.

There were so many lawyers and journalists in the Michelangelo Ballroom, the public had to squeeze into just a few cramped rows of chairs at the back. The commission had hired an RCMP officer for security at the door. He'd been instructed not to allow Saskatoon police officers to attend the inquiry in uniform, to avoid possibly intimidating witnesses. Chief Sabo, wearing a suit, took a seat in the public rows. Jack Warner and Ken Lyons took their places in the first row of public seats just behind the RCMP table. Two elderly white women, known around town as the court ladies, sat behind the tables reserved for the journalists, their pens poised over frayed spiral note-books. They had attended and taken notes during the inquests into the four freezing deaths of 2000, held before this public inquiry.

Erica Stonechild sat with her arms crossed at the back by the door, among her brothers and friends. She still wasn't sure this whole multi-million-dollar production would get them any closer to finding out what had happened to Neil. Jake was coping through cynical humour, and wore sunglasses with a skull and crossbones in their mirror lenses. Dean had managed a day off from his job as a long-distance truck driver to be here. Marcel had brought his wife and three kids to Saskatoon for the opening week. He held his young stepson, Sam, close. He wanted him to hear what had happened to the uncle he'd never met.

Justice David Wright, a dignified man with closely trimmed white hair, wearing a conservatively cut suit and carrying a small hard-shell leather briefcase, entered the room through a side door at precisely ten o'clock and sat down in a formal manner at the first table. The court clerk walked over and gently pointed out to him that he was sitting at the witness table. She directed him to the podium. He climbed the three metal steps to his own table and chair, to chuckles from all assembled.

Justice Wright had come out of retirement to serve as com-missioner to this inquiry. He had begun practising law in 1956 and had been appointed to the Court of Queen's Bench of Saskatchewan in 1981. In 1992 he took education leave and began teaching as a regular faculty member at the College of Law at the University of Saskatchewan, lecturing in civil proce-dure and ethics.

Wright read his introductory remarks with his chin cupped in his left palm. Watching from the back of the room, Erica Stonechild thought it was an underwhelming pose for such a significant moment.

Wright talked about accountability, balance and transparency, and emphasized the broader rules of evidence for a public inquiry. He quoted from a case called *Children's Aid Society of the County of York,* [1934]:

> It is an inquiry not governed by the same rules as are applicable to the trial of an accused person ... This is a matter in which the fullest inquiry should be permitted. All documents should be produced, and all witnesses should be heard, and the fullest right to cross-examine should be permitted. Only in this way can the truth be disclosed.

What Wright did not mention was that, only four days earlier, he had ruled to exclude as evidence that Senger had failed two polygraphs—a second one only weeks before the inquiry—and that Hartwig had refused to take one. No polygraph results, nor the refusal to take a test, would be permitted as evidence. He had banned publication of the details of that hearing, but the polygraphs instantly became the worst-kept secret in the inquiry. Even the court ladies knew. Their exclusion from evidence frustrated and irritated Worme.

On the surface, the ruling seemed to go against Wright's stated principles. But given the established rules of procedure and practice for evidence in public inquiries, Wright had decided that information allowed into evidence had to be both reasonable and relevant. At his discretion, he could admit evidence that might be considered inadmissible in a court of law, but in excluding the polygraph evidence, he had made it clear, based on case law, that this information was not reasonably relevant to the issue of credibility since Hartwig and Senger would both be testifying.

In other words, he would decide for himself whether Hartwig and Senger were lying or telling the truth, based on what they said in front of him. In addition, he considered Hartwig's refusal to take the polygraph not reasonably relevant because "no proper inference can be drawn from the exercise of the right to remain silent in the course of a criminal investigation." In his September 4 ruling, Wright left the door open just a crack, acknowledging that the polygraph is a legitimate investigative tool.

By 10:16 a.m., Joel Hesje, the meticulous commission counsel, had delivered his opening remarks and Stella had taken her seat at the witness podium, near the commissioner. In her red, grey and black short-sleeved blouse, she sat in bright contrast to all the men in dark suits facing her. She blocked out all their faces, except Worme's. He looked directly at her, holding her nervous gaze and smiling encouragingly.

Joel Hesje asked his opening questions in a polite, quiet voice, leading her through the events on the night of November 24 in chronological order. Laughter broke out when he realized he had not read the usual witness cautions to Stella, outlining the legal protections she had for anything she said in the context of the inquiry. Justice Wright joked that the caution was so long it was confusing even to him. Stella decided right then that she liked the commissioner.

After the witness cautions were read, Stella answered very clearly, if slowly, often wiping tears from her eyes with a tissue as she remembered Neil. The room fell silent as she described the last time she saw him alive, while she had been sitting at the kitchen table with her sister, drinking tea.

"Harry, I said, you have to be careful, it's stormy. Please stay inside."

He had come over, kissed her and left.

Somehow she managed to get through Hesje's questions. In just over half an hour, she told the story she had waited thirteen years to tell in public.

Aaron Fox and Drew Plaxton were the first lawyers to cross-examine her. Her nerves were strung so tight she forgot her answers as soon as she said them. Aaron Fox was an accomplished criminal lawyer. A tall, slightly stooping man, he approached her with an understated presence. All Stella could remember afterwards was that he raised the issue of alcohol three times in the first few minutes of cross-examination.

Fox also entered into evidence the first public exhibit of the inquiry. It was the article published in March 1991 in the *Star Phoenix,* in which Stella had first voiced publicly her suspicion that Neil's death hadn't been an accident. The article showed that she had spoken to the media, but hadn't voiced any concerns about the police. Stella calmly explained that Jason Roy had come to talk to her after the March article appeared.

Hesje outlined for Justice Wright how he would like public exhibits marked with a P and any confidential exhibits marked with a C, although he didn't know yet if there would be any of the latter. The article was marked P-1.

Drew Plaxton, a small man who wore a diamond stud in one earlobe, represented the police association. Plaxton had struck Stella as unpleasantly abrupt as soon as he had stood up to speak.

"I understand this is undoubtedly something that's difficult for you and I thank you for coming and being forthright with us today," Plaxton began. "But we all have our interest and we all do have some questions we'd like to ask."

As he continued to ask questions, Stella thought him insensitive, almost rude. But she answered, keeping her responses brief, as she was growing tired.

Shortly after lunch she was relieved to see Don Worme step up to the microphone. He and Darren Winegarden were the only aboriginal lawyers in the room. He approached with a smile and with an informality quite distinct from the tone of the morning's proceedings. The other lawyers had called her Mrs. Bignell, but Worme called her Stella and it put her at ease.

"Stella, we've heard your son described in the media and by others as an aboriginal man, or a man. How does that make you feel?"

"He isn't a man. He was a boy," she said, tears streaming down her face. She wiped her eyes. In the most unassuming way she took control of the situation. "He was only seventeen. He never, he never had a chance to become a man. They never gave him that chance to become a man and have a family of his own, to give me the grandchildren that I would have loved, like my other children."

Afterwards, the journalists joked to each other that this would surely be the last time the other lawyers allowed Don Worme to go last in cross-examination.

— — —

On the second morning, Jason Roy sat listening to Pat Pickard's testimony and trying to keep his confidence from evaporating. Vanessa Kayseas was somewhere behind him in the public seating; she had not given up on him entirely and was driving him to and from the hearings.

Like Neil, Jason Roy had spent time in Pickard's group home. He admired the way she spoke about Neil on the stand, describing how he had come to her home in the fall of 1990, had shown leadership skills and tried to improve himself. She told how Neil had called her on the night he died and had promised to come back, but wanted one more night to party with his friends. She had absolutely believed him and was ready to pick him up the next day, but, of course, he never called.

Pickard had always believed that the real story behind Neil's death wasn't being told. But her supervisors in the government, who controlled her group-home licence, had made it clear that they did not want her to share her suspicions with anyone.

Afraid of losing her livelihood, she kept her mouth shut. But when she saw Neil's name in the paper in 2000, after the other freezing deaths had been reported, she decided to set things right by talking to the RCMP. Her supervisors wanted her to report back to them about what she said, but she had refused. She had reached a point where the bureaucracy no longer scared her, she testified.

"I'm too old," she said. "I mean, you know, I mean basically you just get to the point where right is right and wrong is wrong and that's it."

By noon, Roy was squirming in his seat from the heat and the stress of waiting. Wearing a velour shirt hadn't helped. His spirits sagged when Marcel Stonechild took the stand after lunch. They hadn't seen each other since the early nineties, when Marcel had left for Cross Lake to join his mum.

Several times Marcel broke down in tears and Justice Wright allowed him to take a short break. Drew Plaxton pummelled him with tough questions during cross-examination, suggesting Marcel had been led by the RCMP during his interviews to make a link between the marks he had seen at the funeral on his brother's face and wrists, and perhaps an incident involving the city police and handcuffs.

"No, I—I remembered this as soon as my brother's case was reopened, like not right directly as soon as it was reopened, but the more I—the more I heard about my brother's case, the more it got me thinking about that night, his funeral, how he looked, the condition he was in. I can still see those scars on his nose. I can still see the marks on his wrists. I can still see the bruising."

Until then Marcel had spoken softly, occasionally wiping tears from his eyes, but when Plaxton questioned his memory about the state of Neil's body, he sat upright in his chair, leaned forward and clearly articulated his responses.

"Who helped you remember that?" asked Plaxton.

"No one. I wasn't drinking at his funeral. I can remember that."

It was nearly three o'clock in the afternoon. Under cross-examination by Aaron Fox, representing Hartwig, Marcel confessed the guilt he felt over buying Neil and Jason the bottle of Silent Sam and described how his life went out of control after Neil's death.

"I was—I was too busy blaming myself."

"I understand."

"I was drinking very heavily. I lost my job that I had at the time that—I was working for Saskon Construction. I kept on drinking and drinking. I lost my job with Saskon Construction. And then after I cleaned myself up, I started working with my mum at Eaton's."

Roy found Marcel's testimony painful to watch. His own courage was wilting. Every minute he waited to sit in that chair and face the room felt as long as the thirteen years he had borne the guilt for betraying his friend.

— — —

At 3:37 p.m., Hesje walked with a bearlike gait to the lawyers' lectern in front of Stella, Norman and Don Worme. Chairs scraped as lawyers and spectators returned from a short break for cigarettes and coffee. Hesje paused briefly and then announced, "The next witness is Jason Roy."

An expectant hush fell over the room. The television cameras all pointed at the young man as he took his seat and looked at Hesje. Everyone there knew that Roy, the inquiry's principal witness, was the only person alive who could put Neil in the presence of Hartwig and Senger the night he died.

Hesje gently prompted Roy through basic biographical information.

"I went to St. Mary's for about 95 percent of elementary

school, and after that I went to a few different high schools, Feehan, Bedford, Sion, Nutana, Joe Duquette." The long string of school names sounded like stops on a bus route.

At the back of the room Father André Poilievre twisted his dark blue fisherman's cap in his hands. He was worried for his young friend and had used the break to give him some encouragement. He'd also overheard some journalists gossiping about Roy's suspect credibility.

As part of their seating arrangements, the commission staff had set up a table beside the back door for Neil's family and friends, so they would not have to sit in the public seats. Erica had to take tranquilizers for the stress, but she and Jake were there every day. Others, like Jeff Crowe, came when they could. Conspicuous against the backdrop of the inquiry's staid legal propriety, the small group were unafraid to comment out loud on the behaviour of the lawyers representing the police. As Roy testified, though, the table was quiet.

Roy was carefully listing all the people at the Binnings' house on November 24, 1990, when the back doors of the room banged open. Many people turned their heads at the loud interruption. Roy had been on the stand for only eight minutes.

"It's Hartwig and Senger," one of the reporters announced to his colleagues and rushed to his technician at the side of the room.

Within seconds the television cameras swivelled away from Roy and zoomed in on the two men walking, with heads raised high, down the right side of the room toward their lawyers. Dumbfounded, Erica stared open-mouthed as they passed her.

Hartwig was shorter than Senger but clearly more confident. He took a seat with his lawyer, Aaron Fox, and smiled in the direction of the cameras. Senger's brown hair had not yet begun to turn grey. He was a heavier man, with hefty jowls and a red face that grew redder as all eyes turned on him. He was already perspiring from the heat of the camera lights in the airless room. His green wool sports coat would be as uncomfortable in here as Roy's velour shirt. Unsmiling, he kept his head bowed, only glancing at the cameras out of the corner of his eyes as he sat beside his lawyer, Jay Watson.

"It's no accident," Erica sputtered loudly in dismay and rage to her friends. "Why didn't they come in after the coffee break like the rest of us? They're trying to intimidate Jason."

The commissioner, who had shown an iron hand in enforcing the decorum of the proceedings, showed no sign he'd heard Erica and didn't comment on the officers' entrance. And if their arrival was a bit of nasty stage business intended to upset Roy, it didn't work. He was focused intently on Hesje. The commotion did not distract him in the slightest.

Roy had been telling Hesje about stopping at the 7-Eleven to warm up after leaving the Binnings' with Neil, and then continuing across the street to the Snowberry Downs apartment complex.

Hesje brought a map of the area over to the witness table. Fox and Watson jumped out of their seats and crowded closely around Roy as he pointed to landmarks on the map: Snowberry Downs, the 7-Eleven, 33rd Street to the south and Wedge Road to the east, and the tennis court where he'd been separated from Neil. Crowding a witness like this would never be permitted in a trial. Even hunched over, both men were imposing figures, well over six feet tall. And yet, again, what should have intimidated Roy had no effect as he located the important places on the map with his finger.

He explained how he and Neil had argued about giving up after buzzing apartments in the foyers of the buildings in the complex, looking for Lucille Neetz. Roy had wanted to quit, so Neil said he was going on alone. Roy tripped in the parking lot near the tennis court when he'd tried to follow, and that was when he lost sight of Neil. Unable to find him again, he went back to the 7-Eleven and then started back to the Binnings'. He gave just the facts, repeating none of the teenagers' curse-laden dialogue.

Roy collected his thoughts for a moment.

Erica knew what was coming next. She leaned forward to catch every word, holding the hand of a friend who had come for support.

"I started walking back down Confederation Drive," said Roy, "and I got maybe about two blocks from the 7-Eleven on Confederation Drive and there's an alley approach going onto Confederation Drive right there. And as I approached that alley, a police car pulled in front of me and Neil was in the back."

Roy took a deep breath. He chose his words carefully as he continued. "Neil went to—he saw me, he was—he was very irate. He was freaking out. He was saying, 'Jay, help me. Help me. These guys are going to kill me.'"

"Did you observe his condition?" asked Hesje.

"He had fresh blood on his face across his nose. I couldn't see all that well, but he had his face to the window and he was yelling at me, asking me to help him. Not for one minute did I think that he was in any danger."

To Roy, this was not a contradiction. He could see Neil had been roughed up a bit by the cops, but that didn't strike him as unusual, and he expected Neil was being taken back to Kilburn Hall.

"Was he handcuffed?"

"Behind his back."

"Okay. On this map that's in front of you, are you able to identify where you were stopped by the city police?"

"Yeah."

"I'm sorry, I should have asked that, was it a city police car—"

"That's right."

"—that stopped? All right. Now you've indicated that there was an alley, can you identify which alley that was?"

"These are Twin Gables apartments."

"Right."

"And it is the alley directly behind it."

"Now when you were stopped by the police, which direction was the police car coming from?"

"Down the alley. It cut me off walking down—I was walking down Confed Drive and it pulled in front of me."

It was past four o'clock. Hesje asked for a few more minutes before the inquiry adjourned for the day and Wright granted them.

"And you've indicated that Neil was making—was yelling at you or whatever. What—do you recall what the officers said to you? Did you have any conversation with the officers?"

"The officer stopped me and asked me who I was. At the time I was unlawfully at large from a community home and I gave a fake name. I gave a false name."

Jack Warner rubbed his chin and listened carefully. He knew that apart from him, Hartwig and Senger, and the lawyers who had seen the inquiry's confidential disclosure materials, no one in that room had ever heard Roy speak the name he had given to the police that night. Worme had carefully briefed him never to reveal the name to anyone. Despite numerous requests from journalists over the years, he had heeded the advice, ensuring that this detail would be saved for his testimony. The name had never been divulged and had been corroborated by computer records. It was an unassailable aspect of Roy's credibility.

"Do you recall what name you gave them?"

"Tracy Lee Horse."

"And why did you give them that name?"

"He was somebody that I grew up with and I knew his birthday."

"And what was your concern in giving them your real name?"

"For one, I didn't want to be in that car, and for two, I didn't want to go back to jail."

"Okay. Now what happened, you've given the name, do you recall anything else?"

"Asked me who I was and he punched it into his computer, the name that I had given him, he punched it into the computer and it took a little while for it to happen. So I kind of took maybe half a step back to just wait for this process to go through."

Roy was becoming increasingly animated as he relived the moment. He went on.

"And Neil was freaking out in the car, back seat of the car. And the officer driving asked me, 'Do you know this guy in the back?' I said, no, I didn't know him because I didn't want to—I didn't want to be there in that car with him. The name that I gave came back as not having any warrants or anything like that in order for them to pick me up. I asked, 'Can I go now?' and they let me go."

"And what happened? Where did you go from there?"

"The car pulled out in front of me and started heading down Confederation Drive."

"Which direction did the car go?"

"It was heading south."

Roy's eyes were watery now. His voice wavered slightly as he described that last look at his friend.

"Neil was looking out the back of the window, just staring at me. He looked—he just looked scared. He just looked really, really scared, and my thoughts at the time were, Well, he's just going to go back to Kilburn Hall, that will be it. I'll see him when he gets out."

"And, Jason, where did you go from there?"

"I went back to the Binning residence."

"Did you ever see Neil alive again?"

"No."

In just over half an hour, Jason Roy had testified about the few short moments that had become the driving force behind his entire messed-up life. The clerk asked people to stand and adjourned the proceedings at 4:07 p.m. Stella and Norman hugged each other and quietly wept.

— — —

The next morning, Wednesday, anyone standing on the Broadway Bridge looking north toward the Radisson Hotel would have seen a remarkably black sky over the downtown. Father André Poilievre couldn't help but notice the dark cloud hanging over the city and thought the symbolism was disconcerting.

Father André entered the hearing room thinking Roy had made it through yesterday very well. Now he had to face Fox and Plaxton. First, though, Hesje had a few more questions.

Hesje asked Roy whether he had acted on his concerns after Neil's body was found. Roy explained that he did not talk to Stella about seeing her son in the back of the car until much, much later because the family was in mourning. However, Roy did contact the police immediately after hearing about Neil on the news. He described how Sergeant Keith Jarvis had met with him where Roy was staying. Jarvis had taken out some forms for the statement and told him he was going to write down their conversation, the questions and the answers.

"And we did this for about an hour and a half, maybe two hours, and I basically related to him the last time I had seen Neil alive."

Hesje pushed Roy to be more precise.

"Did you tell him specifically that you had seen Neil, the last time you saw him he was in the back of a police cruiser?"

"Yes, I did, and I also would like to mention that as he was leaving I asked him, 'What are you going to do with the information I give you?' and he said, 'We'll look into it and I'll get back to you.'"

"Did you hear back from him?"

"No."

Hesje continued methodically with questions that probed at the heart of Roy's statement to Jarvis.

"Now, did you advise him that when you saw Neil in the back of the police cruiser he was handcuffed?"

"Yes."

"Did you advise him that he was bleeding and apparently had a cut across the nose?"

"Yes."

Hesje showed Roy a copy of his handwritten statement from November 30, part of the original file Jarvis had created in 1990, the copy of which had been made by Ernie Louttit.

Don Worme sat stone-faced, masking his concern. Roy's credibility around the statement, part of the original investigation file Ernie Louttit had found in his basement in 2001, was open to serious attack by the police lawyers.

Roy studied the document carefully.

In addition to the page and a half of Roy's writing there were a couple of short questions and answers in Jarvis's hand.

Nowhere in the short document was there any mention of Roy having seen Neil in the police car.

In their interview during the late summer, Hesje had showed Roy the written statement. Roy explained at the time that he had told Jarvis everything he knew about seeing Neil in police custody. His memory of talking to Jarvis was totally different from what he saw in front of him.

Hesje gave Roy a moment to read before continuing. "There's a date on the top of this statement. It says, it appears to say, November 30, 1990. Is that statement in your handwriting?"

"Yes, it is. Not all of it though. Not—not the—not everything."

"Okay. Now, Mr. Roy, to the best of your recollection, is this the statement that you provided at the meeting you've described at the house on Avenue P?"

"No, it isn't."

"Why do you say it isn't?"

"Because when the officer came to the house to take a statement I didn't write it."

"Do you have any recollection of the length of the statement that was taken on Avenue P?"

"I'm going to have to guess between three and six pages because it took a long time to—to write." Roy went on to say that he had given the statement under duress at the police station on December 20, a couple of days before his birthday.

"This statement was made the first time I got arrested after Neil's death," said Roy, referring to an incident on December 20, almost a full month after his conversation with Jarvis. "I, I was arrested, for one, being on the run, and I'd also been arrested for something else as well. I was—I was brought in to the Saskatoon police station and I was put into one of the holding cells. The first one—the first—the interview rooms I believe they're—I believe they're—I think they would be. I was asked, 'Do you want to reconsider your previous statement?' At that minute I wasn't aware of what he was actually talking about. And I was told, 'Write down what you—write down what you remember of that night,' and he left the room. As I got to—as I got to the bottom— as I got near the end to the second—as I got to the second page, he came back in, and that's when I finished writing it."

"And is this statement truthful?"

"Pardon me?"

"Is this statement truthful?"

"No, it isn't."

"Can you explain why?"

"My birthday was two days later. I wanted to see it. I felt I was in a position—I was in a place where I did not feel safe. I lied for my life."

"And in this statement you make no reference to the fact that Neil was in a police car on November 24; that's correct?"

"That's correct."

Roy seemed to believe what he was saying about the circumstances under which he gave the statement. The trouble was, it made no sense. The document was dated November 30, 1990. And what Roy did not know, because he had not seen the evidence, was that the November 30 statement was already in the report when Louttit copied it in early December, several weeks before Roy was arrested. His shaky answer provided a perfect target for Fox and Plaxton.

Fox stepped up to the lectern with a stooped, shuffling gait, arms swinging at his side. His humble manner usually lulled witnesses into a false sense of security. But Fox seemed determined to attack Roy from the outset. Within minutes he confirmed that Roy was often in trouble with the law and had been drinking since he was thirteen. When Fox asked when his alcohol-abuse problems started, Roy answered, "Before I was born." He meant that his parents were alcoholics. Without missing a beat, Fox asked if he suffered from fetal alcohol syndrome.

"I've never been diagnosed as that."

When Roy had described to Hesje how he and Neil had gotten separated, Roy had not indicated that Neil was angry or swore at him.

"That was your recollection of what he said? I understand, actually," Fox went on, "Neil was actually quite upset with you and, in fact, was swearing at you. Is that right?"

"Well, like, like I had just said he was—took the basic tone of, okay, you don't want to come with me, fine, but I don't know if I can use the appropriate words that were said at that time."

"Gee," said Fox, rebuking Roy sarcastically, "I sure hope you've been using the proper words that were said because, you know, you're under oath. We want to hear the proper words that were said."

At the Stonechild family table near the back of the room, Erica, Jake and their friends groaned and shook their heads. Father André was furious. Fox was trying to show Roy's testimony could not be trusted, but the priest knew Roy simply did not want to swear in front of Justice Wright, so he had left out how Neil had cursed at him.

Fox read out loud a portion of the statement Roy had given to Jack Warner, in which he'd recounted his separation from Neil in the Snowberry Downs parking lot.

"And you said, 'And when we got to the last, uh, apartment where I told him, "Okay it's getting too damn cold. We should turn around and go back." And he said, "No, we're not. We're not fucking going anywhere," I said, "Fuck that, man, fuck, it's starting to get really cold here" And, uh, he says, "Okay, well, fuck you then, go ahead then. Go back. Go back to Joe's if you want." And I said, "Okay, then, I'll see you later," and I started heading back towards there and I remember him swearing and yelling at me and, "Okay, fuck you then. See ya later then, you're a fucking asshole."'"

Roy was flustered as he tried to ask Fox to hear him out, but Fox was less interested in Roy's testimony than in making a speech.

"Do you agree, sir, that the reason why you didn't mention anything about Neil swearing at you, calling you a fucking asshole, telling you to fuck off, he would go on his own, didn't care whether you came or not, leave him alone, the reason you never mentioned anything about that when you were asked by Mr. Hesje about the conversation was because you thought that wouldn't look good, that wouldn't sound very good coming from your mouth at this commission? Isn't that why you didn't tell us about it?"

Roy tried to spar with Fox by saying he was not as concerned about how he came across as Fox was, but Fox quickly got in his face.

"Well, Mr. Roy, you know what we're talking about here? We're talking about the last conversation you had with Neil Stonechild, the last conversation. Understand?"

Beaten down, Roy struggled to keep what remained of his composure.

"I have nothing to hide."

The commissioner called a short break. As he drank his coffee and huddled with his lawyer on the mezzanine, Roy looked pale and dazed. Erica raged to anyone who would listen about Fox's disrepectful treatment of Roy. Father André feared Roy might break down on the stand. It was a public inquiry, but he thought Fox was handling himself as though it were a criminal trial and as if Roy, not Hartwig and Senger, were the suspect. Under the liberal cross-examination rules of a public inquiry, however, Fox had almost a free hand. And Darren Winegarden's opportunities to object to the police lawyers' cross-examination of his client were few and far between.

Stella did not know or care about those rules, but she wondered why Fox could treat Jason that way. "It's not right," she kept repeating.

— — —

After the break, Fox asked Roy to explain how the statement in his own handwriting, which omitted any mention of seeing Neil in the back of the police cruiser, could have been made on December 20 when Roy had been arrested. Although he had made that claim himself, Roy feebly answered that it was not his job to speculate. Fox pointed out that evidence would be submitted that showed the statement Roy claimed he'd made on December 20 had, in fact, already existed several weeks earlier. A couple of times Roy asked him to repeat the question, once saying it was a big question.

"It is a big question, I apologize," said Fox.

Roy finally admitted he had no explanation. Clearly, the statement had been made on November 30 when Roy had met with Jarvis. Jarvis would appear only later in the inquiry, so it remained an obvious question for Jarvis whether or why he had omitted things Roy told him about Neil. But Fox had used Roy's confusion of dates to make him look evasive, and to deliver the desired blow to his credibility.

Fox questioned Roy about why he hadn't approached Neil's family in the days after his death, despite knowing that they would be worried. When Roy tried to say that he had spoken to Marcel, Fox pointed out that Marcel had testified he did not remember talking to him.

When questions turned to Cheryl Antoine, Roy's girlfriend at the time, Fox found it difficult to believe what Roy said he'd told her after returning to the Binnings' that night.

"You said, 'I told Cheryl that Neil got picked up and other than that, there wasn't much more to tell.' That's what you said. You see your friend in the back of a police car, bloody, screaming, 'They're going to kill me,' but you didn't think that that was maybe important to tell her, that that just wasn't important enough to mention?"

"I didn't think he'd die," Roy replied.

"Oh no, no, no, no, I'm not talking about dying," scolded

Fox. Why, he wondered aloud, would Roy not tell his girlfriend exactly what he had seen?

He then asked about Roy's meeting with Stella at the bingo hall in the spring of 1991. Roy was adamant that he had told her about the gash across Neil's nose. Fox pointed out that Stella remembered only that Roy had told her Neil was in the back of the police car. One explanation for the difference, he concluded, was that Roy simply had never told her this.

By the end of the day, Father André noticed that Roy was retreating, one-word answers replacing the confident replies he had given earlier to Joel Hesje.

— — —

The next day, Thursday, September 11, Drew Plaxton took his turn at breaking Roy down. The diminutive, bearded lawyer frequently adjusted the microphone at the lawyers' lectern. Often he would walk around in front of the commissioner, return to the lectern, look up over his reading glasses and stare into Roy's eyes before unleashing another barrage of questions.

By the end of the day Roy was having trouble understanding Plaxton's questions and said that the lawyer was confusing him. Finally, about four o'clock, Justice Wright adjourned the proceedings. Roy would have to come back on Monday to continue.

As the room emptied, Father André could hear the reporters' malicious talk about Roy's poor showing. One columnist declared that Roy seemed to believe what he was saying, but that his testimony had not held up under scrutiny. The priest worried that Roy would give up over the weekend and go on a binge.

Roy walked slowly out of the room and headed across the mezzanine, past the reporters and straight into the men's washroom. He backed into the furthest corner of the room, slid slowly down the wall and dropped his head between his knees. He wept.

He crumpled onto the floor and pulled his knees snug to his chest. Marcel Stonechild walked in to see Roy rocking gently in fetal position.

But over the weekend, Roy stayed focused and did not go on a binge. He spent some time with friends and surprised everyone by coming back to the hearing refreshed.

Plaxton went now to the heart of the matter, Roy's memory. He wanted to know whether Roy actually remembered what he was talking about or whether he had pieced it together from other information he had received.

"The memories are there, sir."

By the time Roy stepped down from the stand he had spent more time testifying than Jarvis had spent investigating Neil's death. Father André was proud of him.

Jack Warner was used to the sound and fury of cross-examination. To him, all that mattered was that the essential points were established. Roy had been stopped by Hartwig and Senger, had given a false name to avoid being picked up, and had told numerous people since, including Jarvis, that Neil was in their custody at the time. Despite the verbal beating, Roy had held his own.

— — —

On the morning of the inquiry's seventh day, Stella's chair sat empty and Erica took her usual seat, looking as if she'd been crying. The table of friends and family were unusually quiet, concentrating intently as Joel Hesje questioned Graeme Dowling, the Edmonton medical examiner who had examined Neil's body in April 2001 and had helped the RCMP analyze Neil's injuries from the initial autopsy report and photos.

Dowling's thin, bony face was a picture of intelligent concentration, and he spoke with an understated precision befitting his impressive credentials.

Dowling spent some time explaining the "triangle" theory of investigation, in which investigators had to take into account the body itself, the history of the individual and the scene of the body's discovery before drawing any conclusions. In cases of hypothermia, he stressed the absolute necessity of examining all three factors.

Just after eleven, Hesje prepared to project on a large white screen at the front of the room the forty-four colour photographs from the first autopsy and the scene of Neil's death.

Stella had chosen to not see the pictures but had asked Don Worme to insist they be shown publicly. The wounds on her son's face might be one of the only ways to get to the truth, even if she couldn't bear to watch the enlarged images projected for a room full of strangers. That's why she stayed in her room.

Worme approached the microphone in a few quick steps and requested an opportunity to speak to pre-empt any issues his colleagues might make about showing the photos.

"Obviously, the graphic nature of these photographs is deeply disturbing for the family. They have not had an opportunity to see them as of yet." Still, Worme told the inquiry, the family had decided against requesting a publication ban.

"Given the nature of this forum, that it is a public inquiry, they are insisting that, in spite of the difficulty that they have with this, that they wish them nonetheless to be made quite public." The family's only caveat was that they hoped that perhaps the commissioner might say a few words to the media and to others so that the pictures could at least be treated in as sensitive a fashion as possible.

"I understand," said the commissioner, his hands clasped in front of him on the table. He asked to see the photos and studied them for a few minutes. As his eyes scanned the exhibits, his shock was obvious. It lingered on his face, and coloured his voice.

"Mr. Worme, I find those very upsetting, I must tell you.

They're extremely graphic. You say you're not asking that I direct a publication ban?" His words carried a tone of admonition.

"No, my lord, they are not asking for that."

"And you've discussed this with them?"

"I have discussed that with them," said the lawyer, his voice calm.

Erica locked her eyes fiercely on the commissioner. She had seen the injuries on her brother's face at the funeral chapel. The public needed to see them, too. People had to know what had happened to Neil.

"And they have a general sense of how graphic these pictures are?" Wright asked, unable to let this go.

"Absolutely, they do, and I can assure you that it is intensely painful for them."

"I'm sure it is," said the commissioner.

Standing at the lectern, Worme tried to ignore his rising fear that Wright would rule against him and stood firm, stressing again that the family did not want a publication ban.

The commissioner looked intensely disturbed. He again called the pictures "very upsetting and very graphic," and worried aloud about the devastating effect on family members of seeing them in newspapers or on TV. Before Wright could decide, Dowling raised the spectre of the pictures appearing on the Internet. Hesje urged the commissioner to break for half an hour, which he did.

When the inquiry resumed, Worme went to the lectern and found the words he'd struggled for earlier to express Stella's courage. "She has wept and prayed," he said, "and her decision is that this public inquiry, in order to meet and to achieve its mandate, ought to give full public disclosure, including to these images."

"I must say to you," the commissioner replied, "that the willingness of the family to have the pictures disclosed in order to see that the entire story is known seems to me, with respect, a very sensible, intelligent approach, notwithstanding the terrific emotional factors that are built into it." He complimented Stella and the Stonechild family on their "insight and wisdom" and finally accepted their wishes.

Stella had carried the day. The only restriction that Wright placed on the publication of the images was that they would not be available on the inquiry Web site, unlike most other material made public at the inquiry.

Joel Hesje asked the technician to project picture number 41. Erica watched the white screen, wiping her eyes roughly. Once, long ago, riding home on the school bus, she and Marcel had seen Neil in the distance on a snow-covered field swinging his lunch bucket in circles around himself, fending off another boy. The bus driver stopped and they ran down the embankment to help their brother. For Erica, this was no different. She refused to look away, not wanting her brother to go through this ordeal alone.

Abruptly, Neil's injured face filled the two-and-a-half-metre-high screen. Erica breathed in so sharply she felt a sharp pain in her chest. She raised her right hand to her mouth to muffle a cry.

"This photograph depicts the face of this individual from the front view," Dowling began in a dry, clinical tone, but Erica heard none of it. She began to wail, oblivious to the people around her. Friends tried to convince her to leave, but she refused, stubbornly telling them, "No, no." Worme came over to talk to her, but Erica just shook her head and stayed in her chair holding hands with one of her friends.

"—and I think the thing that strikes everyone immediately is the appearance of the nose," Dowling continued, despite Erica's loud crying.

The whole room stared at the large screen. Even seasoned journalists looked at each other, astonished, and shook their heads in disbelief. Two dark parallel gashes slanted downward from left to right across the bridge of Neil's nose. The skin had been split open. The lower wound was almost two and half centimetres long, the upper slightly less.

Roy, who had no idea what was coming, could not stand to see Neil like that and walked out. Kayseas followed him. Gary Pickard, Pat's husband, went out to comfort him.

Dowling had been droning on, seemingly unaware of the severe shock in the room. Suddenly, he addressed the commissioner. "I should point out that if I seem to be cold and clinical I hope that doesn't come across as being the way I am, and I apologize to the family members if that comes across at all."

The commissioner reassured him, saying his professional detachment was critical in the analysis of the photographs.

Dowling explained that a layperson might view the marks on Neil's face as a "significant injury," but he emphasized that his own assessment was informed by regular experience with horrific injuries, such as faces destroyed by shotgun blasts, so from that perspective he considered Neil's injuries to be relatively minor.

Using a laser pointer, the red dot shaking slightly, Dowling focused on the screen and continued to explain that these abrasions were caused by some kind of blunt trauma, as opposed to what he called a sharp injury, such as that caused by a knife.

The commissioner gazed intently at Neil's facial injuries.

As he spoke, Dowling said that the injuries to Neil's face would not have caused a large amount of bleeding, and that the blackening of the lips was a result of freezing to death.

Dowling tried to instruct the commissioner on the nature of a blunt object. He used the analogy that if Wright were to fall against one of the tables in the room and split open his forehead, many people would refer to that as a cut. But in Dowling's world it would be called a "laceration produced by a blunt object," no matter how sharp the corner of the table.

Dowling did not take issue with Dr. Jack Adolph's 1990 assessment of the death as accidental, saying he might have reached a similar conclusion. Dowling's autopsy, which he'd performed in 2001, had been no more helpful. The body was in such a desiccated state that even Neil's tattoos had disappeared. None of the injuries apparent in the original photos were still visible. Dowling had X-rays done, "from the top of the head to the toes." But the X-rays revealed only one slight injury to the bony part of the nose, which in Dowling's estimation had pre-dated Neil's death. Because the cartilage in Neil's nose had dried out, any injury there would have been obscured by time. However, he would not rule out cartilage damage caused by a hard object.

Hesje asked whether the injuries were consistent "with what might be commonly described as a beating."

Dowling chose his words carefully.

"I tend to think of that term, a 'beating,' as being associated with more extensive injuries, both external and internal but that, of course, is in my line of work. So, bearing that in mind, I cannot rule out that these were assault injuries."

"In your opinion, are the injuries also consistent with being inflicted by another person with a blunt object?" asked Hesje.

"They very well could be, yes."

For the rest of the day, the lawyers presented duelling theories on what happened to Neil's face and right wrist. They tried to press Dowling toward asserting what had caused the injuries. Dowling wouldn't budge, beyond allowing that any given explanation for their presence was "consistent," or not, with Neil's injuries.

Drew Plaxton, the lawyer for the police association, began by establishing Dowling's credentials, even joking about his prairie roots. Plaxton then asked that picture number 32 be projected onto the screen. It showed the ditch where Neil had apparently first fallen, several metres to the north of the level area where he was found. The weight of Neil's body had broken the snow's crust into large, smooth slabs. "Okay. If we look at picture 32, again with your experience as a prairie boy, does that appear to be a sort of a shrub, maybe some twigs, that sort of thing?"

"Yes."

Plaxton's familiar tone with Dowling was driving Erica nuts. She could see where Plaxton was going with his bizarre questions about twigs and shrubs. There was nothing of the sort in the photo, just a flat, clear area of snow surrounded by small patches of weeds and grass. Dowling had previously agreed that "twigs" fit his definition of a blunt object. She put her hands over her mouth in disbelief as the lawyer proceeded to the next screen.

"If we could have picture 23, please?" In a serious tone, Plaxton continued. "Now that, I believe, is a picture of Mr. Stonechild after the police had rolled him over from his original position. Assuming that's accurate, and he was located where the imprint in the snow is, does it seem very likely his face would have come into contact with twigs, shrubbery, various small articles, the way he was lying?"

At Erica's table the young people leaned together, mocking Plaxton ruthlessly. "Yeah, right, the grass did it," Erica muttered under her breath.

The medical examiner seemed to be looking at the picture with fresh eyes. Lying on his back, arms clutched to his chest in a frozen gesture of futility, Neil looked helpless. A small patch of grass had been exposed where the boy's face had pressed down. Aside from a couple of other brown patches where Neil's body had lain or fallen, the snow throughout the photo showed no signs of melting through to the ground.

Dowling suggested that the warmth of Neil's face against the snow might have melted the snow and exposed the grass over time, clearly backing off Plaxton's notion that somehow the twigs or grass caused the injuries on Neil's nose when he fell.

One of the photographs showed a skin indentation on

Neil's right wrist. When Plaxton suggested the RCMP had been "encouraging" Dowling toward their theory that the marks had been caused by handcuffs, Dowling grew mildly irritated.

"I wouldn't use the word 'encouraging' on me," he said, increasingly irritated. "They were simply presenting a direction that their investigation was looking at."

Plaxton presented his next theory, that a set of handcuffs would not have caused such injuries to Neil's face.

Don Worme was scribbling notes on his yellow legal pad, waiting to begin his own cross-examination. He watched as Plaxton produced a set of Peerless handcuffs similar to what the SPS used and walked over to Dowling. Worme stopped writing, smiled and looked up to watch. Theatrics in the courtroom were high risk and they easily backfired. He wondered whether Plaxton would fall into his own trap.

Plaxton asked to have one of Gary Robertson's photogrammetric images projected onto the screen. "The one with the handcuffs," Plaxton said. Once again Neil's swollen face filled the projection screen. This time a set of metal bands from a pair of handcuffs overlaid the parallel gashes on his nose.

Erica snapped backward in shock. Other than the lawyers and some of their clients, no one had seen this picture before. She closed her eyes involuntarily for a second, and covered her mouth. The stainless-steel bands appeared to fit exactly into the two parallel abrasions.

"Looks like a perfect fit. That's a pretty amazing picture," said one of the local journalists, who had been very skeptical about police involvement in Neil's death.

Whatever Plaxton had hoped to accomplish by showing the photo, he was now battling the shocking impact the picture had created in the room. At the end of Plaxton's meandering cross-examination, Dowling retreated to safe ground and refused to pronounce on the possibility that Neil's injuries were caused by handcuffs.

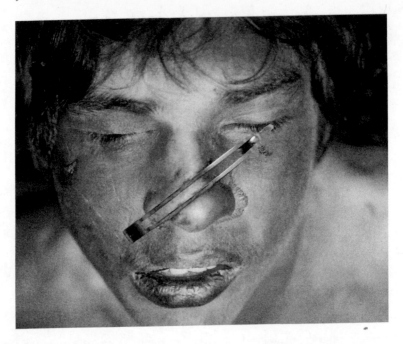

"I think all I can say is that we may have a patterned injury. It's possible that it's grass, it's possible that it's crusted snow, it's possible that it's a handcuff. And as a forensic pathologist, it would be improper for me to say it is or it isn't this or that."

— — —

Don Worme took his time doing up the middle button of his black suit jacket and adjusting the knot in his sky-blue silk tie before proceeding to the podium.

He allowed a moment for the picture of Neil's face to appear on the screen, then asked whether Dowling was familiar with the idea of using handcuffs as knuckle dusters.

"And that's one possible explanation for those injuries, I believe you agreed?"

"Yes."

He asked Dowling whether it might be equally possible for an individual to raise their hands in a defensive movement and have the handcuffs pushed into their face.

Dowling readily agreed.

"Sure," said Worme, "and if one was defending oneself while handcuffed against blows, that certainly might create sufficient force to create those marks? You'd agree with that?"

"That is certainly a possibility, yes."

— — —

At the afternoon coffee break, Si Halyk, the FSIN's lawyer, was talking to a journalist about Dowling's malleable testimony. Tall, angular, distinguished-looking with white hair and glasses, Halyk was one of the most respected members of the Saskatchewan bar and his colleagues often allowed him the opportunity to cross-examine last. As he and the reporter walked back into the room he quipped, "Guess it's time to go nail some jelly to the wall."

Halyk approached Dowling in a relaxed manner. At least once he called the medical examiner "Doc." Holding the handcuffs in his right hand, showing them to Dowling as he spoke, Halyk brought Dowling back to the triangle theory of investigation. One more thing had yet to be taken into account.

"If I put to you as a hypothetical that this person who we're seeing in the photographs right now on the screen was last seen in police custody before he was found dead, would that be an important fact for you?

"It's an important observation, yes." Dowling elaborated a moment later. "It's only important insofar as understanding the circumstances surrounding the death."

— — —

Erica's tranquilizer had kicked in. Halyk had finished with Dowling and Trent Ewart was on the stand. He was the one who'd called the police about Neil ringing buzzers at Snowberry Downs. But Erica was by now so mentally exhausted that she barely cared about what he was saying. All those terrible images of her brother had rubbed her raw all over again. That, and knowing whoever did that to him was still out there.

"A COMMENT MADE IN ERROR"

ON A HOT, HUMID WEEKEND AFTERNOON IN late September, Don Worme's black Jeep Cherokee sped down the smooth blacktop from North Battleford to Saskatoon. After weeks of eighteen-hour days, the few hours alone on the road were a relief.

"Heeee—hee—he—yi," Worme yelled to the rhythm of the four drums blasting from the stereo speakers. He was carrying a cherry-red junior-model all-terrain vehicle in the back, a birthday gift for his eldest son, Donovan. Unable to resist, he had also bought a high-end model for himself, decked out in green and brown camouflage paint, to be shipped home later.

"Hee—yi," he sang. The whoop of the Cree battle cry gave way to the sound of drums that pulsed like a heartbeat. Taking the time to get this gift for Donovan would show Helen that he was not so consumed by the inquiry that he'd forgotten his family. But it also made time for him to do more work without her knowing.

He turned off the song and rummaged through the half-empty packs of Player's Light littering the dash. When he found the cassette he wanted, he slipped it in the tape deck and lowered the volume. A couple of months earlier the commission's investigator, Robert Martell, had flown to the West Coast to interview Keith Jarvis. The drive up to North Battleford had been Worme's first chance to listen to it; and he wanted to listen to it again on the way back.

Since Jason's testimony, he had worried that his nephew had bungled everything. Not mentioning in his written statement to Jarvis that he'd seen Neil in police custody looked especially damaging. After his mauling by the police lawyers, this tape could prove more important than ever.

Worme lit a cigarette. Through the open window sweet smells of earth and prairie grasses baked by the sun mingled with the bitter scent of tobacco.

Martell was a retired RCMP officer who had spent twenty-five years as a crime investigator specializing in professional misconduct. In 1983 he had set up shop as a consultant and had worked as an investigator for several high-profile public inquiries in Manitoba, among them the inquiry that had probed the circumstances surrounding the deaths of Helen Betty Osborne and John Joseph Harper. Both were natives who had died at the hands of whites: Osborne was abducted and brutally murdered by four young men and J. J. Harper was killed in a struggle with a police officer. Martell's credentials as an investigator were impeccable.

For the first twenty minutes of the interview Martell talked about his and Jarvis's shared experience as investigators, carefully building a relationship with his subject. His voice maintained an even pitch and his manner was non-threatening.

Jarvis's own training included statement analysis, a technique for identifying inconsistencies and anomalies as symptoms of deception in witness statements. He talked to Martell about using polygraphs and statement analysis in a rape case around the time of Stonechild's death. His memory of investigating the rape was almost photographic: the alleged victim's name and age, that she and her boyfriend had been on the verge of splitting up, that there had been an argument between them over her pregnancy, that the boyfriend worked at a printing company on Avenue P South. Jarvis even boasted about using receipts from American Express and the Hudson's Bay Company to crack the case.

"Yeah, yeah, yeah," Martell burst out enthusiastically. "But that's when I call investigations fun, when you start talking about the receipts and what have you, and you're going with your gut feeling."

Worme listened to Jarvis dig himself a deeper hole.

Becoming chatty, Jarvis told Martell how he conducted so-called "pure-version" statements. He would start, he said, with a general conversation and then ask the witness to write out a statement in his or her own hand. Finally, he would go over the statement and ask questions on matters that had been left out.

Acknowledging that he had used this approach with Jason Roy, Jarvis had inadvertently explained what could well have happened with the boy's written statement from November 30, 1990. Either Jarvis had failed to ask some key questions—about missing elements of Jason's story, such as seeing Neil in a police cruiser—or he had asked the questions but not put them in the final statement.

Martell cleverly circled away from the issue. He had Jarvis detail his duties, list the names of supervisors and talk about how the shift rotation worked in 1990. Jarvis was helpful and sounded relaxed.

Worme jabbed the fast-forward button. When Martell spoke again, their chattiness had disappeared.

Jarvis was attempting to say that he thought he'd tried to contact Jason on November 30, 1990. Martell questioned this, and Jarvis had to admit that it had been Jason, a troubled boy with a lengthy criminal record, who had taken the surprising first step of contacting the police, which suggested he had been driven by events very much out of the ordinary.

Martell probed further. Did Jarvis know Jason had been checked out by the police that night?

"I don't believe so," said Jarvis at first, sounding unsure.

"You weren't aware that—in reference to a warrant that was out for him?"

"No, and I'm—don't believe that came in the statement. I think that came during the general conversation, and maybe I neglected to put it in the statement, but I did ask."

Worme listened to the last few sentences again. Jarvis had just admitted that he'd left out a key fact that Jason had forgotten to include in his handwritten statement.

"During the general conversation," Martell continued, "did Jason Roy tell you that he had seen Neil in the back of a police car?"

"Yes. Jason and Neil, apparently, when they left Snowberry Downs, had their disagreement, went their separate ways according to Jason."

"Right."

"Jason indicated, I believe, that he was on Confederation Drive walking when the police car pulled up and approached him and basically did a check on him."

"All right," said Martell. Now that Jarvis was providing crucial details, he knew better than to slow him down.

"He indicated that first of all he gave a false name."

"Right."

"Because he was quite, actually quite happy about it," Jarvis recalled.

The boy's glee at fooling the police clearly perturbed Jarvis, and it seemed to be half the reason he hadn't forgotten the interview. Jarvis sounded as if he were talking about something he actually remembered.

"—that fact, that he'd deceived the police because there was a warrant out for his arrest for being unlawfully at large. He also indicated that Neil was in the back seat of the patrol car at the time."

"Right."

"However, he informed the police that he didn't know him because he also knew that Neil was unlawfully at large from the community, or group home in Sutherland. So he declined any knowledge of who Neil was. And that was the last he saw of him."

There it was, what Jason had always maintained: that he had told Jarvis that on the night of November 24 the police had done a check on him, he gave them a false name and Neil was in the back seat of the patrol car at the time.

Worme butted out his cigarette. Jarvis had shown the same grasp of precise detail, the same sort of emotional investment in the memory, as he had with the rape case.

Worme could imagine his nephew talking to Jarvis. Jason would have been scared, anxious to get it over with, wondering if he was going to be taken in. The kid's attendance at school had never been regular and his writing skills were poor at best. Making sense on paper of what he had seen would have been difficult, even impossible, for him. He could easily have assumed Jarvis would be putting facts from the general conversation into his notes and that he did not have to repeat them when he wrote out his statement. Besides, Worme thought, the boy had written only a little over a page, but had been with Jarvis for almost an hour.

Next, Martell turned to Jarvis's questions at the end of Jason's written statement. Jarvis had already known when talking to Jason that police had been dispatched on the night of November 24 to find Neil, so Martell wanted to know why he'd asked Jason what time he last saw Neil and what condition he was in, but did not ask where Neil was when he last saw him. Beyond a feeble suggestion that Louttit may have not copied the entire investigation file, Jarvis had no explanation.

One of the last things Jarvis had done in his cursory investigation was talk to Dr. Adolph on the afternoon of December 5, 1990. Jarvis said Adolph told him then that Neil might have been dead since November 25.

Martell interrupted.

"Well, it was around midnight that you tell us that Jason Roy said he saw him in the police car, is that not right?"

"Yeah, that's right."

"You had information that he was with—that he was in the back of a police car, and he was handcuffed, is that correct?"

"M'hm," said Jarvis, cornered.

"You had information that there was a car dispatched around that same time—"

"Yeah."

"—and the members were Hartwig and Senger?"

"M'hm."

"And that that call came in before midnight . . . and the call cleared at 0017."

"Yeah."

"Is that correct?"

"Yeah."

"All right, the 0017 is on the 25 of November, is that correct?" said Martell pounding his point home.

"M'hm."

By the time Martell's question came, Worme thought, it scarcely needed to be asked.

"Did the information you received from Dr. Adolph not cause you some concern?"

"No, not at that time. I'd—" Jarvis stopped himself for a moment. "I guess not. I didn't think anything of it at the time. I put in a request then through to Hartwig and crew to give me a report on what their dealings with [Neil] were, what they did with him."

Although he had heard it before, Worme listened in disbelief as Jarvis matter-of-factly described how he had closed the file shortly after getting off the phone with the pathologist.

Martell's tone remained neutral and matter of fact, but any trace of friendliness had vanished. Nothing existed in Jarvis's notes or report about contacting Hartwig and Senger after he'd learned they had been dispatched to Snowberry Downs. Worme remembered exactly what Jarvis had told Jack Warner in an earlier interview: "I am sure I would have approached them either personally or by virtue of a memo. I think I approached them personally."

For the first time in the conversation, Martell challenged what Jarvis remembered and suggested he was being deceptive. "And I believe," said Martell, "that you approached them personally, and I believe you know you approached them personally."

Earlier he and Jarvis had talked about statement analysis. Now Martell showed his hand, saying, "I've had your statement analyzed," referring to Jarvis's October 12, 2000, interview with Lyons and Warner. The analyst had concluded that Jarvis was waffling about the nature of his dealings with Senger and Hartwig as a diversion to avoid talking about his conversation with them.

Jarvis denied what Martell was saying, his anger beginning to show. Complaining that the events happened thirteen years ago, Jarvis said he had nothing to hide. Martell reminded him that he'd recalled minute details of the rape case without difficulty.

"He lied about who he was. He lied about himself," Jarvis whined. Martell reminded him that Jason's effrontery was not the issue. The question was why Jarvis had decided not to investigate further when he'd learned that Jason Roy, Larry Hartwig and Brad Senger may have been the last three people to see Neil Stonechild alive.

When Martell raised Ernie Louttit's name, Jarvis flew into an angry tirade. "I don't know what he's got to do with this though—He wasn't involved in the investigation at all—He had absolutely nothing to do with it—He just had a bad habit of sticking his nose in other people's files." He raged about Louttit's lack of "common courtesy," then promptly denied having talked to him. "I don't recall meeting with him at all."

"Is it possible that that meeting could have happened?"

"I have no idea."

"Is it possible?" Martell persisted.

"Anything's possible, Bob." The sarcastic familiarity was a signal from one cop to another: Jarvis had had enough of being treated like a suspect.

Martell offered to show Jarvis the analysis of his statement; Neil Parker, a polygraph trainer and teacher at the Canadian Police College, had conducted it. Jarvis refused, saying it didn't matter.

Martell ignored him.

"It says, 'Probe the area where he states he isn't sure if he sent a memo to Hartwig, Senger, or spoke to them in relation to their dealings with Stonechild . . . Becomes vague here.' Any reason why you'd become vague?"

"I'm not becoming vague. That's exactly what I can recall."

The conversation turned to Neil's injuries. Jarvis suggested that, in showing him photos from Neil's autopsy, Jack Warner had been "trying to get me to say that the markings on the wrists of the deceased were from handcuffs."

Jarvis admitted now that they might have been caused by handcuffs, but he sounded dismissive. "However, I didn't see them at the time. They could also have been caused by a watch, they could have been caused by a rubber band, who knows. It's not my, you know, it's not my field of expertise."

Parker's analysis also questioned Jarvis's incongruous laughter during his statement to Warner. Martell read from the analysis again. "'And the part where laughter is noted is where he's nervous in editing. The topic in these areas bothers him and he doesn't have an answer so he covers up with a laugh.' Any comment on that?"

"No, I don't know what he's talking about."

"'Jarvis has convenient memory lapses and yet recalls other areas in detail,'" Martell continued.

Jarvis denied this opinion, too, but softened his tone slightly when Martell allowed that they might be referring to his lack of memory about Hartwig and Senger.

"That could be. That's thirteen years ago. There's some things stick with you some things don't. It doesn't matter how you want to look at it with memory, I—"

"We're talking of death and policemen being involved, Keith."

"I know we're talking of death—"

"And you're saying you can't remember."

"—and I'm talking from memory from thirteen years ago. When I retired from the police department, I retired from the police department."

"No, you didn't," said Martell, reminding him again about the rape case.

"Yeah, I remembered her," Jarvis conceded.

When Martell tried to discuss Hartwig and Senger again, Jarvis threw a tantrum.

"It's one or the other. As I said, I don't know how many times today in this interview, interrogation, whichever it is, I'm not sure what it's leading to here."

"Yeah."

"But I'm getting to the point where I'm saying enough's enough and I'm not going to talk to you anymore."

"Okay."

"Because this is either an interview or an interrogation. Which? If it's an interrogation, then I'll phone a goddamn lawyer."

Martell asked if he would take a polygraph. Jarvis said that it didn't matter to him one way or the other, but he wanted to consult with a lawyer first. He did, however, need to know if he was being accused of anything. Martell assured him that he was not and that he was offering the polygraph as an investigative aid, the way Jarvis himself would have used it during his own time on the force.

"We're attempting to get to the bottom of this."

"Yeah."

— — —

The low skyline of Saskatoon was coming into view. Worme had heard how Jarvis had gone to his doctor after the interview. Martell's approach had upset him so much he was afraid of having a heart attack. A few days after his meeting with Martell, the Saskatoon Police Association had hired a lawyer for him. Worme took these as warning signs. As badly as he wanted to believe he had the retired investigator right where he needed him, Worme's gut was telling him Jarvis just might deny almost everything he'd said when he took the stand at the inquiry.

— — —

The long hours of sitting in the inquiry room had worsened Stella's pain. It shot up her legs and stabbed at her back. To her right, Norman had dozed off while the lawyers and a witness were droning on about something she could barely follow. He was snoring gently. To her left, Don Worme was reviewing his notes. She wished her table were near the high windows with the view of brightly coloured leaves falling on the banks of the river. A few minutes after eleven, on October 10, she leaned toward Worme and whispered that she needed to leave to get a coffee.

At the same time, Joel Hesje rose to his feet. He spoke with an unusual sense of urgency.

"Mr. Commissioner," he said, "if you would like to take a break at this point, I have a witness I need to speak to."

The commissioner agreed to a fifteen-minute break without asking for an explanation. At the back of the room, in front of the public seating, Gary and Danny Pratt stood side by side, looking like two toughs awaiting sentencing. As taut as a coiled spring, Gary shifted from foot to foot, dressed in jeans and a silver and black hoodie. Standing protectively beside his younger brother, Danny wore a blue and green hockey sweater with the sleeves pulled up to expose his tattooed forearms. He was shorter and stockier, with black hair and a darker complexion, and long hours in the weight room at a federal penitentiary had added authority to his already menacing presence.

But Father André smiled at the men, walked over, shook Gary's hand vigorously and patted him on the back. All morning the priest had been worrying aloud that Gary was not going to show and the lawyers would declare he had something to hide.

Despite the RCMP's having eliminated him from suspicion when he'd passed his polygraph, the police lawyers at the inquiry still had their sights on Gary. They dropped his name repeatedly, creating a sense in the room that he remained a suspect. And now he'd come to face them without legal representation.

Gary spoke briefly to Hesje and then walked out to the mezzanine toward the tables set up with the coffee urns. Stella had settled into one of the few cushioned armchairs nearby. Jake, Erica, Norman and their friends crowded around her. Gary and Danny, and Danny's girlfriend Tamara, had no choice but to walk past as they headed for a clearing near the elevators. Gary and Stella's eyes met. Gary nodded, then stopped a respectful distance away with his head lowered. Tamara consoled him with a hand on his shoulder. He wiped at one eye.

Grabbing Norman's brawny arm for support, Stella struggled to her feet from the deep chair. The back pain made her sway as she walked directly to Gary. People balancing coffee cups and saucers, including a couple of lawyers, moved aside to let her pass.

When she reached Gary she did not hesitate. Her head

only reached his chest, but she reached up and hugged him as fiercely as if he were her own son. He looked as though he were eighteen years old again and tears flooded his eyes. Stella didn't speak, but her message was clear.

Moments later the inquiry resumed. Hesje rose to address the room. Without being asked, Gary walked up the centre aisle and stood in front of the commissioner, motionless, arms clasped in front.

"Mr. Commissioner," said Hesje, "we had subpoenaed Gary Pratt to attend today. He has appeared in response to that subpoena in a timely fashion. I have spoken with him. He has been very cooperative, but there are some problems in terms of having him testify today." Hesje asked the judge to release Gary from the subpoena until a later date, when he could appear with a lawyer.

Father André was disappointed. Every time Pratt was forced to return, the chances of his actually showing up dropped. The commissioner dismissed Pratt, and in a stern tone reminded him he was still under subpoena. Pratt strode out of the room without saying a word, his brother at his back.

— — —

Gary Robertson took the stand on Monday, October 20. After Hesje walked Robertson through the basic facts of his involvement in the RCMP investigation, Fox wasted no time in challenging his professional qualifications.

In his curriculum vitae, the photogrammetrist stated, "1976 to '77 under government sponsor attended Ottawa University to complete credits for certification in civil engineering." The courses were not directly related to photogrammetry, nor did Robertson advertise them as such, but the entry in the CV was still misleading. After a lengthy, argumentative cross-examination, Robertson was forced to admit that he had never completed any of the courses in civil engineering and had not passed any of the exams.

Fox mocked him. "See, we got a—we got a fellow back home, you know. We ask him how far did you go in school and he says, well, I got halfway through grade twelve, I got my grade six, you know."

Fox also challenged Robertson's expertise when it came to analyzing imprints made on human skin. Robertson had previously alluded to using live pigs to test the imprint patterns of different materials such as rope because of the similarities between human skin and pigskin.

"You—how many studies have you been involved in where you implanted a mark on a pig and then made an interpretation of it? How many pigs have you worked on?"

Robertson worked through the various studies he had been involved in.

"I think it was four," he said finally. "We did four."

"Four?" asked Fox.

"Yeah."

"That's the extent of it, four pigs?"

— — —

Late that night, unable to sleep, Don Worme paced barefoot on his main floor. Most of the lights were off and his family was asleep. He sipped the last of some Merlot from a tall crystal glass and tightened the belt of his thick terry-cloth robe.

As he had feared, Jarvis was now claiming to have been browbeaten by the RCMP and the commission's own investigator, Robert Martell. Since that interview, Jarvis had been granted standing and was now represented by his own counsel, Kenneth Stevenson.

Worme was terrified that Justice Wright would refuse to admit the Martell tape, which Stevenson was calling an interrogation. Furthermore, by turning the recorder on and off several times as they'd talked, Martell had opened himself to complaints that parts of the interview were missing.

Worme didn't believe that this was the case, but the math so far gave him cold comfort: polygraph evidence excluded, Jason refused standing, his credibility badly bruised by Fox and Plaxton, no mention of Neil in Jason's handwritten statement, his botching the dates when trying to explain that omission.

Jarvis's admission to both the RCMP and Martell that Jason had told him about seeing Neil in the cruiser was critical for Worme to prove that Hartwig and Senger had taken Neil into custody. But worse than Jarvis changing his story, it was now looking to Worme as if the tape of his admission might never go public.

Sitting in the dark, he felt defeated. Neil's case seemed to be slipping away. "Something bad is happening. That's it," he said to himself. "Now they're going to drive hard to the end."

— — —

The next day at the inquiry, as Gary Robertson began his Power-Point presentation, Stella restored Worme's courage to continue, if not his hope.

Despite the challenges to Robertson's credentials, Wright ruled that he would listen to Robertson's testimony in the narrow area of the measurements of the wounds themselves and of comparisons of those measurements to a specific object. However, only after hearing the testimony would he decide what weight if any to give it, he said. Everyone in the room knew the object Wright was referring to was a set of handcuffs.

Suddenly the commissioner noticed with alarm that Stella was still in the room and would be exposed in a moment to the image of her dead son projected onto a giant screen. Whenever this had been about to happen, Stella had left the room.

From the beginning of the hearing, Wright, who showed the gruffness of long experience with almost everyone else, had treated Neil's mother with sensitivity. Stella appreciated this and always spoke about the judge with respect and trust.

Wright abruptly interrupted Hesje.

"Excuse me, Mr. Hesje. Mr. Worme, would you like to excuse..."

Don spoke to Stella for a moment, then addressed the commissioner.

"I've canvassed this with Mrs. Bignell and she has elected to—"

"Is she all right?" Wright interrupted.

"—remain present."

It was a defining moment.

Near the beginning of his testimony, Robertson had made it clear that he'd done his original measurements of the injuries without knowing the RCMP's suspicions that they might have been caused by handcuffs. Only later, when he had finished measuring the wounds, was he asked to compare the handcuffs to them.

Speaking much of the time in jargon that merged mathematics, forensics and photography, Robertson showed a close match in dimensions between Neil's injuries and the Peerless handcuffs. His findings suggested the marks on the wrist were likely to have been caused by similar handcuffs and that the cuts on the nose were consistent with being hit hard by such handcuffs.

At one point, the picture depicting Neil's nose with the superimposed handcuffs was projected again. Stella had refused to believe that the police used handcuffs on Neil. Seeing this image finally changed her mind.

"Why?" she said quietly to herself, unable to turn away. "I was so naïve."

The lawyers for the police quickly went on the offensive. Plaxton demanded to see Robertson's working papers, although

Hesje pointed out that they were not comprehensible to the layperson. He then tried to joust with Robertson regarding his mathematics and methodology.

SPS lawyer Barry Rossman emphasized that Robertson had not measured with the actual handcuffs used by Hartwig and Senger in 1990. The bands on the two officers' cuffs measured two and a half millimetres while the bands on the cuffs used by Robertson measured two millimetres. Robertson replied that if the actual cuffs were wider, they would, in fact, be an even better fit. Either set of cuffs was well within his margin of error.

On the third day of Robertson's testimony, Worme was depressed again by the way things were going. Robertson could well be tainted for the rest of his career by the ridicule of his CV. Studying the commissioner's impassive face, Worme worried about whether Fox, Plaxton and Rossman had successfully challenged the accuracy of his findings and the link Robertson was making between his measurements and the handcuffs.

When his turn came to question Robertson, Worme tried to bring the jargon down to a level everyone in the room could follow, his sense of humour showing through his dark mood.

"Now, I don't have Mr. Plaxton's enormous mathematical abilities, so I'm going to try to reduce this into something I've seen on TV. The other night I was watching David Caruso on *Crime Scene Investigations* and there was apparently a fingerprint that was located on a round bottle, and I believe it was a tequila bottle or something, and through the, what they had called photogrammetry—which I found to be rather coincidental— they took that fingerprint and flattened it out so that they could compare it against the database of all the fingerprints that would be in, I guess, two dimensions?"

"Right," said Robertson.

Worme had showed Robertson's measurements were really a simple matter in the end.

— — —

Jarvis began the bulk of his testimony on November 24. He had been examined briefly by commission counsel in late October before the inquiry had taken a one-month break.

As Jarvis walked up to the witness table on the thirteenth anniversary of Neil Stonechild's death, his jaunty gait and odd masklike smile aroused an instant dislike in Worme. To think that the former sergeant had not bothered to look closely at Neil's frozen body in the morgue the night police had brought him in from the field filled Worme with disdain. Jarvis had gone there with the ID officer, Sergeant Bob Morton, to get a formal identification for the body. When he had testified in October he'd said that if he had seen the marks on Neil's face he would have done more. To Worme these were mere excuses.

"The guy stood less than a metre away from the frozen body of a seventeen-year-old boy found dead in a field wearing only one shoe, but he never bothered to even so much as look at him. What's up with that?" he'd grumbled to friends at the Freehouse pub. "I'll tell you what's up. The kid didn't matter to him. Not a bit."

For the next several hours, Plaxton and Fox lobbed easy questions at Jarvis. Jarvis looked too comfortable, almost smug. His glib answers infuriated Worme. Roused from his gloom by smouldering animosity, he began scribbling questions on his yellow legal notepad.

Plaxton homed in on a key issue from Jarvis's interview with Martell. "I think you do state that you had received information about Stonechild in a police cruiser. Was that accurate?"

"No, sir. That was a comment made in error."

"Right, 'a comment made in error,'" thought Worme cynically. It was the exact phrase Jarvis had used several times on the first day of his testimony in October to recant what he had said to both RCMP Corporal Jack Warner and commission investigator Robert Martell in separate interviews three years apart.

On the stand that day, Jarvis claimed the police had created false memories for him by suggesting scenarios to him during the interviews. He also implied that he might have answered questions when Martell had briefly turned off the tape, which provoked a sharp argument among the lawyers about the tape's admissibility. In the end, though, Jarvis could not provide a single example of a question or answer that was missing. Through Don, Stella inisted that the tapes be heard. Finally Wright ruled they could be played for the inquiry.

Now, in November, Jarvis picked up where he'd left off, explaining the cause of his "error" to Plaxton.

"My way of thinking, sir, it was through the initial contacts that I'd had, several contacts with officers Lyons and Warner, in their attempt to refresh my memory, confusion arose. Had I had the opportunity to have my notes and the police file available at the time, it would have been much clearer, because had that information been brought to my attention at that time it would have been in my notes, in the report, and certainly in Mr. Roy's statement."

"Okay," said Plaxton. "There's nothing in any of that to indicate police officers were involved?"

"No, sir."

"Okay. And there would have been if you had that information?"

"That is correct, sir."

Warner shook his head in disbelief. He remembered quite clearly showing Jarvis a copy of his notes and the autopsy photos the night before he and Ken Lyons had interviewed him in Burnaby.

— — —

Worme's chance to cross-examine Jarvis came after the afternoon break. He began by telling Jarvis that the retired officer had offended his client by approaching her that morning and calling her by her first name, as though he knew her well. Jarvis looked slightly nervous.

Then Worme asked Jarvis how he had won a promotion to the rank of staff sergeant in 1991, despite stiff competition. Jarvis reluctantly admitted that the performance evaluation leading to that promotion would have closely considered how well he'd kept his notes and files.

At an almost leisurely pace, Worme got around to referring Jarvis to page eighty-one of his notebook.

"You have a reference there at the bottom of, I guess, the upper portion to Lucille Neetz. Do you see that?"

"Yes, sir."

Long ago, in his grandfather's kitchen, Worme had heard many stories about the legendary skill of Cree hunters. One of their favourite tactics for hunting buffalo was to erect a pound, a large corral three to five metres high and disguised to blend into the landscape. A long chute, sometimes a hundred metres long and typically made by lashing saplings across standing timber, extended obliquely out from the entrance. A sharp turn concealed the enclosure from the onrushing buffalo until they were too far in to turn around. The hunters began pushing the herd toward the trap by slapping the ground with clothes or sticks. Startled by the sharp noises, the animals would run off. When they settled down again, the men made more noise, gradually pushing the animals toward the mouth of the chute. When the animals were close enough, an experienced hunter on one of the swiftest horses guided them in.

Worme slowly built his trap. He took Jarvis through his considerable training, in everything from leadership and motivation to interviewing and interrogation. Whenever Jarvis seemed threatened, he eased off. He allowed Jarvis to describe

proudly his instrumental role in having CPR training introduced to the Saskatchewan Police College. He indulged Jarvis's
nostalgia, his being seconded to serve as a kind of "den mother"
for the recruits at the police college, where he had taught, of all
things, the art of note taking.

"All right," began Worme. "I believe you've indicated to us
repeatedly, Mr. Jarvis, that if it is not in your notebook or if it is
not in the reports then it didn't happen. Is that what you're
telling us, sir?"

Jarvis replied, "That I had no knowledge of it, that's correct, sir."

Worme carefully emphasized the accuracy of Jarvis's note
taking. That was critical because now he was denying what he had
already told investigators twice, namely that Jason Roy had told
him during his November 1990 interview that he had seen Neil
in the cruiser. Roy's brief handwritten statement contained no
reference to Neil in a police car, and Jarvis himself had no such
notation in either his notes or reports made at the time.

"But you're not asking us to believe that in fifty-five minutes the only thing that was discussed is what's recorded in that
page and a half?"

"That is the information that I was provided by, or given by,
Mr. Roy," Jarvis replied. And he held to his story, despite the fact
that his own interview with Warner and Lyons had lasted about
and the same length of time as Roy's but yielded a transcript that
ran fifteen pages.

Worme moved on. Jarvis remembered Stella and Erica visiting him two or three times. Although they testified that they
had gone to get Neil's clothes, Jarvis now claimed he could not
remember the reason for their visits.

"You have no independent recollection of that?"

"No, sir."

"And you made no notes of that?"

"No, sir."

Worme kept pushing Jarvis on his note taking. He turned to the reference in Jarvis's notebook about Hartwig and Senger being sent to Snowberry Downs to look for Neil. Jarvis had already testified about going to Central Records to look up the dispatch cards for the night of November 24, 1990, which had resulted in his learning which officers had answered the call. But he never could definitively say what or who had triggered his search.

"And you were told at that point in time, from the records that were maintained by the police service, that it was Officers Hartwig and Senger that attended at about four minutes before midnight."

"Yes, sir."

"And that they had cleared at about seventeen minutes past midnight."

"Yes, sir."

"Okay. Now, you told us that you had asked them for a report?"

"That is the best of my recollection, yes, sir."

"You have no notation of having asked them for a report in your notes."

"No, I don't."

"And there was no notation of having asked them for a report in any of the reports that you would have filed and prepared under P-61?" said Worme, referring again to Jarvis's investigation file.

"I don't believe there is one in there, sir."

By this time, the table reserved for Neil's family and friends was in fine form. They were enjoying watching Jarvis stumble. They whispered and chuckled loudly enough that Aaron Fox and Drew Plaxton glowered at them severely.

"You go, Don," said Erica under her breath. "After what they did to Jason on the stand, let him have it."

Worme moved forward a few pages in his folder of notes. He had no intention of letting up.

"And, without a notation, you have no independent recollection."

"Independent recollection of?"

"How you contacted them?"

"That's correct, sir."

"You'll agree, though," Worme pressed, "that that's a pretty important point, is it not? Not only in retrospect but indeed at the time, that would be a fairly important part of the police work you were obliged to do?"

"You could call it that, sir, yes."

And yet, Worme pointed out, Jarvis had told Warner, Lyons and Martell that he had been satisfied with whatever Hartwig and Senger had told him.

"And you have no indication anywhere in the reports that you've created, P-61 or in your notes, as to what response, if any, you received from these two individuals."

"No, I don't, sir."

"And you'll agree with me that that's pretty important information?"

"Yes, sir."

"Do you have an explanation why there's no indication of that?"

"No, I don't, sir, other than this is a partial report."

"Do you have any recollection of ever seeing a response from officers Senger or Hartwig?"

"No, I don't, sir."

"Okay. If you had received such a report, do you think you might remember it today?'

"Yes, possibly."

In the stories, once the Cree hunter had funnelled the buffalo into the chute, up the ramp and into the pound, the hunters shot the animals with arrows as they milled around in a clockwise direction. Then a few daring young hunters would jump into the pound and pluck the arrows from the sides of the dying beasts. Each arrow they retrieved then belonged to them.

The retired officer reacted defensively to Worme's questions about why he'd concluded the file so soon, on December 5. Jarvis said he had spoken to the pathologist, who had indicated there were "no signs of violence."

"Just on your comment that there was no sign of violence," Worme challenged, "you're aware that we've had evidence before this inquiry that that is not at all what was reported to you, but rather that there was no trauma sufficient to cause death?"

"'Trauma' would have been my choice of word, sir, in the report," said Jarvis, "but my indication when I spoke with Dr. Adolph, and the indication given by him, that the only injury was a minor . . . and I repeat, it was described as a minor abrasion to the nose."

"But you see what I'm getting at?" said Worme, doing his best to remain patient. "I mean there's a difference between 'no trauma sufficient to cause death' and 'no trauma whatsoever,' which I think is what your notes indicate?"

"That would be my interpretation of how I wrote my notes out, sir. My choice of words."

"So you admit that you didn't record what it was that was told to you; rather, you put your own interpretation on that?"

"I believe I had it earlier in the report, sir, that it was a minor abrasion."

Seeing that Jarvis was doing his best to avoid answering the question, the commissioner interjected. The issue was the difference between what Jarvis had entered in his report, "no trauma," and Dr. Adolph's actual pronouncement, that the trauma was not the cause of death.

Jarvis had always maintained that the file on the Stonechild death could be reopened if new information came forward. So Worme turned to Jarvis's telling Morton he could destroy the clothing in 1993. It would be pretty tough to continue with the investigation once the exhibits were destroyed, Worme suggested. "And one of the first things that you told us today, sir, is that the death of this boy was in a location that could not be explained?"

"Right."

"It was an inexplicable death, in your own mind?"

"Yes."

"And not withstanding that, you give the go-ahead for the exhibits to be destroyed."

"There had been no other information come forward, sir, to suggest any further investigation on the file, to my knowledge," said Jarvis.

"And while I appreciate no information came forward, nor did you do any actual investigation to seek out that information; that's true isn't it, Mr. Jarvis?"

"I don't know, sir. I was—I was not—"

"Well, you were there," Worme rebuked him. "You must know whether you did further investigation or not."

"Let him answer the question," Jarvis's lawyer, Ken Stevenson, shouted.

"I wasn't in Morality at the time, sir," said Jarvis.

A little over an hour after beginning his cross-examination, Worme concluded, sarcasm lacing his voice.

"Okay. And so the buck stops where, Mr. Jarvis?"

"I don't know, sir."

— — —

That night Stella had dinner in the Sheraton restaurant with Erica, Jake and his girlfriend, Dawn. Her passing glance at a nearby table turned into a stare: Jarvis was eating with a woman who looked as if she might be his daughter. Stella didn't have the energy to find a new restaurant, but she wished they were elsewhere.

"What do you think he's on?" said Erica. "He just looks too frickin' happy to my eyes. Do you see that weird grin on his face?"

Stella chuckled at her daughter's irreverence.

"Jarvis," said Stella, shaking her head. "He didn't have anything to say to me all these years. All of a sudden today he comes up to me."

"He came up to you?" said Erica, staring at Jarvis, who seemed unaware that the Stonechild family was taking turns glaring at him.

"Yeah, he comes up to me, smiling, just like he was on something."

They all leaned in to hear.

"'Hi, Stella, how are you?' he said, just like he knew me."

Erica flicked her long hair in disgust.

"Knew you? The gall of the guy!"

Stella's determination had never been about bitterness or casting blame. But sitting there all day listening and watching the stiff, grey-haired man answer questions with that strange smile rarely leaving his face had been unnerving. Several times Jarvis had repeated how he had moved on from being a police officer, how he did not remember the articles published about Neil's case. It was as though he had lived the past thirteen years in another time and space, not hers, never troubled by all the questions she'd refused to let go of, questions he could have helped answer.

Stella's suspicions around Jarvis always had to do with Neil's clothes. "Why did Jarvis tell the police to get rid of Neil's clothes? Why did he do that? He knew we wanted them, especially the jacket," she asked.

Stella stabbed at her food without much interest. The man had destroyed a valuable opportunity for investigators to harvest forensic evidence.

"Why not pack them up and give them to us? Instead they threw them in the garbage. That always bothered me about him."

"He's coming over here," Erica said, seeing Jarvis stand up.

Back straight, eyes forward, Jarvis went by the Stonechilds without the slightest sign of recognition.

"Trip him for me, will you?" Stella joked as he passed. She couldn't help herself.

In an instant he was gone.

SHADOW GAMES

ON WEDNESDAY, JANUARY 7, GARY PRATT FINALLY took the stand.

Joel Hesje led Gary through a brief description of the gun incident of August 1990. Pratt said he had been released from remand in October 1990 after the charges resulting from the incident were dropped, in part because other witnesses, including Neil, had never testified.

"Okay, were you ever in a physical altercation with Neil Stonechild?"

"No."

"Do you know in November of 1990 the whereabouts of your brother Danny?"

"I do believe he was in the federal penitentiary."

"Did you ever transport Neil Stonechild to the north industrial area?"

"No." Pratt also answered that he did not own a vehicle in 1990.

"Mr. Pratt, were you in any way involved in the death of Neil Stonechild?

"No, I wasn't."

"Now, you were contacted by the RCMP, is that correct?"

"Yes, I was."

"And do you remember who that was?

"Corporal Jack Warner."

"And did he indicate that he wanted to speak to you about the death of Neil Stonechild?

"Yes."

"And were you prepared to meet with him, and did you cooperate in dealing with Mr. Warner—Constable Warner?"

"Yeah, I did everything they asked me. I took a polygraph test, I passed. Done deal."

There it was, on the public record, the word every lawyer in the room had been ordered to avoid. After waiting months to testify, and in the most straightforward manner, Pratt had let the secret out and there was nothing anyone in the room could do about it.

It was difficult for any lawyer to match the impact of that moment, but it didn't stop Drew Plaxton from vigorously cross-examining Pratt the next day. He spent considerable time exploring the details of the fight over the guns. Pratt reiterated that Neil had come out of the bedroom and had had nothing to do with the fight with Eddie Rushton.

Pratt also acknowledged he was aware of a booze can operating around 46th Street in the north industrial area.

"And, okay, you'd been there. Had you ever been up there with Neil?" asked Plaxton.

"No."

"Do you know if Neil knew about this place?"

"Not to my knowledge."

"How about his brother Marcel?"

"Not to my knowledge."

Fox went over the same ground again during his cross-examination, trying to establish whether Neil had possibly shown up to testify against Pratt. Pratt insisted he had never seen Neil.

Mark Brayford was fed up with the suggestive language Fox and Plaxton had used during their cross-examinations as they rooted around for any reason Gary might have had to hurt Neil. So he succinctly laid the innuendo to rest.

"Mr. Pratt, I'll be quite brief. I just want to focus my questions in two areas. The first area is the suggestion that you might have had some motive to kill Neil Stonechild. To very briefly recap the evidence in relation to the incident at Eddie Rushton's house, the person that threatened you there was Eddie Rushton, not Neil Stonechild, correct?

"Correct."

"And when you in fact were charged, you were charged as follows: 'That you did steal monies and jewellery from Eddie Rushton, and immediately before did beat Eddie Rushton and did thereby commit robbery'?"

"Correct."

"And when you were ultimately discharged from that charge by the proceedings being stayed, did you consider that Neil Stonechild had hurt you or helped you?"

"Helped me," said Pratt, referring to Neil's not testifying.

"So at the point at which you were released, in that month preceding his death, how would you have characterized your friendship at that point?"

"Hadn't changed."

Brayford ended his brief questions by repeating the central questions.

"And did you ever hear of anybody, as part of street justice, simply being driven to another part of the city and dropped off?"

"No."

"Just in conclusion then, did you have anything to do with the death of Neil Stonechild?"

"No, I did not."

— — —

The highest-ranking active SPS officer called to testify at the inquiry took the stand on the afternoon of January 8, 2004.

Deputy Chief Daniel Leonard Wiks had joined the SPS in 1972, and had served as administrative deputy to three consecutive chiefs. In 2000, he was appointed as the administration liaison between the SPS and the RCMP. Later, he coordinated the SPS links to the Stonechild inquiry.

The next morning, Wiks's testimony elaborated at painstaking length on the operational history of the force. His lawyer, Barry Rossman, prompted him through lengthy explanations of dreary administrative matters, things like the ratio of officers on staff to Saskatoon's population. By mid-afternoon Wright was urging Rossman to move it along.

Wiks began detailing for his lawyer the activities of the so-called "Issue Team," a group Chief Sabo had asked him to establish to prepare for the inquiry. In Wiks's telling, the group seemed benign. Composed of several members of the SPS, including a representative from the police association, it began its work around July 2, 2003. Wiks said the group was assembled to discuss things like security for the inquiry venues and how to share information with the media and the rank and file. They also set up a public hotline.

Wiks was well prepared to lead the Issue Team. He had been briefed on the RCMP evidence years before the inquiry had been called, not just upon the arrival of its disclosure material. From his numerous meetings with Darrell McFadyen, he knew that the RCMP had long considered Senger and Hartwig suspects, and that they had tapped both men's phones. Wiks himself had appointed Murray Zoorkan and a colleague to review the wiretap transcripts. He had been briefed before Senger's RCMP polygraph test and knew the full content of the investigation file long before the justice department had seen it. He'd even met with Ken MacKay from the Saskatchewan department of justice in Regina to review whether there existed reasonable grounds to believe Hartwig and Senger had committed a criminal offence.

Rossman led Wiks through statements he'd made to the press in May 2003. Wiks had spoken to James Parker, a reporter from the Saskatoon *Star Phoenix,* and said there was no reason to suspend Hartwig and Senger while the RCMP conducted their inquiry. Parker's article quoted him: "The only reason we would suspend someone is if we had some indication that there was some wrongdoing. We had no indication of that whatsoever. And we still don't."

Perhaps still dozy from Wiks's lecture on the administrative intricacies of the SPS, the commissioner had not yet asked the obvious: How could Wiks have said this knowing what he did about the RCMP evidence at the time?

Instead, the commissioner's alarm bells were ringing over Wiks's Issue Team. Wiks said that the team had discussed Gary Robertson's photos showing handcuffs superimposed over Neil's nose. Unhappy with the conclusions of the RCMP's expert, they had contacted an anthropologist at the University of Saskatchewan, the FBI attaché in Ottawa and a medical examiner from Minnesota to help them out. The RCMP and commission counsel Joel Hesje, he claimed, were aware of what the SPS was doing. At this, Wright interrupted Rossman. He was clearly perturbed.

"Excuse me, Mr. Rossman. I'm not sure I understand this, Deputy. I understood you to say that the Saskatoon Police Service left the entire investigation in this matter to the RCMP. Well, with respect, it seems to me, in light of what you said a few minutes ago, that you had assumed the function of investigating also and gathering evidence from other sources that you thought had a bearing on the question of the handcuff evidence. Am I missing something here? How did that happen?"

Wiks tried to deflect the commissioner's concern. If they had come up with anything, he assured Wright, they would have forwarded it to the RCMP immediately. But Wright did not let go so easily.

"If you had doubts about it, why wouldn't you have simply got hold of McFadyen, or somebody, and said, 'Look, as a peace officer, I have trouble with this version of what happened for these reasons. I think that you people should look at this again. And we've been told that there are experts available to assess this, so to be fair about it, we think that you people should have another look at this, or follow this up.' What frankly is worrisome to me is, it seems to me, with respect, that you, on behalf of the Saskatoon Police Service, started into your own investigation because you were unhappy about Robertson's opinion. And I'm not saying Robertson was right, not for a moment, but I find that, frankly, puzzling."

The commissioner dropped the matter for now, and the inquiry adjourned again, until March. Justice Wright was not charged, after all, with the task of investigating the SPS.

But come March 8, Si Halyk was on his feet before Rossman could get back underway with Wiks, bringing something urgent to the court's attention.

Halyk had been forced to apologize much earlier in the inquiry when he had suggested the SPS were engaged in a "shadow" investigation. There was "no crow like fresh crow," another lawyer had quipped at Halyk's expense. Now Halyk relished the turnabout Wiks had inadvertently provided. Call it a shadow investigation, parallel investigation, investigation of the investigators, the deputy chief himself had made cross-examination on the subject possible.

With dramatic flair, Halyk attacked the secrecy of the Issue Team, showing the room a piece of paper that had been almost entirely blacked out. It was a page from the team's meeting minutes, which had recently come to all the lawyers as disclosure material. Was it satisfactory, Halyk challenged, given how the police had handled things, that they should get to judge for themselves what should or should not be shared with the commission?

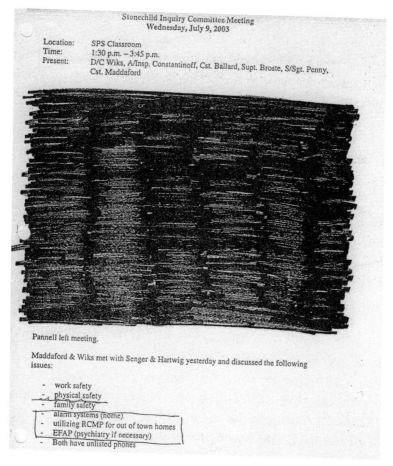

Pannell left meeting.

Maddaford & Wiks met with Senger & Hartwig yesterday and discussed the following issues:

- work safety
- physical safety
- family safety
- alarm systems (home)
- utilizing RCMP for out of town homes
- EFAP (psychiatry if necessary)
- Both have unlisted phones

One of many heavily edited pages from the SPS Issue Team meeting minutes.

There had never been anything secret about the Issue Team, Rossman replied, and in large part the blacked-out text included phone numbers, maps of where Hartwig and Senger lived, where their children went to school and where their wives worked. The commissioner took Halyk's subsequent suggestion and agreed to study the documents and determine personally what should be allowed.

— — —

At Rossman's prompting, Wiks continued in great detail about new directives put in place during the lead-up to the inquiry, everything from how to respond to sudden deaths to how notebooks should be maintained. But one thing caught Stella's attention.

"With respect to 1990," said Wiks, "the property should have properly been seized, tagged, put in our exhibit control, and at the end of the investigation that property should have been returned to somebody who had—who it could properly be turned back to. And, quite frankly, that policy hasn't changed much from then to today. If at some point in time property is seized, today the property is turned back after it's done or has no investigative purpose, it's turned back to the people who they rightly belong to."

Hearing Wiks acknowledge that Neil's clothing should have been returned to his mother was some comfort.

Halyk had to wait until late afternoon for his cross-examination, but when he got his chance he wasted no time attacking. Referring to the minutes, he questioned the approach of the Issue Team in its very first meeting on July 2, 2003.

"The first thing I want to ask you, in terms of the issues, why was it necessary to know who Neil Stonechild's parents and siblings were, and why was it necessary that it be noted that he went to school at Bedford but dropped out? Why was it necessary to know why Constable Louttit kept the file? Why was the Issue Team concerned about these things, instead of being grateful that the file was in existence, for example? Just why did you care?"

Because he thought he might be asked about it at the inquiry, Wiks said.

"Okay. So—but let me just follow you here. You thought that you needed to know the information as to who Neil Stonechild's parents and siblings were for the purpose of giving evidence today?"

"I thought I needed to know all of the information I possibly could, yes."

"You thought that somebody seriously would ask you why Neil Stonechild dropped out of Bedford School, is that what I'm understanding?"

Jay Watson, Senger's lawyer, objected, demanding to know how this was relevant to the inquiry, but Justice Wright was clearly interested in Halyk's direction.

"Well, before you leave the microphone, Mr. Watson," Wright said, "the impression I have is that Mr. Halyk is saying, I believe, that the inclusion of this information suggests there was another agenda, not just to gather information in anticipation of testifying. And that that agenda was a good deal more worrisome, if I could put it that way."

Halyk did not mince his words.

"I think by the time we look through this whole thing we'll see a pattern here of the Saskatoon Police Service trying—it appears that one can submit—to discredit some of the investigation conducted by the RCMP, discredit some of the victims involved. And whatever means they used should be disclosed."

Halyk kept working through the minutes, picking at sections to build his case that the SPS had actually been mounting a campaign to defend their own officers.

"'Hartwig and Senger dropped Stonechild off at north end, records show they were dispatched and attended another call within about ten minutes, therefore no time to drive to north end.' Excuse me," asked Halyk, "when did you decide that, that there was no time to drive to the north end?"

"I knew that from—from where the incident happened at Snowberry Downs to the—to where the body of Neil Stonechild was found, there's no possible way to drive there in ten minutes and return to another call."

"You came to this conclusion... First of all, did you run any tests at this point in time, before you made this statement, that they had no time to drive to the north end?"

"No."

"And did you know the exact distance from point to point before you made this statement, that there was no time to drive to the north end?"

"No, but I've driven from that area—from the area of Snowberry Downs to the north end—quite often, actually."

"And you've timed it quite often?"

"No, I haven't."

"And is this what you call investigation or police work for a senior police officer, that kind of conclusion based on that kind of information?"

Halyk then attacked the credibility of that ten-minute gap itself.

"And if you were the police officers who had just dropped off a male in the north abandoned location and you get another dispatch, do you expect that those police officers are going to say, excuse me, we need a little more time to finish this drop off? Do you?"

"No."

"No. So what significance is the time?"

"It was significant to me at the time."

"But what you're doing, you talk about, Deputy—tunnel vision. You know what tunnel vision is?"

"Yes, I've heard the expression before."

"And do you realize what that means in this setting? It means that you had a preconceived notion when you were going through this information with your committee as to what the result should be and everything should fit the result you desire. That's what you were doing. Weren't you?"

"No, I wasn't."

"You think that this is good, objective statements that you

made in this committee report?" Halyk asked, referring to the minutes.

"I don't believe they were objective, no."

Halyk continued through the minutes to establish that the Issue Team had also sought out ways to discredit Jason Roy's testimony.

"Because the next question is, 'What is Roy's motivation? Persistent in reporting to several people.' So in other words, folks, this guy's got to have some bad motive here, let's go find it so we can discredit him; isn't that what that's saying?"

"I can't remember what the context of that question was in my mind at the time."

"But it could be read that way, couldn't it?"

"Yes, it could."

Halyk pressed on. Finding a way to protect Hartwig and Senger seemed clearly to be one of the main concerns of the Issue Team's discussions, he put to Wiks.

"Again, as I alluded to yesterday, as an employer we had a responsibility to look after our employees' concerns as best we could. That's what that's alluding to," Wiks said, trying his best to hold the team's line.

The FSIN's attorney and the deputy chief battled over other issues, including the coordination of the SPS's and the Saskatoon Police Association's media strategy through the Issue Team. But Halyk had only been building toward his finishing move. The lawyer began by quoting from Jack Warner's report, which Wiks held a copy of in his hands.

"'I believe Neil Stonechild was in the custody of Senger and Hartwig on the evening of November 24, morning of November 25. Neil Stonechild died on the morning of the 25th. Indicates that RCMP believe Hartwig and Senger had involvement in his death.'" Halyk looked up from the page. "So is not the question, sir, suspension? How can you keep people working on a police force who may have been involved in a wrongful killing?"

Plaxton and Fox jumped up to object that Halyk was straying into areas beyond the scope of the inquiry. Justice Wright said he understood what Halyk was probing for, but suggested he ask more focused questions. The commissioner added dryly, "All good cross-examiners tend to overstate their case, I suppose both of you know that. And that's not a criticism."

"I've only witnessed it, Mr. Commissioner," responded Fox, sportingly setting up the commissioner to deliver his punchline.

"Which means you've never looked in a mirror, is that what you're saying, Mr. Fox?" said Wright, much to the amusement of the room.

Reading from the minutes of the Issue Team meetings, Halyk revealed that the force had discussed offering Hartwig and Senger paid leave while telling the media they were still working in Community Services. The police, he was trying to establish, were prepared to lie.

— — —

As the day wrapped up, Halyk asked what in the evidence compiled against Hartwig and Senger troubled Wiks the most. Wiks acknowledged two concerns. The first was Jason Roy's account that he had seen Neil handcuffed and bleeding in a police cruiser. Second was Gary Robertson's finding that the marks on Neil's wrists were caused by handcuffs.

Halyk suggested there might be a third, a piece of RCMP investigative evidence related directly to Senger. Senger's lawyer jumped up and objected.

Stella smiled as she watched the lawyers' argument nosedive into full-fledged legal mumbo-jumbo meant to avoid mentioning the very word Halyk was pushing Wiks to say on the record. The commissioner issued a temporary publication ban on the discussion that ensued. Once again there was an elephant in the room. And not a single person there didn't know that it was all about Senger's polygraph test.

After a day's break in proceedings, Wiks continued his testimony on March 11. Halyk came back to the *Star Phoenix* article written by James Parker in May 2003, which had already been entered as exhibit P-140. Halyk began reading aloud from the article.

"'Two Saskatoon police officers'—I'm reading—'considered suspects in the 1990 freezing death of Neil Stonechild remained on the job while the RCMP conducted an investigation into the case. Acting City Police Chief Dan Wiks said Thursday there was no reason to suspend or reassign the officers during the 2000 investigation which was forwarded to the provincial Justice Department and resulted in no criminal charges. Constable Larry Hartwig and Constable Bradley Raymond Senger will be key witnesses at a public inquiry into Stonechild's death to be held this fall. "They remained on their regular duties," said Wiks, "the only reason we would suspend somebody is if we had some indication that there was some wrongdoing. We had no indication of that whatsoever and we still don't."'"

Plaxton tried to object, but the commissioner allowed Halyk to continue.

"Now, the first question, Deputy, is, is that an accurate quote of what you said at the time?"

"That's an accurate quote of what I said, yes."

Halyk read aloud again, this time from the minutes of a meeting held by the Issue Team on July 22, 2003.

"'Can we be respectful of the process but not respectful of the media, e.g., if the media distorts the truth, don't get into an argument with them, it's their job to cause alarm, and a lot of what is stated the general public are able to see through this. The media's job is to sell newspapers; people trust less what they see and hear in the media.'"

Wiks accepted the veracity of the minutes.

"Did it ever occur to you, Deputy," continued Halyk, "that it's possible that the public get misinformation through the media because the media has been misled by responsible organizations providing the wrong information? Do you think that's a possibility?"

"And who are you speaking of?"

"I'm speaking of the police department in this particular example."

Erica watched from her usual seat at the back of the room, looking on with fascination as Halyk's cross-examination tied Wiks up in knots. After days of listening to mind-numbing talk of proper procedure and policy, and precise detail on what he knew about the RCMP investigation, she was happy to see Wiks on the hot seat.

One of her friends, a local activist, was growing increasingly agitated listening to Wiks's testimony. After having been stabbed in 1998, John Melenchuk felt too little had been done to investigate the crime. Since then, he had become a thorn in the side of police, organizing over the years several protests against incidents of police injustice. He had spent many days at the inquiry, mostly sitting with Erica and Jake.

"You agree with me now that—let's start with the kindest term possible—that what you said to the press in May of 2003 to Mr. Parker was an absolute untruth and misstatement?"

"I—it was misstated, yes."

The commissioner then directly addressed Wiks, apologizing to Halyk for the interruption.

"What he's asking you very specifically—"

"Yes."

"—is whether your statement to Mr. Parker was accurate? Let's begin with that, was that an accurate statement?"

"No, it wasn't."

Melenchuk was fuming. Whatever legal euphemism Halyk

was forced to use, in Melenchuk's world it was simple. He had just listened to the most senior police officer at the inquiry caught out in what he thought seemed a pretty obvious lie. Throughout the events that followed the freezing deaths—the protests, unsatisfactory inquests and the media attention—Melenchuk had papered the city with posters complaining about the police. This time, he decided, he'd complain about Wiks directly.

Later that day, the inquiry hit one of its lowest points. A public exhibit was entered showing a picture of a ruined, soiled running shoe accompanied by an envelope with the handwritten words "Neil Stonechild's shoe?" On October 16, shortly after the inquiry had begun, someone had left the running shoe and the note on a desk in one of the interview rooms of the SPS station.

Someone was playing a callous, cruel joke since the shoe was not Neil's, Wiks admitted. Wiks said the lab had been contacted, but he was not sure whether an analysis was being done on the handwriting. The Identification Section had done some analysis, including checking for fingerprints on the envelope and the shoe. Wiks was at a loss to explain how the items had come to be in the interview room. He became defensive when Don Worme suggested that the rooms were accessible only to members of the SPS.

"And to the people who are—who are actually in the rooms when they're being interviewed," Wiks replied.

But in such cases individuals are always accompanied by a police officer, Worme remarked. Wiks, however, was unwilling to admit the likelihood that one of his officers had planted the shoe and the note.

"They're accompanied to the rooms but on occasion, many occasions, people are left in the rooms by themselves," Wiks said, grasping at straws.

— — —

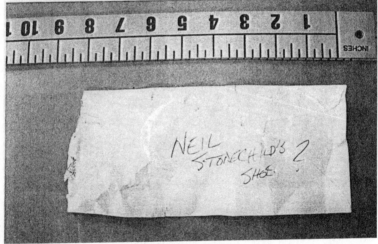

That night, John Melenchuk wrote a letter asking the SPS to formally charge Deputy Chief Dan Wiks with perjury and obstruction of justice.

The next day, he told Jason Roy about the letter. He was still trying to get up the nerve to hand-deliver it to the station. Roy agreed to go with him for moral support. The two men walked the short distance from the Sheraton to the police station and straight to the front desk. By coincidence, they handed the letter to Bruce Eholt, the officer who three years before had first heard from Darrell Night about his experience of being dumped near the power station. The two men walked out, satisfied they had spoken truth to power, no matter what happened.

Wiks had told a reporter that Hartwig and Senger were not suspects in Neil Stonechild's death when he clearly knew the opposite was true. Within a few days of Wiks telling the inquiry under oath that he had misled the public, Chief Russell Sabo had little choice but to put his deputy on administrative leave.

"I DO NOT RECALL"

NO SOONER HAD LARRY HARTWIG WALKED
briskly to his seat at the witness table under the sombre
yellow lights than Stella knew his heart was closed. He seemed
too sure of himself. It was now the fortieth day of the inquiry,
March 15, 2004.

The night Neil died, Hartwig explained when prompted
by Aaron Fox, he was working Saskatoon's west end. His regular
partner, Ken Munson, had been seconded to a special project,
so, some time after ten o'clock, he partnered up with rookie
Constable Brad Senger in Car 38.

Answering his lawyer's questions about that shift, Hartwig
said he had only two independent recollections, unprompted
by referring to things such as notebooks or computer records.
The first would have been hard to forget. He and Senger had
gone to a house at the end of their shift early on November 25
where they'd had to tell a woman that her husband had killed
her two young sons and then shot himself in a failed suicide
attempt. He also remembered a young man named Jamie being
punched in the face on the dance floor of Confetti's nightclub—hardly a remarkable event for Saskatoon on a Saturday
night.

Referring to his notes, Hartwig acknowledged being dispatched to handle an intoxicated person on the 3300 block of
33rd street at 11:51 p.m. He had written at the time, "Neil

Stonechild causing problems," followed by "GOA," or gone on arrival.

CPIC records showed that he and Senger were dispatched to Snowberry Downs at 11:51, and that they'd pressed the "at scene" button on the mobile data terminal of Car 38 at 11:56. Also at 11:56 they'd run a CPIC query on Tracy Horse and Tracy Lee Horse, whose birthday was indicated as 74–4–19. At 11:59 they'd queried "Neil Stonechild," entering no date of birth but an age, eighteen. Both CPICs were entered by Senger, badge number 80.

Fox referred Hartwig to a notation at the bottom of page eleven of his notes for the night of November 24, 1990, where the officer had written the name Tracy Horse, and added the middle name Lee. Hartwig said he no idea who Tracy Lee Horse was prior to the RCMP investigation in 2000, and that he assumed the notebook entry showed that he had done a "person check" on that individual. As for the missing date of birth on the Stonechild CPIC, Hartwig said that meant the boy had not been there when the computer query was made. Otherwise, he and Senger would have asked him for it when they'd searched the computer database for any warrants.

Hartwig said he would also have recognized Neil Stonechild. His only prior independent memory of dealing with the teenager had been of a street check in 1989, but records and notes showed he had taken a statement from Neil about the August 1990 Rushton gun robbery and issued him a traffic ticket for driving without a licence only a month before he died.

The CPIC records showed a query for Bruce Genaille at 12:04, entered by badge number 332, Larry Hartwig. The entry included a date of birth, 67–04–21. At 12:17 "clear" had been punched into the MDT. One minute later they were dispatched to deal with a suspicious person a couple of blocks away on O'Regan Crescent. The records show that it took them six minutes to get to the scene, which they'd cleared at twenty-seven minutes after midnight, and had indicated that the complaint was unfounded. Hartwig couldn't remember anyone he'd talked to.

At twelve-thirty, the two officers CPICed the man who had made the complaint against Neil, Trent Ewart. Strangely, Hartwig suggested they had done this so long after being at the scene for "intelligence applications," cop talk for checking out Ewart and seeing who his associates might be. The entry was significant for another reason: it showed that the timing of CPIC entries could not prove whether the subject was present or not.

Fox pointed out that the CPIC on Neil would have shown a warrant for being unlawfully at large from Pat Pickard's group home. Hartwig agreed, saying he would have arrested the boy and brought him to jail.

Stella stared directly at Hartwig as Fox continued.

"Constable Hartwig, did you ever have Neil Stonechild in your car on that night, handcuffed, bleeding, screaming at Jason Roy, 'They're going to kill me'?"

"Absolutely not."

Fox went back to the CPIC records. After the Ewart check at twelve-thirty, the next relevant entry was at 1:39, the initial dispatch to a property-damage complaint at 111 Wedge Road, right next to Snowberry Downs.

In the hour and nine minutes between those two entries there was nothing to show what Hartwig and Senger had been doing—no dispatches, no notebook entries, no CPIC queries.

Fox asked his client if he had made any connection between his search for Neil at Snowberry Downs and the boy's body being found in the north end only a few days later.

"No, I did not," Hartwig replied. It seemed curious for Hartwig to have had dealings with the Stonechild family and to claim to know Neil well enough to be able to recognize him, but not to make such a straightforward connection. Fox didn't ask.

Aside from notions and stray facts picked up through locker-room chat and the media, including the theory that Neil had been trying to turn himself in to the Saskatoon Correctional Centre, Hartwig denied categorically having any personal knowledge related to Neil's death.

He told Fox he did not recall Jarvis talking to him sometime in 1990 or 1991 about the dispatch to Snowberry Downs.

"No, I do not," Hartwig also replied when Fox wanted to know if he recalled anyone investigating Neil's death who had approached him and asked him what had happened that night when he went looking for Neil.

"Is it possible someone spoke to you?" asked Fox.

"Yes."

Hartwig also drew a blank went it came to whether or not he had later received a memo about the dispatch to Snowberry Downs. He could not say one way or the other.

He did recall having had a conversation with Constable Ernie Louttit, whom he described as a friend, about the case back in 1991, when theories about Gary Pratt's possible involvement were swirling around. He remembered Louttit being upset about the investigation.

"I left it with Ernie," said Hartwig, explaining why he did nothing to follow up on the conversation, "as Ernie is a very good police officer and he would do the right thing."

Fox raised the series of interviews conducted by the RCMP's Ken Lyons with Hartwig in May of 2000. When Lyons had begun talking about the Rodney Naistus and Lawrence Wegner investigations, Hartwig had told Lyons that he knew nothing about those cases beyond rumours. Hartwig had mentioned Neil's name in the conversation without being asked. Now on the stand he explained to Fox that he did not know either Naistus or Wegner, and brought up Neil's name because he knew him. Hartwig had stated that in that first interview with Lyons he didn't even remember being on shift on the night of November 24, 1990.

Hartwig grew visibly angry when Fox turned to the May 18, 2000, RCMP interview, when Hartwig had realized he was a suspect. His treatment by the RCMP during the interview still infuriated him.

"Quite frankly, sir, I felt like I was raped."

— — —

Don Worme stepped forward to begin his cross-examination. He and Jack Warner had both noticed that Hartwig was quick to anger when anyone challenged him. As Warner put it, Hartwig's head and mouth were not in sync. So, Worme posed his questions like a matador waving his cape in Hartwig's face.

Worme directed his questioning to Hartwig's May 7, 2000, interview with Ken Lyons. Before going far though, he backtracked, needling Hartwig some more, this time prodding his hostility towards Lyons. Worme gathered that Hartwig had some problem referring to Ken Lyons by his official title, Sergeant, which it had been at the time of the investigation.

"Actually, Staff Sergeant Lyons," Hartwig corrected him.

Worme said Hartwig had used the title only once in answering Fox's questions, and he wondered aloud what that meant. Hartwig simmered.

"Sure, I can call him that if that would make you happy."

"Well, I don't care if I'm happy or not."

"Okay."

The commissioner signalled he'd had enough.

"I think it's clear, Mr. Worme, there's some animus here. I get the point."

When Worme questioned him about his earlier testimony, Hartwig admitted that his description of feeling as if he had been "raped" could have offended some women who had experienced that "detestable violence." Still, Hartwig refused to change his description.

Before the inquiry adjourned for the day, Worme focused again, more closely this time, on the interview with Lyons on May 7. Hartwig had been the one to first mention the name Stonechild when Lyons had begun talking about Naistus and Wegner, hadn't he? Worme asked.

"I don't know, you'll have to ask him," Hartwig snapped.

The commissioner stepped in. He asked Hartwig to confirm that he was the one who had introduced Neil's name in the conversation. He agreed that he had. Moments later though, Worme suggested Hartwig had used the words, "Why don't we talk about Stonechild, that's the one I know about?"

"No," Hartwig said categorically.

"All right. So is he lying to us when he records that and attributes that to you?"

"I don't know, maybe you should ask him that," Hartwig said again.

And according to Lyons's summary of the interview, Hartwig had called Neil "a nice kid but real bad." He now denied saying those specific words.

Worme pressed on. He wanted to know about Hartwig's next comment, recorded by Lyons as "All I know is that the guys arrested him in the 3300 block 33rd Street." Hartwig again denied saying that.

"Well, what did you say?"

"Mr. Lyons was asking me to—I was referring to the . . ."

"You mean Staff Sergeant Lyons, I'm sure," interrupted Worme.

"—newspaper." Hartwig caught himself. "Sorry, Staff Sergeant Lyons. I was referring to the newspaper article of February 22, and I did not mention the 3300 block 33rd Street, I mentioned Confed and 33rd."

"Confed and 33rd?"

"Correct."

Barely pausing Worme asked, "Is that the 3300 block of 33rd Street?"

"Yes, it is," Hartwig conceded.

Later in his testimony, Hartwig would say he prided himself on his memory. He'd argued with Worme about minuscule details; he had shown impressive command of precise details from an interview that had happened almost four years earlier. But he still couldn't remember more than a scant few details about the night of Neil's death.

Worme continued to question Hartwig about the rest of what he'd claimed to know about the Stonechild incident back in 2000. He read verbatim from Lyons's summary: "They were going to a call of a suspicious person or a B and E in progress. They found Neil. He was drunk at the time. They arrested him for intoxication. (paused) Then in a questioning voice: 'Why would they have driven him around trying to find out who he was?' Then they found some guy and asked him who he was. Then some guys are saying things like they're going to kill me or they're going to beat me up all the time."

Hartwig claimed the knowledge came from newspaper articles, and that Lyons's summary had mistakenly attributed the recollection directly to him.

Justice Wright was growing increasingly troubled by Hartwig's repeated suggestions that the RCMP had misstated what he had said and that Lyons had characterized his comments incorrectly, or worse.

Like any good lawyer, Aaron Fox stepped in to minimize the damage his client was on the verge of creating. Gesturing with his arms for emphasis, Fox explained that the RCMP report showed that Lyons had reviewed the newspaper article with Hartwig. In any case, his client was not suggesting that Lyons had done anything improper.

Warner was amused. The lawyer looked like someone trying to stuff the shit back into a horse, he thought to himself.

— — —

The next day, as proceedings got underway, Justice Wright warned everyone in the room to avoid interfering with the witnesses. It had been reported to him that during one of the breaks someone had spoken "in an aggressive fashion" to Constable Hartwig.

Worme had already found out from Stella that it was Neil's older brother, Dean, the former U.S. marine, who had approached Hartwig as he was exiting the room. They had exchanged words, but Erica had pulled Dean away before the situation could escalate. She began lecturing her brother about the stupidity of his actions even before Hartwig continued on his way.

From the lectern at the front of the room, for all to hear, Worme assured the commissioner that Stella had nothing to do with what had happened.

At this, the commissioner allowed himself a personal observation about Stella. "Your client strikes me as a respectful, quiet person quite prepared to see the process go forward in an orderly fashion, and I can't imagine for a moment that she would have any knowledge of this or anything to do with it. It never even crossed my mind."

Worme picked up where he'd left off: Hartwig's animosity toward Lyons. Again they jousted over the fact that it was Hartwig who'd first raised Neil's name in conversation with Lyons. Hartwig's explanation was that he simply knew Neil and was aware from newspaper accounts that the boy was part of the RCMP investigation.

Even Wright appeared puzzled by this. He interrupted to ask Hartwig, "What earthly reason would there be for you to mention the name Neil Stonechild in this context?"

"Because I knew the RCMP were investigating the death of Neil Stonechild, and they asked me about people I did not know about. The only person that I knew was Neil Stonechild," Hartwig answered.

"All right," said the commissioner.

Worme attacked Hartwig for saying that his knowledge at the time of the Lyons interview about Neil's having been driven around, or about the name Tracy Lee Horse, had come from the media. These details did not appear in any of the many media reports presented to the inquiry.

He next got Hartwig putting X's on a map showing the possible routes between 33rd and Confederation Drive, and the field near 57th Street where Neil had been found.

"I appreciate your testimony that you've never driven that route," said Worme, "but I can tell you that I have. And although I'm not going to give evidence here, would you agree with me that drive is actually less than six minutes?"

"I'm not certain," said Hartwig. Then, showing how well he knew the area, he recounted in precise detail the stoplights anyone would encounter driving the route.

Throughout the morning, Worme prodded and poked at Hartwig, his tone mocking and incredulous. At one point he focused on Hartwig's notes for the night of November 24. Between an entry for a property check at 11:34 and the dispatch to Snowberry Downs at 11:51 were a couple of untimed notations—"Tracy Horse" with the name "Lee" added after it, along with an address and birthday, and then the name "Neil," which was crossed out and followed by "Genaille Bruce" and an address and birthday.

Hartwig said he had no idea why he'd crossed out Neil's name, but he agreed with Worme's assertion that the placement of the untimed notations between the entry at 11:34 and 11:51 was "pretty curious."

Hartwig seemed to be contradicting himself, Worme suggested, in that he had previously claimed that it was his practice to note things when they happened.

Hartwig denied doing anything different from his usual practice. "Calls in progress are generally written down in the

Aeit Grenaille.
Bruce
118-3308 33rd
67/04/21

2361 10-25
      306-3308 33rd
      Neil Stonechild
      causing problems

      GOA.

0155 10-23,
      III   Wedge Rd

      Someone damaging
      a truck.

notebook after the call is cleared," he stated, adding that that was likely what had happened in this case.

— — —

After going through the Snowberry Downs CPIC queries in detail, Worme returned to Hartwig's having stopped Bruce Genaille. Why, he wanted to know, would Hartwig have mistakenly stopped Bruce Genaille and called him by Neil's name if the officer already knew Neil? Hartwig replied that it was dark and Genaille might have been facing away from the car.

Evidence, including Genaille's own testimony, showed that Senger and Hartwig had stopped him much earlier than the 12:04 a.m. CPIC query, probably between ten and eleven o'clock, well before they were dispatched to Snowberry Downs. When he was stopped, Genaille said, there was no one in the car other than the two officers. He claimed that when he asked why they were looking for Neil they'd replied that they were checking into a disturbance at the 7-Eleven across from Snowberry Downs.

The Trent Ewart CPIC query showed that Hartwig followed a practice of sometimes querying individuals after his encounters with them. In his testimony, though, Hartwig downplayed as "very unlikely" the possibility that he and Senger had contact with Genaille earlier in the evening and had queried his name after the fact.

Earlier, Hartwig had said the CPIC for Neil at 11:59 indicated that the boy hadn't been present, because no birth date had been entered. Worme saw another possibility: Neil had simply refused to give his birth date.

After clearing Snowberry Downs at 12:17, Hartwig and Senger were dispatched at 12:18 to O'Regan Crescent, a few blocks away. They arrived at 12:24, six minutes later. By Hartwig's own admission, the drive should have taken about one minute. He could not account for the difference.

At least once during Hartwig's testimony, Worme became belligerent. He asked Hartwig whether he was in the habit of cleaning his cruiser at the end of a shift or checking it to see if anything, such as a wallet, had been left behind. Hartwig agreed the car would be cleaned or checked as required. Worme pursued the point with vicious sarcasm.

"And I know this probably sounds foolish, but did you find a shoe in your vehicle at the end of your shift?"

"I don't recall ever finding a shoe in my vehicle at the end of my shift," Hartwig replied matter-of-factly.

Worme concluded his cross-examination by saying that Hartwig's characterization of the interview with Lyons troubled him. He had the sense that Hartwig was not unduly concerned about Neil Stonechild's death, and that his indifference resembled that of almost every police officer who had testified. Hartwig denied this assertion, saying he was very much concerned.

"I mean the rightful indignation that I saw yesterday," Worme said, "it seemed to me that the only thing you were concerned about was the alleged rape of Lawrence Hartwig."

— — —

On the second to last day of testimony, Dr. Emma Lew, a forensic pathologist from Dade County, Florida, who had been born in Saskatoon, took the stand. Hesje had conceded to pressure from the SPS to have her testify.

Wiks and others had first heard of Dr. Lew in November 2003, when she had made a presentation at a forensic seminar on child abuse in Saskatoon. Police invited her to the station afterwards to view photo enlargements of Neil's autopsy. Lew had concluded that the marks on Neil's face and wrist were not caused by handcuffs and could have been caused by any number of objects.

The police lawyers were resolutely deferential to everything Lew said on the stand, but she did not fare so well with Halyk and Worme's associate, Greg Curtis, a former school teacher with a biting wit that rivalled Worme's. Both men portrayed her appearance at the inquiry as shabby opportunism on the part of the SPS.

Halyk and Curtis questioned Lew as to whether she was qualified to speak authoritatively about freezing deaths, since her only experience of dealing with a frozen body turned out to have been in Turks and Caicos. Authorities there had put the body of a murdered man in a freezer until she could arrive to examine it.

Lew defended her authority on the subject, declaring in essence that freezing temperatures tend to preserve injuries better than warm ones. That, Curtis retorted, was only common sense, "otherwise we wouldn't have freezers in our kitchens."

Lew claimed to see marks or striations within the cut on Neil's right wrist. She suggested that they were inconsistent with the smooth surface of handcuffs and may have come from the pressure of his clothing, the cuff of a jacket, for example. Neither lawyer could see any such striations. Even Wright, usually poker-faced, seemed perplexed as he looked on.

During Halyk's cross-examination, Lew made the mistake of theorizing that the grass might have caused the cuts on Neil's nose. Halyk immediately got in her face.

"And you see, you've got to understand why there might be some degree of skepticism. You're back in farm country, all right? And there's lots of farm folks out there who've seen lots of grass, lots of hay. Okay?"

"Yes."

"And they've fallen down in the snow lots of times face first and I don't think any of them have ever seen two parallel cuts across the nose. They would think that that was a bit of a joke, with the greatest respect."

Finally, Lew had to admit that she'd never seen injuries like the ones she was looking at caused by grass.

Halyk next convinced Lew to try on a pair of Peerless handcuffs, like those used by Hartwig and Senger, to help determine what might have caused the indentation in Neil's right wrist.

"So," he said taking hold of one handcuff, the other one attached to her wrist, "let me just put it to you this way: if he was in that police car and was resisting, the police will take one cuff off and get him out of the car and take the cuffs off."

"Yes."

"He's resisting going out because he's going to be thrown out in the middle of nowhere."

"Yes."

"And he's pulling back and resisting."

"Yes."

"If they're pulling on the cuff, you might well get the kind of the mark that's shown on the wrist then."

"Yes, that's possible you would get some sort of a mark, yes."

"Yes, and in that location?"

"Yes."

Halyk thanked Dr. Lew and had the cuff taken off her wrist. But he was not finished.

"Now," he continued, "you've got the police officer who's pulling on him, gets him out of the car, then with the other one holding him, takes the cuff off."

"Yes."

"Gets it off his hand."

"Yes."

"And then when it's off his hand it's unlocked," Halyk went on. "The police officer goes like that at Stonechild." He began swinging the one loose cuff while holding the other.

Wright himself interjected to make it clear that Halyk was swinging the cuff as though at the face of Neil Stonechild.

"That would leave possibly the exact marks that you have," Halyk concluded.

Lew did not agree, but Halyk's performance had made its point.

— — —

That night Stella was excited. They were all going to have dinner with Neil's old wrestling coach.

The doorbell rang. Everyone arrived at once. Jake and Erica, Jason and Vanessa, and the guest of honour, Geoff Wright. Wright had brought along his wife, Gail, his daughter and his brother. Even the food was delivered just as they'd arrived. The landlord leaned over his balcony, worried the crowd might mean a party.

Wright's back was so bad that he clutched the banister for support, struggling to pull himself up the two flights of stairs to the apartment. After several operations to repair degenerating discs, a pump strapped under his shirt delivered experimental pain killers to his body at timed intervals.

Any awkwardness at the reunion did not last past the handing out of pizza, chicken wings and pop. Soon everyone was talking at once.

From the moment Wright had heard about Neil's death he had scoffed at the idea of the boy turning himself in to the Saskatoon Correctional Centre. He had worked there himself. He knew the area and figured Neil could only have been dumped there. He felt the police had been covering up their involvement from the beginning. The whole business disgusted him.

One day after the inquiry had been called, he had been flipping TV channels in his living room when it occurred to him that he should do something to commemorate Neil's life, and not just his death, which seemed like the only thing anyone was going to remember about the boy. He began rifling through old boxes of videotapes and then spent months reviewing, minute by minute, hundreds of hours of footage he had shot of the wrestlers he'd coached.

After dinner, he presented Stella with the video and DVD he and Gail had produced of Neil's wrestling career. They'd made it look quite professional, with a grainy cover photo of fourteen-year-old Neil dressed in a wrestling singlet and facing the camera confidently. Before playing it, Wright gave a short speech. He called Neil "a founding champion" of the Wolverine Wrestling Club.

For the next seven minutes, everyone huddled around the TV. In a few frames Neil's thick black hair could barely be seen hidden among the other club members as they rallied just before a tournament. In another shot he simply walked quickly across the mat and was gone. They cheered for him as he leaned into his opponents in his trademark way. They laughed out loud when Erica noticed that he was chewing gum while he wrestled, which was strictly forbidden. They watched him come back on points against the favourite in Moose Jaw. Stella did not know the name of the move, but she watched Neil lift the other boy over his head and throw him down on the mat. And there was the moment when, too euphoric to care, he'd comically tugged the singlet from where it was wedged in his behind while raising his other hand in victory. Stella hadn't felt happier in years. What was it about her boy, she wondered, that, despite his terrible fate, his spirit could still move people?

Wolverine Wrestling
salutes

Neil Stonechild
A Founding Champion

When the video was over they immediately wanted to watch it again. This time Stella let the narration wash over her in soothing waves: "founding champion ... a quick study ... thirty matches ... five gold medals, one silver ... a winning percentage of .900 ... led the Wolverines to the provincial championship ... establishing a Neil Stonechild Award for Wolverine rookie of the year ..."

— — —

The next day, Stella's spirits were still buoyed by the video as Constable Bradley Senger took the stand. It was the last day of testimony. He picked up where Hartwig had left off, replying "I do not recall" to question after question. But he did not share Hartwig's confidence.

Senger had still been on probation on the night of November 24, 1990, barely out of police college. While on the day shift later that week, he was the officer who had taken the call about a body found in the north end.

Like Hartwig, Senger clung to the absence of a birth date in the CPIC records to show that Neil was not present when they'd queried his name. He, too, couldn't explain why they had CPICed Trent Ewart after leaving the scene of his complaint, beyond suggesting it was an afterthought done for "criminal intelligence purposes."

Whether it was a question about contact with Jarvis, looking for Neil, taking the call about the body, or press reports at the time, Senger continued to say he could not recall. Of the night he and Hartwig went looking for Neil, Senger remembered only the incident near the end of the shift when they'd had to tell the woman about the murder of her sons. And, as expected, he flatly denied taking Neil to the remote industrial area and said he did not know who had.

From the moment he'd arrived in the hearing room that morning, Don Worme had steeled himself for the coming confrontation with Senger. He brushed by journalists with whom he usually chatted and radiated his foul mood.

While he waited for his turn to cross-examine Senger, he remembered his visit to the Court of Queen's Bench shortly before the inquiry began. Worme had wanted to see what he had said on the stand as a four-year-old during the trial of Francis Littlechief. He was surprised that they had been able to find the court transcripts in the basement archive. It had been almost forty years. Many were handwritten on thin, nearly transparent onionskin paper. He'd stood at the counter reading his decades-old account of Littlechief striking down his mother, his sister, his brother; hiding under the kitchen table; begging the man not to hit him; a terrified Marleen running out the back door into the alley, abandoning him and Kim; finding the courage to open the front door when everything was finally quiet to go to the neighbours for help.

"Pretty good for a four-year-old," Worme had said to himself.

This was going to be good, too, he thought, focusing on his plan of attack. When he got his chance with Senger, he fought to introduce the transcripts of the RCMP wiretaps from 2000. Worme had to admit to Justice Wright that he was not suggesting there was any incriminating evidence on the tapes. Wright said he would consider the matter over the break. Knowing he was going to lose that argument, Worme, acting helpful, pointed out to the commisioner that in the transcripts "Heartless" was a reference to Hartwig. Senger confirmed the nickname.

Worme then had Senger describe the "screen test," which Hartwig had told Lyons about during his formal interview four years ago. In Senger's description, the driver of a police car hits the brakes and the momentum slams a suspect, unbelted but handcuffed, into the metal barrier or screen between the front and rear seats. While Senger said he had heard of the term, he denied ever having done it himself.

Conscientious, hard-working, diligent: Worme described Senger's character as he ran through the constable's record. "And then on the other hand," he said, suddenly changing direction, "the other side of that is just this other thing, a dishonesty about you, a cheater, legal cheating."

Worme seemed to take everyone by surprise, even Senger's lawyer, Jay Watson. He was referring to Senger's admission, during Sergeant Charles Lerat's polygraph exam a couple of years earlier, that he had once falsified a subject's breathalyzer test, lowering the results of the second test to avoid having to do the third. In other words, he had changed the results and breached his duty out of laziness.

Watson jumped to his feet trying to stop Worme's line of questioning. The information about the breathalyzer was a separate incident and not relevant to the Stonechild case. In the process of objecting, Watson inadvertently put another unpleasant story on the record.

"There's another incident," said Watson. "I'm not sure if he's prepared—my friend is going to talk about it. It refers to an incident at the Canadian Tire when Officer Senger inadvertently left with a rake, thinking it was paid for when it wasn't. If he proposed to go into that, I have the same objection."

Amused, Worme said, "Sounds to me like Mr. Watson wants to give evidence." He added that he was not going to pursue the Canadian Tire matter.

Wright had ruled against admitting Senger's polygraph as evidence. By using an admission from the test for his current line of questioning, Worme had managed to ensure that the transcript of the test, with some blacked-out sections, could be entered as a public exhibit.

— — —

Halyk couldn't believe that Senger hadn't remembered the name Stonechild on November 29, just a few days after looking for Neil in the west end.

"Why?" Senger wanted to know; it was just a routine call and they'd never found him.

But, Halyk pressed, the news of Stonechild's death should have stood out even more to Senger for the very fact that he was a rookie.

"Surely at some point in time you would have heard, as a police officer, that this was Neil Stonechild, or should have connected that in your mind and said, by gosh, that's the young fellow we were out looking for. Gosh, if we would have found him we might have spared his life. I wonder what happened. Wouldn't you think that train of thought would go through your head?"

"Sure, it could have, yeah."

"But you don't remember it happening?"

"No," said Senger.

Was it going to be as simple as that, Worme thought to himself as he listened. Just a matter of saying that Neil was GOA on November 24, to deny any knowledge about the boy's disappearance and death and to say they could not remember associating the discovery of his body with the call to Snowberry Downs? Worme felt his anger and cynicism build as he thought through the strange mathematics in a commission of inquiry that made denying and forgetting add up to nothing happened.

Senger was the last witness. As he finished, all that remained was for the lawyers to come back to make their final arguments. Then Wright would spend several solitary months compiling the final report.

Stella had said repeatedly that she only ever wanted to know how her son had died. As she walked out of the hearing, she grabbed Erica and hugged her in full view of the television cameras. She held her close until the worst of a huge wave of sadness had passed her by, until she felt calm enough to speak with the reporters. When the inquiry started she had been terrified of testifying and of talking to media. But now, standing in front of the cameras, she spoke firmly and with conviction.

"They'll have to pay eventually, they will. Whoever did this. We all have to answer to one God—they're going to have to die, too, one day." All the cameras were rolling. "When you answer to God, you can't take a lawyer with you. No lawyers where they're going."

— — —

Six months later, on October 25, 2004, Don Worme took Stella and Norman to lunch at the Mandarin on 20th Street. Afterwards they would be going to a private meeting with Saskatchewan's justice minister, who would hand over an advance copy of the *Report of the Commission of Inquiry into Matters Relating to the Death of Neil Stonechild*. Fogged in at Cross Lake, Stella had endured an eleven-hour bus ride and a flight from Winnipeg not to miss the meeting.

Waiters wheeled carts loaded with delicacies to the table. Worme was at his most attentive. It had been more than four years since that first call to Stella and his subsequent commitment to getting where they were today. Given how much was on the line, having lunch at a familiar place was the only way he could pretend to feel even slightly relaxed. He was now commuting between Saskatoon, a new office in Toronto and Forest, Ontario, where he was spending two weeks out of every month as co-counsel for the Ipperwash inquiry into the shooting death of native protester Dudley George at the hands of the Ontario Provincial Police. Between numerous cellphone calls from both his offices, he was talking his way through the preparations for the meeting.

"If the report is any good, Stella, we'll go down to the Cabinet offices once it's released," he said, while at the same time imagining how unlikely that would be. Privately, he expected a report full of lame recommendations.

"If, on the other hand, the report is no good, we'll have our own news conference back at the firm, and throw rocks at it from there." He laughed, trying to keep the mood light.

He was filled with admiration for Stella, watching her laughing at his jokes. He could hardly fathom what continued to buoy her battered spirits. He always saw hope in her. She had demonstrated it throughout the inquiry, walking in each day with an open mind.

Worme thought about Darrell Night, Lawrence Wegner and the other men. Dan Hatchen and Ken Munson had received only eight months in jail for dumping Darrell Night, and they both got out early. Night's fear kept him living in poverty at the elders' lodge on the Saulteaux reserve rather than coming back to Saskatoon. Worme had accompanied Mary Wegner to four Round Dances since Lawrence's death in 2000. Like Stella, Mary still did not know who had left her son to die.

The drive to the cabinet offices from the restaurant took five minutes. Worme scanned the formidable entourage surrounding the new justice minister, Frank Quennell. It included the deputy minister, the head of the prosecutor's office, as well as the justice department's chief civil litigation lawyer. For a moment Stella looked overwhelmed, but as usual Worme had only to touch her arm lightly and she relaxed. Stella, Helen Semaganis and Tamara Starblanket, a new member of his legal team, were the only women settling in around the boardroom table full of men, including Norman Bignell and Worme's associate Greg Curtis.

Stella took a good look at Minister Quennell. He was a wiry man, very solemn-looking, faint-spoken, with not a hint of brash. Had she passed him on the street she would not have taken him for the justice minister of the province. He had been a classmate of Worme's at law school and Worme had always thought of him as a decent man.

Quennell immediately apologized to Stella for the loss of her son, and on behalf of the people of Saskatchewan he also apologized for what she had been put through. He told her he accepted all findings and recommendations of the inquiry report. She could tell from the tone of his voice that he was moved.

As he opened a spiral-bound copy of the report, Stella glimpsed the book's cover, a glossy sepia-toned picture with the small figure of Neil lying in the field near the Hitachi building, with his legs slightly drawn up toward his chest. She willed herself to keep her composure.

Quennell went immediately to the end of the report, to Justice Wright's "Summary of Findings" on page 212. He read each one of the thirteen conclusions aloud in a quiet, deliberate voice, shaking with emotion.

"Number one, Neil Stonechild was the subject of two complaints of causing a disturbance on the evening of November 24, 1990.

"Two, Constable Bradley Senger and Constable Larry Hartwig, members of the Saskatoon Police Service, were dispatched at 11:51 p.m. to investigate a complaint about Neil Stonechild at Snowberry Downs.

"Three, Hartwig and Senger arrived at Snowberry Downs within minutes and carried out a search of the area. In the course of doing so they encountered Neil Stonechild."

"Number four, the constables took Stonechild into custody."

Stella started to cry when she heard those words. What he read to her next was the crux of what she had been dealing with for fourteen years.

"Number five, in the early morning hours of November 25, 1990, Stonechild died of cold exposure in a field in the northwest industrial area of Saskatoon."

"Number six, Neil Stonechild's frozen body was found in a field in the northwest industrial area of Saskatoon on November 29, 1990.

"Seven, there were injuries and marks on Stonechild's body that were likely caused by handcuffs."

Worme's tongue had gone dry. Expecting to lose, he was overwhelmed as each of Wright's findings seemed to build on the strength of the one before.

The eighth finding described how the SPS's preliminary investigation "properly identified a number of suspicious circumstances surrounding the death." But from there, Wright's findings cast the work of the SPS in a dismal light. Quennell read on.

"Number nine, the principal investigator assigned to the case, Morality Sergeant Keith Jarvis, carried out a superficial and totally inadequate investigation of the death of Neil Stonechild.

"Ten, Jarvis was informed by Jason Roy that Neil Stonechild was in the custody of the Saskatoon Police Service when Roy last saw Stonechild on the night of November 24/25 1990. Jarvis did not record this important information in his notebook or investigation report."

For all his failings, Roy had never once wavered in recounting the last known words of the friend he'd betrayed. He was vindicated at long last.

Findings eleven through thirteen described the inadequate police response.

"Jarvis and his superior, Staff Sergeant Theodore (Bud) Johnson, concluded the investigation almost immediately and closed the file on December 5, 1990, without answering the many questions that surrounded the Stonechild disappearance and death.

"Jarvis dismissed important information provided to him by two members of the Saskatoon Police Service relating to the Stonechild disappearance and death."

The thirteenth and final finding described how the SPS had ignored the suspicions surrounding Neil Stonechild's death for fourteen years.

"In the years that followed, the chiefs and deputy chiefs of police who successively headed the Saskatoon Police Service rejected or ignored reports from the Stonechild family members and investigative reporters for the Saskatoon *Star Phoenix* that cast serious doubts on the conduct of the Stonechild investigation. The self-protective and defensive attitudes exhibited by the senior levels of the police service continued, notwithstanding the establishment of an RCMP task force to investigate the suspicious deaths of a number of aboriginal persons and the abduction of an aboriginal man. These same attitudes were manifested by certain members of the Saskatoon Police Service during the inquiry."

Wrapping up, Quennell told Stella he had asked the head of prosecutions to look at whether criminal charges should be laid, based on the report. The test, he told her, would be the likelihood of securing convictions. He had been told that the evidence to date did not meet that test. He assured her the RCMP were continuing to investigate and that the Stonechild case was not closed.

By this point both Stella and Norman were quietly weeping. Worme asked the minister for a few moments in private to digest the findings with his team and his clients, effectively dismissing the minister.

No sooner had Quennell and his colleagues left the room, than Worme reached for Stella and embraced her wholeheartedly. Then he put his left arm around Norman, pulled him close and shook his hand at the same time. Then he turned to Helen and to Greg Curtis.

"We won," said Worme with some hesitation. After all, they had spent four years fighting this case, feeling often as though nobody believed in the value of finding justice for one seventeen-year-old boy. He hugged Curtis, elation on both their faces.

Thinking ahead to the tight timeline, Helen Semaganis was the only one keeping her emotions in check. She knew they still had to read and digest the report in full. In twenty-four hours it would be publicly released and they'd be facing the local and national media about Wright's damning conclusions.

— — —

Later in the afternoon, Worme drove Stella and Norman back to the hotel to rest. They had dinner plans with Jack Warner. Worme's cellphone was ringing every few minutes. Journalists from all over the country wanted interviews, each station competing for him and Stella to come on the air.

The reporters who had descended on Saskatoon for the release of Wright's report had all signed a confidentiality agreement with the justice department. The only people they could discuss the report with were other parties bound by the same agreement. When they talked to Worme, they seemed shocked at the strength with which Justice Wright had expressed his findings and his dismay at the police service's attitude during the inquiry.

Assembly of First Nations Chief Phil Fontaine called to offer his congratulations. Annette Ermine, one of the investigators for the FSIN, called too. Worme had also received several calls from Jack Warner, who was in his car on the way from Regina to collect his own copy of the report.

"I can't tell you what's in it, Jack, they might shoot me. You better sign that undertaking," Worme joked.

"I'll sign it as soon as I get up there." Warner cared about a few critical points. Did the judge believe Jason Roy? Did the judge find credible Robertson's photo of Neil's cuts superimposed with the Peerless handcuffs?

"Let's just say you'll be blown away when you get here," Worme said.

Around five, Worme picked up his sons Donovan and Eli and their thirteen-year-old sister, Tannis. After agreeing they'd all meet up later for dinner at Chianti Café, the kids' favourite

Italian restaurant, he dropped Donovan off for a piano lesson and Tannis at hockey practice. He had an unexpected hour to kill.

Eli had fallen asleep in the back seat, his head drooping over the seatbelt. The sky outside had darkened. Inside the Jeep it was quiet, the only light visible in the cab coming from the green LED display on the rear-view mirror, showing the Jeep had 480 kilometres worth of gas left in the tank.

Worme drove by instinct to the dark fields at the edge of the city. It wasn't often in his life that he could say "I'm just plain happy." For a rare moment though, he felt an unparalleled joy.

He had spent so many hours in his Jeep during the past four years while working on this file. It was on the highway that he'd first heard the tape of Jarvis's interview with Martell, and he had spent many long cellphone calls with Warner discussing the investigation. Or he'd just crank up Bob Marley CDs and sing along, or chant to the sound of native drummers.

Worme stopped the car, rolled down the window and allowed himself a cigarette. The engine clicked as it cooled. He looked out into the darkness and thought of Neil. This boy he'd never met, whom he'd spent four years getting to know, had died alone out here.

Justice Wright had spoken, but Brad Senger and Larry Hartwig were still fully employed. Worme inhaled deeply and blew a small smoke ring out the window. The fight was not over; the blue wall of denial the SPS had put up for fourteen years was still standing and wasn't likely to come down anytime soon.

By eleven, the kids had had their spaghetti dinner, and were at home and in bed, giving their parents some time together. Since their move to the Eagle Ridge acreage, sitting on the stools around the kitchen counter while they reviewed the day had become an evening ritual. Worme poured his wife a glass of Merlot.

As exhausted as they were, they began reading through their separate copies of Wright's report, Helen marking passages of interest with a yellow highlighter, Don blurting out entire sections aloud as they caught his attention.

"Listen to what he says about Hartwig's search for Neil. 'Constable Hartwig's silence as to his search for Stonechild on November 24 is even more incredible in light of the fact that he discussed the death with Constable Louttit in early January 1991. He was aware that Constable Louttit had concerns about the circumstances surrounding Neil Stonechild's death, but did not disclose his search for Stonechild at a time close to his disappearance and death.'"

Helen half-listened to her husband as she traced her highlighter across her copy.

Don jumped ahead. "'I cannot accept that Constable Hartwig simply forgot about the search for Stonechild when he learned of the death, or that he failed to recognize the complaint might have some significance to the investigation into Stonechild's death. In all of the circumstances, his assertion that he did not recall what happened is simply not credible.'"

Don looked up to make sure he had Helen's attention, then continued. "'I conclude that he recalled what happened and his assertions are a deliberate deception designed to conceal his involvement.'"

Both of them sat still for a moment, thinking about what he had just read aloud.

"I do not recall" seems to cover almost anything, they'd joked with each other throughout the inquiry. And here, the judge was so struck by how many times Senger said "I do not recall," that he had cited them. Don started reading, following the lines on page eighty-three with his right index finger. "'I was struck by Senger's numerous responses that he had no recollection. He had no recollection of looking for Stonechild, no recollection of receiving the call reporting the finding of the body, no recollection of being contacted by Sgt. Jarvis and no recollection of any press reports of the death in 1990 and 1991.

It is not surprising that Senger or any other officer would not recall the details of a routine call ten or more years after the event. It is however difficult to accept that he would not have recalled the search for Stonechild when within a matter of days—on his next working shift—Stonechild's body was located. It is also difficult to accept that he did not recognize the potential significance of their earlier search for Stonechild to the investigation into the death of Stonechild. The discovery of Stonechild's frozen body made the call on November 24 anything but routine. I would expect it to impress the search for Stonechild in the memory of both Hartwig and Senger.'"

"Don, I can't read if you keep talking," said Helen, with a bit of a laugh, suspecting her protest would win her at best only a few seconds of quiet. Don quickly proved her suspicions right.

"This is just incredible, I can't believe this," he said. "Listen to what he says about why neither Hartwig nor Senger went to Jarvis the day Neil's body was found." He paused finding his place on the page. "'Why would Senger keep quiet? I can only conclude that he chose to conceal his involvement with Stonechild on November 24/25.' He's using language like 'deliberate deception' and 'conceal,' when he talks about both Hartwig and Senger; a judge couldn't be any more scathing."

He read through the sections outlining the lengthy cross-examination of Jason Roy, looking for the judge's conclusions.

"'While Roy's testimony contained errors and contradictions, this does not prevent me from finding credible his testimony relating to what he observed on the evening of November 24 and the morning of November 25 1990.'"

He sped through the next line in silence before continuing. "'The existence of corroborating evidence does of course make my task a good deal easier. I conclude by commending Jason Roy for his tenacity in pursuing this matter over many years.'"

Incredible. Not only had Wright believed Jason, he had praised him.

Don's wineglass was empty. He refilled it and topped off Helen's with the last of the bottle. He could not go to bed without reading what Wright had to say about Jarvis, who had originally not even wanted to testify, citing health issues. He'd winced as the counsel for the commission had given the lawyers instructions to go easy on Jarvis because of his heart problems. No one had shown similar concern for Jason Roy.

Worme hadn't forgiven Jarvis. "I told Jack that Jarvis would turn," he announced, suddenly remembering a bet they'd made. "Jack owes me a golf game at the course of my choice." He giggled. "It's gonna be expensive. Golf in Hawaii, whadda ya say, Helen? Hawaii in February sounds so *gooood!*" He smiled. "I love it." He sipped his wine more slowly now; Helen would not let him open another bottle tonight.

"The judge clearly doesn't believe him." he continued. Helen hadn't made much headway with the highlighter. "'I do not accept that Sgt. Jarvis and Roy only discussed what was in Roy's written statement.'"

Flipping forward to page 114, he read Wright's final comments on Jarvis's evidence.

"'As I have already noted, the interview with Roy lasted some fifty-five minutes. I believe Sgt. Jarvis did press Roy for further information after he had provided the written statement, as any competent investigator would have done. I am satisfied that in so doing, Roy did reveal to Sgt. Jarvis that he last saw Neil Stonechild in the back of a police car, as Roy testified and as Sgt. Jarvis recounted in his interview with Martell. Sgt. Jarvis did not record this important information in his notes or reports. This cast a totally different light on Sgt. Jarvis's actions as an investigator. What might have seemed inexcusable incompetence or neglect now took on a more serious focus.'"

"Smokin'!" Don said playfully. Few could get away with quoting signature Jim Carrey lines, or any other such goofy clichés, with as much enthusiasm as Don.

"Don, be quiet for a minute, will you," Helen said. "Listen to the final line in Justice Wright's overview about November 24. He says Hartwig and Senger had Neil in the car. 'The evidence did, however, establish on the balance of probabilities: a) that Neil Stonechild was last seen in their custody at approximately 11:56 p.m. on November 24, 1990; b) that he died of cold exposure in a remote industrial area in the early hours of November 25, 1990; and c) that there were injuries and marks on his body that were consistent with handcuffs.'"

She looked at him sternly. If the evidence was so clear to this judge, then why didn't the justice department lay charges?

"That's gonna be the first question at the newser tomorrow," Don replied.

Thinking for a moment, he added, "It's the only thing people will want to know, that and what happened in the twenty-seven minutes between the CPIC with Jason and the officer's arrival at O'Regan Crescent. Where were Hartwig and Senger and what were they doing?" Don thought nobody could have answered it better than Wright himself, in his report, who was "satisfied that Cst. Hartwig and Cst. Senger had adequate time between the Snowberry Downs dispatch and O'Regan Crescent dispatch to transport Stonechild to the northwest industrial area of Saskatoon."

— — —

Within hours of the nationally televised afternoon news conference that made Justice Wright's report public, Chief Russell Sabo suspended Hartwig and Senger, pending a decision on their future.

Don Worme decided to hold a dinner for his entire law firm at John's, the most famous steakhouse in Saskatoon, only a few steps from the courthouse and the Sheraton Hotel. He drove to the restaurant in his big Sequoia, which comfortably accommodated Norman and Stella. As soon as Norman got in the car, Worme turned around to him, offering up his right fist in greeting.

"I'm happy. I'm truly happy. Pure joy, this is what it feels like, Stella. We won, we actually won!"

He reserved a private room with a big wooden table running down the middle, seating at least twenty people. He'd invited all his staff. Helen was bringing Tannis, and Greg Curtis had promised to bring his own teenage daughter. Don and Helen wanted the kids to experience the highs, having too frequently put up with the lows that followed their parents home from their work on the freezing-death cases.

Worme had seated Stella to his right and Jack Warner on his left. He ordered plenty of red and white wine. Worme was a paradox. He clearly loved the luxury that came with success but he was never completely at ease with it. A crushing fear of failure drove him, a feeling he often summed up in a phrase that echoed his grandfather: "Never, never, ever let them win." Tonight he was living his maxim.

He held court like a patriarch in the panelled room of the expensive restaurant, but he was acting out a more matriarchal tradition, assembling his brood to tell the story of what they'd been through to win, the first telling of the story that would now be a part of the lore of the young aboriginal law firm.

He was a cynic but believed he was an optimist, refusing to give up on his idealism. The inquiry's conclusions had left him reeling, happily. He was still a bit stunned. As he rose to speak, he was desperate to avoid tears.

"Bringing you all here tonight was important. It's been a long haul, a long road we've travelled with Stella. But tonight we are celebrating a moment which is rare in the life of a firm. We may never experience it again in this same way. We want to thank Stella for her patience. She never gave up her will to get answers and she is the one who inspires us all to fight on."

Helen stood to offer her own thanks and to remind them what a special night this was.

"When we become lawyers we dream about making a difference, experiencing something like this. Some people might go through their entire career and never experience this, and we need to remember that as we gather with Stella and Norman tonight. Stella lost Neil, but she doesn't have to feel alone anymore."

— — —

Stella turned over to her left side and slowly raised herself to get out of bed. She was exhausted. She and Norman had flown home after Justice Wright's report was released. After getting back to Cross Lake, the adrenaline faded and her fatigue set in.

No sooner did she put her feet on the ground than she collapsed onto the floor. Norman asked her what was wrong.

"I feel so dizzy. Every time I try to stand up my head starts spinning."

The dizziness had arrived along with the fatigue. She could lie in bed comfortably, but as soon as she raised her head the spinning began. She'd close her eyes, hoping it would get better, but often that only seemed to make it worse. Now she'd fallen and she was scared. She caught herself imagining the worst. She really had to make an appointment at the nursing station.

Don Worme had been phoning her almost every day. She looked forward to his calls, for distraction. Usually, he made her laugh as he told her about the latest turn of events in Saskatoon. The police had been under constant media attack ever since the report had been made public. Regional talk shows debated whether the two police officers should be fired.

"You've been busy then. What do you tell them on those radio shows?" she said.

"I tell them we have nothing but sympathy for the officers' families and children, and the pain which has been inflicted upon them by the actions of these two."

The officers had rallied, though, he told her. Their lawyers declared they would fight any discipline issued under the Police Act. The police association called the inquiry a comedy of errors. Almost half the police officers in the city supported Hartwig and Senger, and had signed petitions to voice their outrage. They had organized marches to protest. The other half, however, were silent, as was most of the town.

Behind the scenes, Worme worked the phones encouraging the city and the province to settle with Stella to avoid a civil suit. "I've called them all, Stella, telling them to do the right thing."

He was hoping for a quick settlement for Stella's sake. So far, the city had been playing games. Reporters kept asking the mayor of Saskatoon what he thought of the report, and he kept saying he hadn't read it yet.

"Just like the papers, none of those police officers ever reads the paper, at least that's what they kept saying on the stand." Stella chuckled at that. She read the paper, why didn't they? Every senior officer who testified at the inquiry had denied reading the *Star Phoenix* front-page article in March 1991, in which she had complained about the lack of investigation into Neil's death.

— — —

Within two weeks of the report's being handed down, Stella found out she had positional vertigo, likely caused by an inner-ear infection, something the doctor felt would go away if she rested. Her phone rang all the time, family, friends and reporters. On November 12, 2004, Don Worme called her again with an update. The moment he heard her voice his entire bearing shifted, as if he were a son calling his mother with unexpected good news, knowing he won't be able to hide the emotions about to follow.

"Hope you've been feeling better."

"You get used to it," she said. "I just try not to look up or bend forward. Usually it goes away if I just sit up in bed for a few seconds before I stand up."

"I got a call from the chief's office. He wanted you to be the first to know."

"Know what?"

"The chief will be firing Hartwig and Senger today."

"Bless the Lord" was all she said as she cried quietly into the receiver.

POSTSCRIPT

OUR CONVERSATIONS WITH THE MAIN CHAR-acters of this story are ongoing as events continue to unfold.

Larry Hartwig and Bradley Senger are appealing their firing through a disciplinary appeal hearing. On the fifteenth anniversary of Neil Stonechild's disappearance, Larry Hartwig and his lawyer filed papers asking the Saskatchewan Court of Appeal to overturn findings of the Stonechild Inquiry.

Saskatoon police chief Russell Sabo issued two notices of formal discipline against Deputy Chief Daniel Wiks for giving misleading statements to the media and for dishonourable conduct. The hearing officer found Wiks guilty of negligently making inaccurate oral statements to a Saskatoon Star Phoenix reporter. However, the hearing officer was not satisfied, on the balance of probabilities, that Deputy Chief Wiks made the inaccurate statements wilfully. Wiks awaited a decision on how he would be disciplined until March 2006, when he was allowed to retire, ending all disciplinary proceedings against him. The City of Saskatoon decided early in 2006 not to renew the contract of Chief Sabo.

Jason Roy is moving on with his life, but continues to struggle with the trauma and fallout of his teenage friend's death.

No criminal charges have been laid in connection with Neil Stonechild's death. As she awaits further developments, Stella Stonechild Bignell is determined to continue speaking to the media and asking questions of the police until she gets the answer she still has not found: How did Neil Stonechild die?

Acknowledgements

We would like to express our gratitude to the many people without whom this book would not have been possible: to the mothers, Stella Stonechild Bignell and Mary Wegner, and their families, for offering us their trust, sorrow and joy and helping us understand the many questions that continue to drive their quest for answers to how their sons died; to Jason Roy for his persistence in telling his story and sharing it with us; to Vanessa Kayseas for her understanding patience; Darrell Night for his courage in coming forward and then again for sitting down with us for many hours to tell us how he survived; Jeffrey "Bluesky" Crowe for helping us better understand Neil, and for the use of his stunning mural depicting their friendship. We are also deeply grateful to Don Worme and Helen Semaganis, his partner in life and law; Darren Winegarden; Greg Curtis; and Dayla Mousseau—who all helped us document and navigate the many years they have dedicated to the families who came to them for help.

Thanks to Sophia Male and Bilbo Poynter for long evening hours of research. Thanks also to Brooks De Cillia, Dan Zakreski, Geoff Wright, Father André Poilievre, Jack Warner and many others in Saskatchewan whose generosity and expressions of kindness helped us better understand the context of this story and the city of Saskatoon, and to the staff of the Broadway Café for providing us with nourishment and encouragement during our many visits there.

We would like to thank Anne Collins for her faith and enthusiasm in taking on our team; our agent Denise Bukowski; Craig Pyette and the staff at Random House for helping us fine-tune the complexities and keeping the lights on in the boardroom; Carole Melanson for keeping the focus on the day job; Mary Rogan and David West for their photos; Anne Holloway and Erika Krolman for added editorial acumen.

Above all, our love and gratitude goes to our families, without whose patient encouragement this book would not have been possible: Rowena Conti, Haven, Leo and Monica; as well as Simon, Isabelle and Danielle; Christina, Mark and Julie; Reiner and Evi; Jill, Mike, Caroline, Huw and Rebecca.

PART I: SWEET CHILD

PROLOGUE

Many of the details about Don Worme's early years come from our interviews with him and our visits to the house on Avenue J North and the Kawakatoose reserve. Further information on the history of the Kawakatoose First Nation and the warrior Kawakatoose can be found on the website www.collections.ic.gc.ca/bands/bkawacl.html. The narrative reconstruction of the murders of Don Worme's mother and sister is based on testimony given at the trial of Francis Littlechief in 1964, recorded in handwritten trial transcripts in the archives of the Court of Queen's Bench, Saskatoon. Other details about the murders come from accounts published in the Saskatoon *Star Phoenix*.

VANISHED

The story of Neil's early years in Saskatoon draws heavily on our many interviews with Stella Stonechild Bignell; her children Dean, Erica, Marcel and Jake; and Neil's friends, including Jeffrey "Bluesky" Crowe and Jason Roy. The portrait of Neil's wrestling career was drawn from conversations with his coaches Geoff Wright, Wendell Wilkie and Gil Wist. The source for information about Cree traditions and ceremonies, including the disciplining of children, was *The Plains Cree* by David G. Mandelbaum. Stella heard stories similar to those related by Mandelbaum while growing up and believed in the traditional Cree style of parenting. Interviews with Jason Roy, Stella, Marcel and Pat Pickard helped us reconstruct Neil's last night. Witness testimony, transcripts and public exhibits from the Commission of Inquiry into Matters Relating to the Death of Neil Stonechild were an invaluable resource for this reconstruction.

Constables Larry Hartwig and Brad Senger declined to be interviewed, but fortunately, we had access to their testimonies at the inquiry as well as public exhibits of their computer records and notes from the night of Neil's disappearance.

The Memory Box: One Hundred Years of Policing in Saskatoon by Susan Grant provided a history of the Saskatoon Police Service, and testimony and public exhibits from the Stonechild Inquiry provided further historical insight.

Our description of Neil's last moments relies on testimony at the inquiry, a study of the police video taken when his body was found and information on the effects of hypothermia from the textbook *Forensic Pathology* by Dominick J. DiMaio and Vincent J.M. DiMaio.

Finally, throughout the book, we were guided by the evaluation of the evidence and findings of the Honourable Mr. Justice David H. Wright in his *Report of the Commission of Inquiry into Matters Relating to the Death of Neil Stonechild*.

The re-creation of the disturbance at the 7-Eleven is based on Wright's findings and the testimony of Bruce Genaille.

THE INVESTIGATION

The discovery of Neil Stonechild's body and Keith Jarvis's investigation are based on transcripts from the Stonechild inquiry, public exhibits and police notebooks, as well as several interviews Jarvis gave to the RCMP in 2000 and his testimony at the inquiry in 2003. Jarvis declined to be interviewed for this book.

Descriptions of the weather during the events described, here as elsewhere in the book, rely on a combination of transcripts, first-person recollection and the excellent database maintained by Environment Canada online at www.climate. weatheroffice.ec.gc.ca.

Extensive personal interviews with the Stonechild family, Pat Pickard and Jason Roy, as well as their testimony at the Stonechild inquiry informed our portraits of Neil's family and acquaintances at the time of his disappearance, death and funeral. The description of Constable Ernie Louttit's involvement is based on his testimony at the inquiry.

Descriptions of St. Paul's Hospital morgue, the Westwood funeral home and Saskatoon's Woodlawn Cemetery were drawn from our visits.

CASE CLOSED

As elsewhere in the book, events and conversations have been drawn from a mixture of our interviews and reporting, and from the forty-three days of testimony at the Stonechild inquiry, much of which we attended.

Don Worme's memories of his beloved grandfather Edward and Stella's recollections of police officers Ernie Louttit and Eli Tarasoff are the result of the exclusive access Don and Stella provided us.

Although in his testimony Jarvis did not recall the meetings he had had with Louttit and Tarasoff, he did not deny they took place. Both Louttit and Tarasoff clearly recalled the meetings, substantiated in Louttit's case by his notes from the time. In his report, Commissioner Wright concludes that Louttit and Tarasoff did meet with Jarvis.

Stella Stonechild's meeting with Eli Tarasoff at the Saskatoon police station is based on interviews and also inquiry transcripts, in which Stella testifies that this meeting took place. Tarasoff confirms this in his own inquiry testimony. In his testimony and in a statement he provided to the RCMP (which became exhibit P-134), he describes Sergeant Jarvis as "an Englishman with a colonial attitude" and further stated that "When Natives were involved he did not take it serious." Justice Wright quoted Tarasoff's comments in his final report, page 124. He further wrote that when Tarasoff had suggested to Jarvis that the investigation could have been more in-depth, Jarvis was rather flippant about it. Wright also notes, on page 106 of his report, that Jarvis claimed to have no recollection of the meeting with Tarasoff.

Background regarding Terry Craig's March 4, 1991, *Star Phoenix* article comes from Stella and our interview with Craig. Former Saskatoon Police Chief Dave Scott did not agree to be interviewed for *Starlight Tour*. We were guided by his testimony at the inquiry. On page 125 of his report, Commissioner Wright notes that Scott's comments, which were reported in Craig's article, were "untrue." "The public was seriously misled," according to Wright. While Wright said the evidence did not establish that the deception was intentional, he added that Scott had a duty to provide accurate information to the public, concluding: "If he had carefully reviewed the file, the matter may have been investigated further in 1991." On the stand, Scott did not suggest he had been misquoted.

Neil's friend Jeffrey Crowe described at length for us the meaning and inspiration behind the four-panel mural he painted as a sixteen-year-old at Kilburn Hall following Neil's death, as well as the significance of his artistic signature of the medicine wheel turning backwards. Although the mural is not accessible to the general public, we were fortunate to be given access to Kilburn Hall to see the painting, which stretches the length of one wall of the gym. Panels one, "Crowe and N. Stonechild Bros," two, "Depression," and three, "Brothers," were named at the time the mural was painted. Crowe did not name the fourth panel until 1997 when he overcame his substance-abuse problems. He called it "Hope." A fire exit sign has been cut through the lower-left portion of the painting, and from time to time officials have discussed painting over the mural.

GIVING UP AND GOING HOME

Commissioner Wright's report confirms that computer records from the Saskatoon Police's Information Service's Management System (SIMS) show that Morton destroyed Neil's clothing and belongings at the request of the original investigating officer, Keith Jarvis.

The record, which was entered in evidence as P-59, reads in part: "93 January 12 The following exhibits which have been in exhibit storage were destroyed. S/Sgt. Jarvis indicated the case is closed and exhibits could be destroyed."

Wright noted in his report that Morton did not follow the procedure outlined by former Superintendent Frank Simpson who worked in the Identification Section in the '60s and '70s. According to Simpson, general practice at that time was to obtain clearance from the family before destroying clothes. In his testimony Jarvis did not say why he told Morton to destroy the clothes in 1993 despite repeated visits from Stella and Erica requesting the clothes be returned. Wright pointed out in his report that Morton had adequately discharged his responsibility to provide support to Jarvis in the collection and preservation of evidence. As for what happened to the clothing itself, Morton, when cross-examined by Don Worme, indicated they were most likely disposed of "in a fashion" that would have seen them taken to a garbage dump.

PART II: HIGHEST POWER

PROLOGUE

This is a narrative recreation of a documented case. In the summer of 1976, an SPS officer, Constable Ken King, was fined a week's pay for driving a pregnant woman and her companions along Spadina Crescent, dropping them off near the South Saskatchewan River and forcing them to walk back. Native people in Saskatoon told us the area near the power station was the destination for dropping off natives because it was so isolated; houses were far enough away so that someone who was dropped there wouldn't be heard by anyone.

STARLIGHT TOUR

Darrell Night and the family of Lawrence Wegner gave us their full cooperation, inviting us to visit their homes on the Saulteaux reserve in Saskatchewan on many occasions to document their stories. We also relied on public documents and transcripts of testimony from the inquests of Lawrence Wegner and Rodney Naistus, as well as from the trial of police officers Hatchen and Munson.

The details of Lawrence Wegner's life and his last days come from numerous interviews and conversations with family and friends, as well as with Jocelan Shandler.

Historical details on the Cree *ehmaykwanowake*, the Give-Away ceremony, which Lawrence was studying, come from *The Plains Cree* by David G. Mandelbaum.

Numerous conversations with Darrell Night and testimony transcripts from Hatchen and Munson's trial in 2001 form the basis for the narrative of Darrell Night's starlight tour. One area of dispute during the trial concerned how Night was put into and taken out of the police cruiser. Night says he was thrown in. Hatchen and Munson say they simply placed him in the car. Night also says he was dragged out and hit his head. Hatchen and Munson also say that from the beginning Darrell Night pleaded to be let out of the car. Night says he didn't until he thought they were going to kill him.

FROZEN BODIES

The descriptions of Lawrence Wegner's last night and the discovery of his body are based on interviews, testimony transcripts and public exhibits from the inquest into his death. The inquest jury decided that Lawrence Wegner died of hypothermia, but by undetermined means. Despite the testimony of witnesses who say they saw Wegner put into a police cruiser, precisely how he came to be in the field where he froze to death, still wearing clean socks, remains a mystery. To date no one has been charged.

THE SECRET GETS OUT

Personal interviews and transcripts from the inquests and from Hatchen and Munson's trial form the basis of the sections describing Darrell Night's interactions with Saskatoon police officer Bruce Eholt and the eventual reporting of Night's drop-off to authorities. Deputy Chief Daniel Wiks's testimony during the Stonechild inquiry described his attempts to track down the officers who had dropped off Darrell Night. Although Wiks does not use the expression "knocked heads" in his testimony concerning these attempts, the term represents the vernacular used by Saskatoon police officers we met during our research.

Descriptions of the events that took place after Darrell Night's drop-off and the media reporting of the deaths of Lloyd Joseph Dustyhorn, Lawrence Wegner and Rodney Naistus were based on public records and transcripts and our interviews with former Saskatoon *Star Phoenix* staff Dan Zakreski, Les Perreaux and Gord Struthers. Don Worme, Helen Semaganis and Gregory Curtis allowed us generous personal access to help recreate the shock and upheaval in their lives during the chaotic few weeks in February 2000 when the freezing deaths and Darrell Night's drop-off first came to light. These events would shape their legal careers and family lives for years to come. Numerous exhibits and witness statements compiled by Project Ferric were also invaluable.

"DECADE-OLD DEATH RESURFACES"

Stella Stonechild granted the authors full access to her legal files, personal records and family mementoes, and allowed many personal interviews with her and members of her family. Combining these personal records with public records provided us with a historical time frame for the events and details of Don Worme's interactions with his clients, Stella Stonechild and Jason Roy, and others connected to them, including Vanessa Kayseas and Father André Poilievre; and RCMP officers Jack Warner, Ken Lyons and other Project Ferric task force investigators. The legal files also contained some documentation of Worme's correspondence with the RCMP and SPS regarding Neil Stonechild's case.

PART III: LEGAL CHEATING

BIZARRO WORLD

A detailed description of the RCMP's Project Ferric task force and its activities was given at the Stonechild Inquiry by Chief Superintendent Darrell McFadyen. At one point, thirty-two investigators and support people were working on the task force, the total cost of which was $750,000.

Mobile data terminals, or MDTs, which were installed in SPS cruisers in the late 1980s, allow officers mobile access to the SPS computer system, and give police access to criminal records. In connection with the inquiry, Justice Wright describes them in the following way on page 73 of his report:

> The MDTs in 1990 gave patrol officers full search access to the Canadian Police Information Centre database, a national records database commonly referred to as CPIC. It can be searched by local police departments such as the Saskatoon Police Service. The CPIC national office has the ability to determine what queries were conducted by police officers in 1990. This is referred to as an offline search. The RCMP conducted a number of offline searches in relation to the RCMP investigation into the death of Neil Stonechild. The documentary results of some of these offline searches were made inquiry exhibits, and they established that Cst. Senger and Cst. Hartwig made a number of CPIC queries in relation to their search for Neil Stonechild.

The passages describing Project Ferric's interviews with SPS officers is based on exhibit P-134, which became public during the testimony of Chief Superintendent Darrell McFadyen at the Stonechild inquiry. P-134 contains witness statements taken by McFadyen from various SPS police officers. Specific comments about Sergeant Jarvis in *Starlight Tour* attributed to Staff Sergeant Tom Vanin and Sergeant Dennis Read can be found in these documents. On page 138 of Justice Wright's final report he discusses the more than 200 witnesses interviewed by the RCMP investigators regarding Neil Stonechild's death.

TRUTH AND LIES

The foundation of the section detailing the RCMP's interviews with Hartwig and Senger in May 2000 includes inquiry exhibit P-184, a transcript of Hartwig's interview with Lyons on May 18; P-185, summaries of other conversations between the two men in the same month; and P-195, a handwritten letter of complaint from Senger to Chief Scott, dated May 29, 2000. Hartwig and Senger's testimony at the inquiry was also used.

Valuable context and perspective about the RCMP's meetings with Hartwig and Senger in May 2000, its contact with Jarvis and the elimination of Gary Pratt as a suspect come from our conversations with RCMP investigator Corporal Jack Warner and Gary Pratt.

Although Keith Jarvis declined to be interviewed for the book, we had access to his notes and testimony, as well as to summaries, transcripts and cassette tapes of his interviews with the RCMP and commission investigator Robert Martell.

Physical descriptions of the SPS station on 4th Avenue come from our tour of the building. In addition to testifying at the inquiry, Sergeant Murray Zoorkan talked to us about the Cold Case squad, finding Jarvis's missing notebook, his role as liaison for the SPS with the RCMP and his encounter with Larry Hartwig at the water fountain.

On page 172 of his report Justice Wright mentions Jarvis's suspicion, expressed to the RCMP—and expressed as an experienced officer—that handcuffs had caused the marks on Neil Stonechild's wrist and face. Wright indicates that Jarvis's suspicion is consistent with "that which is obvious to the naked eye" and confirmed by Robertson's photogrammetric evidence that "established the origin of the marks on a balance of probabilities."

LUCKY SHOES

Constable Ernie Louttit spoke briefly to us about some background issues, but declined an interview. We relied on his and other police testimony from the Stonechild inquiry, and a compilation of public exhibits, documentation of contacts between Don Worme and the RCMP from Stella Stonechild's legal file to describe how the original Stonechild investigation file came into Jack Warner and Project Ferric's hand. In conversation with us, Louttit maintained that he delivered all of the pages he'd copied to the RCMP.

P-184, the transcript of Larry Hartwig's interview with the RCMP, and P-197, the transcripts of Brad Senger's polygraph test with Chuck Lerat in December 2001, inform our description of the RCMP's attempts to get Senger to undergo a polygraph examination and the examination itself. Other records about the test, obtained independently of the inquiry process, provided further details and background.

In the spring of 2005, Chief Russell Sabo testified publicly before a police disciplinary hearing into the conduct of Deputy Chief Daniel Wiks, which followed the Stonechild inquiry, that Senger had agreed to two polygraph examinations, the first one with the RCMP. The second took place in the summer of 2003 and was conducted by the SPS. Senger failed both tests.

NO CHARGES

The Saskatchewan justice department did not lay charges in the Stonechild case in light of the RCMP's report. The justice department refused for a second time to lay charges after Commissioner Wright's findings from the public inquiry were published in the fall of 2004. This prompted a strong public rebuke from James Stribopoulos, an assistant law professor with the Faculty of Law at the University of Alberta. He wrote that the Crown was making "a serious mistake in dismissing the possibility of criminal prosecution." In an op-ed piece published in the *National Post* on November 11, 2004, Stribopoulos wrote, "In any other case, evidence that the deceased was last seen alive in the company of a suspect, that the suspect was in possession of an implement that could cause the unusual markings found on the body of the deceased, that the suspect had ample opportunity to commit the crime, and that the suspect lied about being with the deceased, would undoubtedly be considered enough to bring charges."

PART IV: WHERE DO WE GO NOW?

PROLOGUE

This is the verbatim testimony of Donald Worme, delivered at the age of four in April 1964 at the murder trial of Francis Littlechief, who had killed his mother and sister. This was Worme's first experience with the legal system and he remembers details of the trial and the prosecution to this day.

FAMILY AND FRIENDS

We spent much of the summer and fall of 2003 in Saskatoon researching. Jason Roy, Vanessa Kayseas, Roy's lawyer Darren Winegarden, and Roy's friend and confidant Father André Poilievre were very generous with their time as they prepared for the inquiry. Public documents on standing applications and rulings, testimony transcripts and exhibits provided by the inquiry's public affairs staff members Candace Congram and Irene

Beitel, and an exceptional website (www.stonechildinquiry.ca), guided us throughout the inquiry process and in the writing of this book.

As the inquiry hearings continued through September, October and November 2003, we also experienced and documented events in and around the hearings through continued access to Stella Stonechild Bignell, her lawyer, Donald Worme; and their families. We also met with many other people who knew Neil, among them Jeffrey "Bluesky" Crowe, Pat Pickard, Warren Davis from Kilburn Hall and Neil's wrestling coach Geoff Wright.

"A COMMENT MADE IN ERROR"

Testimony transcripts, tapes of Robert Martell's interview with Keith Jarvis, played during the hearings, and conversations with Martell, Jack Warner and Don Worme about the public exhibits, guided us in writing the sections about Jarvis. Personal observations during testimony and meetings with Stella gave us access to the family's reactions to Graeme Dowling's and Keith Jarvis's much-anticipated testimonies.

Background on Cree hunting practices comes from Mandelbaum's *The Plains Cree*.

SHADOW GAMES

We witnessed Gary Pratt's multiple appearances at the inquiry and also met him and his companions as he tried to hire a lawyer.

The illustration from the confidential Issue Team meetings chaired by Deputy Chief Daniel Wiks was entered as a public exhibit at the urging of Silas Halyk, representing the FSIN. Large sections of the minutes of meetings held just before and during the inquiry, and which Halyk was initially reprimanded for calling a "shadow investigation," remain blacked out.

"I DO NOT RECALL"

Officers Hartwig and Senger were among the last witnesses to testify at the inquiry. Through their lawyers, both officers declined opportunities to speak with us. Our re-creations of their roles in these events are guided by their testimony, public exhibits and other documents.

Don Worme attempted to get more RCMP evidence from Project Ferric's investigation into Neil Stonechild's death admitted as evidence and on the public record. Transcripts of the wiretaps on Hartwig's and Senger's phones were ruled confidential by Justice Wright; however, Wright did allow the transcripts of Senger's RCMP polygraph test in December 2001 to enter the public record. These exchanges form the basis of the sections on Senger's testimony.

Justice Wright's report on his findings from the inquiry as well as our interviews and meetings with Don Worme, Helen Semaganis, Greg Curtis, Jason Roy, Stella Stonechild Bignell and their families inform the final sections of our narrative.

Index

"Sergeant McCaffrey" and,
167–68, 270
Skakum, Ron, 174, 270
Snowberry Downs, 35–36, 37–38,
200, 234
SPS. *See* Saskatoon Police Service
Starblanket, Tamara, 383
starlight tours, 182. *See also specific
people involved*
media coverage of, 173, 182,
209, 357
Night and, 128–35
protests against, 203–4
SPS and, 64–65, 113–15,
166–67, 181, 285
threats to witnesses, 201–2,
204–5, 206–7, 296
victims of, 113–15, 177–78
Star Phoenix
articles on Neil
1991, 95, 97, 291, 395
2000, 186, 192, 193
Louttit and, 92, 166
and Night case, 175
SPS and, 349, 357, 386
and starlight tour cases, 173,
182, 357
Trainor column, 199–200
statement analysis, 320–21, 325
Stevenson, Kenneth, 331–32, 342
Stonechild, Brenda, 250
Stonechild, Dean (Chris), 26, 269,
288, 369
Stonechild, Erica, 17
as child, 19–20, 24, 311
at inquiry, 288, 295, 339, 358,
369
and autopsy photos, 308,
310, 311, 314, 315, 318
and Jason Roy cross-
examination, 297, 304, 305
on Wright, 289

Jarvis and, 218, 338
and Neil's death, 69, 218
exhumation/reburial, 249,
250
at funeral chapel, 70, 71
Stella and, 21, 87, 381
Warner and, 210
Stonechild, Gabriel, 250
Stonechild, Jake, 17, 20, 21, 24
girlfriend (Dawn), 342
at inquiry, 295, 304
at Kilburn Hall, 15, 67–68,
100, 101, 107
and Louttit, 73–75
and Neil's death, 67–69
exhumation/reburial, 249,
250
Warner and, 209
Stonechild, Marcel, 17, 24
as child, 18–19, 20, 311
and Cross Lake move, 107
family life, 250, 288
and inquiry, 250, 288, 293–94,
306
and Louttit, 87–88
and Neil, 26, 30, 59–61
and Neil's death, 57–58,
59–61, 71, 80–82
guilt feelings, 59, 61, 80–82,
96–97
and reburial, 250
and Neil's disappearance,
42–43, 46, 56
and Gary Pratt, 80–82, 346
and Jason Roy, 306, 308
Stella and, 96–97
stepson (Sam), 288
Warner and, 209
Stonechild, Neil, 17, 20, 311. *See
also* Commission of
Inquiry; Stonechild case;
Stonechild investigations

and autopsy photos, 242–43,
    309–18, 326
exhumation by, 248–50,
    276–77
Hartwig and, 240–41, 369–70
and injuries, 211–15, 239–40,
    243, 247–48, 333
SPS and, 193, 219–20,
    247, 274–75, 348–50, 353
Wiks and, 209, 240, 242,
    274–75
wiretaps by, 222–23, 260–61,
    348, 379
Stonechild investigation (SPS).
    See also Jarvis, Keith;
    Morton, Bob
and clothing, 54, 88, 105–6,
    341–42, 343, 352
and discovery of body, 47–53,
    55, 56–57
missing shoe, 48, 50–51, 52, 53
examination of body, 52,
    53–55, 59
autopsy, 59–60, 75–76, 235,
    249, 313, 326
and injuries, 82, 239–40,
    326, 341
file on, 78–79, 86, 89, 218, 341
destruction of, 194–95,
    197–98
Louttit and, 78–79, 86, 184,
    352
Tarasoff and, 89–90, 219
Struthers, Gord, 163, 167,
    168–69, 183
Sun Dance, 84
Sunshine, Dinah, 46, 64

Tarasoff, Dion, 89, 219
Tarasoff, Eli, 88–90, 219
Thomson, Glenn, 164, 165–66,
    167, 168

Trainor, Brian, 199–200, 241
Truro, Marjorie Pratt, 203

Valiaho, Brenda, 104–5
Vanin, Tom, 219–20

Waghray, Ranjit, 161
Warner, Jack, 197, 210–11. See also
    Lyons, Ken; Stonechild
    investigation (RCMP)
and Hartwig, 222–23, 225–28,
    366
at inquiry, 288, 298, 308, 368
Jarvis interviews by, 205–6,
    217–18, 233, 236–40,
    325–27, 336
and Louttit, 246–47
Lyons and, 197
and Gary Pratt, 244, 346
report by, 251–53, 271–72,
    355
and Jason Roy, 207–8, 304
and Senger, 225, 226, 230–31,
    260–66
and SPS, 247
and Stonechild family, 209–10,
    271–73
and Stonechild investigation,
    197–98, 209–13, 215–16,
    219, 271–73
and protection, 204–5, 206
and Worme, 197, 206, 207,
    247–48, 391, 393
Washington Post, 205
Watson, Jay, 287, 296, 353, 380
Waywaysecapo reserve (MB), 73,
    249, 250
Wegner, Bailey, 121, 163
Wegner, Gary, 145–46
Wegner, Lawrence, 116–22,
    137–45, 164–65. See also
    Wegner investigation

ROBERT RENAUD is Regional Director, CBC Ottawa, and SUSANNE REBER is Executive Producer, Investigations, CBC News. They worked together for over seven years leading CBC National Radio News, winning several awards for investigative journalism, and have been researching the Neil Stonechild case since 2003.

A NOTE ABOUT THE TYPE

Starlight Tour has been set in Janson, a misnamed typeface designed in or about 1690 by Nicholas Kis, a Hungarian in Amsterdam. In 1919 the original matrices became the property of the Stempel Foundry in Frankfurt, Germany. Janson is an old-style book face of excellent clarity and sharpness, featuring concave and splayed serifs, and a marked contrast between thick and thin strokes.